THE BREAD LOAF ANTHOLOGY

of Contemporary American Short Stories

PUBLISHED FOR THE BREAD LOAF WRITERS' CONFERENCE

Middlebury College

BY UNIVERSITY PRESS OF NEW ENGLAND

Hanover and London

THE BREAD LOAF ANTHOLOGY

of Contemporary American Short Stories

Edited by Robert Pack and Jay Parini

UNIVERSITY PRESS OF NEW ENGLAND

Brandeis University
Brown University
Clark University
University of Connecticut

Dartmouth College
University of New Hampshire
University of Rhode Island
Tufts University

University of Vermont

Printed in the United States of America   5   4   3   2

LIBRARY OF CONGRESS CATALOGING-IN-PUBLICATION DATA

The Bread Loaf anthology of contemporary American
  short stories.

  Bibliography: p.
  1. Short stories, American.   2. American fiction—
20th century.   I. Pack, Robert, 1929–   .
II. Parini, Jay.   III. Bread Loaf Writers' Conference
of Middlebury College.
PS648.S5B7   1987   813'.01'08   86–40387
ISBN 0–87451–392–8
ISBN 0–87451–401–0 (pbk.)

Acknowledgments

Some of these stories have appeared in periodicals. To their editors, acknowledgment and thanks are due: •
"Gypsy Moths" by Ann Beattie first appeared in *The Washington Post Magazine*.
"Falling and Ascending Bodies" by Harold Brodkey first appeared in *Vanity Fair*.

(continued on page 331)

FOREWORD

Like its companion volume, *The Bread Loaf Anthology of Contemporary American Poetry*, this book gathers what might be thought of as a particular moment in American fiction. The stories brought together here have been written within the past five years, and none have yet been published in collections by their authors. The writers included have not necessarily attended the Writers' Conference that has taken place on Bread Loaf Mountain in Vermont for more than sixty years, though most of them have studied or taught there. We, the editors, simply have tried to create a representative anthology, one that would reflect the variety and scope of fiction in this country in the late 1980s.

The short story is our most native form, one that has always attracted our best writers. Poe, Twain, Hawthorne, James, Crane, Cather, Hemingway, Fitzgerald, Porter, O'Connor, Welty—the reader's mind pauses before such a list. Each writer has added something to the form. The good news is that, in spite of a shrinking market for stories in large, national publications, writers of talent continue to find the form a challenge and an inspiration. As we think this anthology ably demonstrates, it remains possible for story-writers to "make it new," to modify and extend a durable American form.

We have tried to include a variety of styles and approaches to the short story. At one extreme, we have the so-called Minimalists, with their popular, pared down, "cool" style, and with what John Updike recently referred to as their "resistless immersion in the stoic bewilderment of a generation without a cause." On the other, we have our share of what Rosellen Brown has called Maximalists, writers who luxuriate in the sheer physical presence of language. Between these extremes, one sees at work a multiplicity of influences, from the post-Freudian "psychological" story to the fantastic (which has drawn new life from the Magic Realists of Latin America). As ever, the straightforward, realistic, "well-made" story continues to thrive, as it has from the beginnings of the genre.

What these stories have in common are an allegiance to fiction as a preserve of human intelligence and feeling, and a dedication to values handed down by serious writers over generations. These concerns inform the literary fellowship of Bread Loaf each summer, and we hope to pass them on in these twenty-three stories by some of our most accomplished writers.

ROBERT PACK
JAY PARINI

CONTENTS

THE BREAD LOAF ANTHOLOGY

of Contemporary American Short Stories

GYPSY MOTHS

Alice and her brother-in-law Lem are on their way to Billy's apartment so that Alice can get her daughter Nicki and take her to Connecticut. Since Alice and Billy separated, she and Lem have become even closer. When Lem isn't traveling with the band, she always tries to round him up to go to Billy's with her. He can make small talk about anything. He has a calming effect on Billy.

Trucks rattle by on Ninth Avenue. A greengrocer, standing on the sidewalk, pries open crates of tomatoes with the concentration of a child opening a present. A couple of blocks down, young men with wild hair, wearing T-shirts with Donald and Mickey cavorting, walk past the iron fence and turn into the seminary. Lem has a key to the side gate of the seminary. The story he told her about how he got it was as complicated as the way the key works: it only turns the lock from inside, to let people exit, so Lem has to stand outside and stick his hand through the bars to turn the key counterclockwise to get in. Lem often calls her at night, when they're less likely to be seen, and they meet and sneak into the grounds. It's beautiful inside—hard to believe such a place exists in New York. Alice let Nicki's grandfather, Randolph, assume that the photograph she gave him of Nicki for his birthday taken inside these grounds was taken at his farm in Connecticut.

On the brass plate around the door handle of Billy's building, someone has scratched "Find Jesus." At the Chelsea Central, this message is also on the doorplate. Perhaps if Jesus isn't to be found at Billy's, he's at the Chelsea.

Alice pushes Billy's buzzer. Muffled machine-gun fire comes through the intercom. "Alice," she says. More gunfire, then a shot: a quick buzz, and they're in. The war dies out behind them.

Billy looks down from the top of the steps. Head tilted over the banister, his face looks fuller than it is. He's wearing one of his ugly shirts: this one has cowboys twirling lassos, seated on horses rearing up like charmed snakes.

"The gang's all here," Billy says, and turns and walks into his apartment.

On the second-floor landing, Alice looks into the large mirror tipped against the wall. Years ago it fell, pulling down several nails and a lot of plaster. The landlord refused to hang it again, or let them get rid of it. This is the apartment that Alice used to live in with Billy. What she sees in the mirror is a surprisingly proper-looking woman in a blouse and skirt with a ruffle at the bottom. Before he went in ahead of her, Lem was a streak in the mirror.

Alice never tries to describe what's happened to the apartment to anybody. Who'd believe it? Where there aren't cabinets or rows of chifforobes, there are shelves: shelves added between the already existing shelves of the floor-to-ceiling bookcases. And boxes: boxes opened and unopened, everywhere. If she moves her head quickly and takes in the whole panorama of the long front room, she feels like she's watching some mad sequence in a Disney film in which inanimate objects, piled precariously, suddenly shuffle into a silly dance. The boxes and shelves and new pieces of furniture are to accommodate Billy's collection of rubber stamps. He has thousands of them. It would be as pointless as counting raindrops to try to guess the total: Victorian bouquets; horses jumping; strutting penguins; puffing trains; pirouetting ballerinas; pointed firs; Boy Scouts around the campfire; wood-block stamps with the letters of the alphabet on them.

He orders them from California, from Europe, from stamp-makers he hears about by corresponding with other stampers. The medicine cabinet is filled with stamps that have something to do with medicine or sex: naked ladies; anatomical close-ups; tourniquets; crutches. In the kitchen, the dishes are stacked in a box, and he has removed the old metal cabinets and put in shelves four inches apart. Some of the stamps are arranged alphabetically, some by subject, some by artist, his favorites kept in a big mahogany wardrobe with shelves added inside, exactly three inches apart. He has sold his stock to buy the stamps and the shelves and furniture to keep them in. Billy considers stamping the as yet unrecognized art form of the 20th Century—what Warhol would have moved toward if he hadn't gotten sidetracked.

"Look," Billy says. They're never there a minute, before he starts talking about the stamps, showing them what he calls "images." He turns toward one of his drafting boards. A couple of stamps fall on the floor, into open boxes containing more stamps. He touches a stamp to an ink pad, carefully imprinting something on a card. It's Nicki. Somehow he's had her reproduced on a stamp. Clipped to the piece of rope that stretches the width of the room are pieces of paper of varying sizes. Alice sees a pelican, rising out of what seems to be a brain; a tree toppling into the Queen Mary—a tree that must somehow have been rooted in the ocean; a chain of men on motorcycle, all slightly overlapping, blurring into the gray haze of a cloud of hornets spiraling off the ground. Marie Antoinette is nose-to-nose with a horizontal Empire State Building. Alice stops looking. He has succeeded in making the world seem improbable. She remembers how frightened she was when Billy first started stamping, and she came to pick up Nicki. She saw the smudges of ink all over her and mistook them for bruises.

"Where's Nicki?" she says.

"Upstairs. New people moved in who've got a kid a year older than her. Mother's got green hair."

"Who moved out?" Alice says.

"Mrs. O'Neill. Her son came and got her and moved her to Ohio. Quite interesting: notice that big antique crock the landlord had in the front hallway's gone? She took it and left some peacock feathers leaning up against the wall."

"Well," Lem says. "Speaking of moving—have you given any more thought to relocating to the farm?"

"Oh, come on," Billy says. "How am I going to move out of here? I couldn't transport this stuff. It's still coming in—cartons every day from the coast. You two think I can just pick up and do what I want, but come on—I'm *working*. Do you know what I'd have to go through to transport this collection to Connecticut? Do you think I could trust movers? *I'd* have to pack the stamps and transport them—come on."

Alice's father has announced that he intends to put his farm on the market if Alice and Billy don't want to patch up their differences and live there. She and Billy were married at the farm. When she was growing up, she spent all her summers there. She's worked it out with the magazine she works for that she can spend a week a month there now, instead of at the office. Randolph wants to spend winters with a cousin in Florida, and he's convinced that if the farm is unoccupied, it will be vandalized. "I'm not trying to talk somebody into the family business," Randolph said. "All I'm trying to do is offer you a brook, some trees, some land. Seems like you've all claimed such independence for yourselves that if you love this place as much as you all say, you ought to be able to find a way to live here." All of them tried to talk him out of it but, as usual, he stopped the argument. "Just think of me as Walter Brennan, in some movie," he said. "The way he acts when he's a maniac and he won't do anything for anybody."

Lem finds a small corner of the sofa packed with boxes that he lowers to the floor. He sits down, lights a Camel. Billy never invites them to sit. She hears from friends that he's stopped inviting them over. He was a graphic designer until he quit a few months ago. The specifics are quite different, but it seems to Alice that she has married her father. It seems to her a truth that men who admit to liking sensual things will be the most likely to go crazy.

Billy leans against his drafting table and holds a rubber stamp, fingering the top of the wooden handle. He does it gently—the gesture of a person who can't resist touching a delicate flower. He used to give her flowers and gently touch his fingertips to the unopened buds. He used to be obsessive about his love for her, her body. Flattering herself, she took it to be a particular obsession. Then he started acquiring other things.

The next day, Saturday, she's walking through the field with Lem. How strange, what's happened to all of them. Lem dresses in punk pink shirts and plays in a band called "Flamingos." In his time off, he wears the same shirts preppies wear. She's stopped having two wardrobes—one for work and one for the rest of her life. It isn't even necessary anymore. Billy has remained the same. Billy and Randolph, of all things. Only both of them have become more excessive. Back at the house, her father is teaching Nicki to play the fiddle. Nicki's riveted attention is much like Billy's passionate concentration when he deals with what he's interested in. This keeps recurring: intensity carries away the people she loves.

"Nicki wouldn't come on the walk with us," she says.

"Don't be sad," he says. "Or hell—at least you realize what's wrong. Look at the years I spent speeding, pretending that everything was a joke. I didn't even want to try."

Alice remembers hiding the Dexedrine, driving Lem around all night until he calmed down.

"What are you thinking?" he says.

"Remembering. Remembering all the potholes we drove over. Thinking we were going to go into orbit from the West Side highway."

"Jersey was a blur across the water," he says. "Jersey looked like an out-of-focus streak of lightning."

"Stay and talk to Randolph," she says.

"I have to play tonight," he says. "You know it's Saturday."

"It's funny when you think about it," she says. "Billy's gone back to being a child. He sits there with his stamp pads and his stamps, and you're leaving to *play*."

The apples aren't on the trees yet—the dozen trees still standing, after the huge lightning storm at Christmas. Poison ivy has curled up one tree.

"You're blaming me because I've used 'play' as a synonym for performing music?"

He shakes his head, sits down on the dry grass. Far away, on the road, a car drives by. Around them are dandelions. Thistle. Big weeds, more lush than the foliage of any of the nearby flowers. That had been one of Billy's passions: extremely expensive posters, imported from Germany, of unrecognizable flowers with a column at the side of the poster showing cross sections of pistils and stamens. They're no longer hung in the apartment; the last time she saw them, before he converted the space to shelving, they were leaning in a closet.

"Listen," Lem says, closing his eyes and tilting his head back. "Randolph's a prick. He's selling this place out from under you to punish you for not being a perfect little girl. You know how calculating he is? Why do you think he's nicer to me than to your husband? Because he knows how to create dissension." He sits up, makes confetti out of a handful a dry grass, then throws it away, takes her hand, kisses her knuckles.

She wonders if Walter Brennan has made any movies lately; if this could happen in a 1983 movie with Walter Brennan. They sit in the field a few minutes longer, until he looks at his watch—the big round watch that he can dive in, that probably also tells him atmospheric conditions if he wants to go into orbit—how ironic that he's looking to see how long he has before he has to be back in New York City.

Back at the house, the music lesson is over. Randolph is inside, frying chicken for dinner. Nicki is on the front porch, drawing, and Alice is suddenly amazed: those knobby knees make the rest of her leg beautiful by comparison. Her skirt is tangled under her, and Alice can see the pink flowers on Nicki's underpants. She's wearing the same pants, the same white shoes Alice wore when she was a child. The tips of the leather straps that go through the sandals are still cut so that they look like an arrow.

Lem hugs Nicki and sits on the step by Nicki's rocker. What is Nicki going to remember about all of them? She remembers her own mother's wavy hair—Rita Hayworth hair—and this tableau: her father holding a kitten to his face, her mother's head bent, curls sweeping around her cheeks, her chin touching Randolph's shoulder, both of them huddle in the room that has become the library. It was unfinished then, and the cat had had kittens under the shelf, on a pile of gift-wrapping paper that her mother always carefully unwrapped from packages she was given and smoothed out and put in a pile. Her earliest memory of something her mother said to her was about the paper—that Alice needed to be careful; that she should smooth it and fold it but not tear it.

"Nicki," Alice says, sitting beside her daughter, "in September when you go to kindergarden—if you don't tell them your nickname is Nicki, you can be called Nicole. It's all right if you want to be Nicki, but if you'd rather be called Nicole, you're sort of getting a chance to start over."

"I don't want to start over," Nicki says.

Nicki is using an orange crayon, adding something to her picture. Lem tries to figure out what it is: bird? butterfly? moth? He has to drive back to New York, but looking at Alice as she looks at Nicki, he's not sure what he can say that won't sound lame and falsely encouraging; saying a simple goodbye gets harder and harder, but he already told her everything he knew, in the field. He's wanted to kiss her for a long time, but that would probably be a mistake, too. He's been making too many mistakes. He blundered the night before, when they walked through the field to the edge of the woods: she listened to the millions of gypsy moths crinkling in the trees and said that it sounded like rain; he said it was the leaves disappearing.

Harold Brodkey

FALLING AND ASCENDING BODIES:
FOUR PASSAGES

ONE

Take, for example, me and Jimmy Setchell.

Me at age almost fourteen, James S. the same, yet two grades behind, because of the month his birthday is in and because of my rushing my passage in school. We are American Jews, essentially undefined in the category of falling and ascending bodies.

Jimmy shouts, "Woo-hoo! Whoopsy-daisy—" We are on bikes; the wind twists and edits syllables. The words sound odd and young. He wants to sound more grown-up, and, so, in a tougher manner, he says, "Upsy-daisy—" That's no good; so, he persists, "Up we go—" Still not the way he wants to sound. He tries "Wowee," and "Geronimo-o-o." He thinks the last one is O.K. He smiles like a juvenile paratrooper and sails down a declivity and starts uphill.

I am looking out of my eyes at that moment. This moment. I am slouching in my biggish, skinny body, at the edge of a weedy field of the whole moment.

I intended to end a remainder of innocence in me from my childhood that day. I intended to end my vow not to kill anything, or harm anyone, if God made things reasonably O.K. for my father—my father by adoption—who had been a youngish man, in his early forties then, and let him live for a while unterrorized and undespairing, not

8

shamefully. That had been the grounds of the vow. Now my Dad was dead, but that wasn't it: I was glad he was dead and probably wouldn't have done much to stop his death—this was five, nearly six years after the vow, which I had pretty much kept. It was that I was tired of the way I had been good; it had been a foul way to live. So, I intended to kill something in the course of the day. I had a disassembled .22, borrowed, extorted, from another boy. Jimmy carried it for me in a canvas pack on the bike rack in back of him.

Or I might decide not to kill. I might still refuse to kill. I might choose to remain solitary and pure, relatively undefended, even if that maneuver, of retreat, retreat inside my self, had gone so sour in the failures of the world and of my fathers that it had ruined the angle of the line of my inner fall—or ascent—for a long time. My desire now to use the rifle—well, I feel it as this thing that propels me toward life, perhaps fake, perhaps real, life. I proceed in a famine of companionship toward companionship. After my years as a child, I see companionship as a blood deed. I intend, today, to play with guns as a step toward acquiring social abundances and social knowledges. Let actuality begin—that kind of thing. Of the young man I was, it can be said, *he has an edge like a guillotine.*

This is meant to describe my mood, the killing something; and the question won't be resolved in this account.

I grin, I grimace as I pedal. I am very bookish. I name the non-transcendence, the non-thought of this excursion, *a day off,* a no-day, all-real, nothing much, a tilted day (from the ordinarily moral and busy, from the sense of the future that is *not* secret). This is a form of private gaiety. My forehead and my mouth and my mind, my legs, and my genitalia enter the next moment. I remember the sense of enlistment. I remember the brute intoxication of irrevocability.

I take the declivity and more or less shout "Geron-i-m-o-o" too. Then I start pedaling furiously as I think I saw Jimmy do. My heart has trebled, quadrupled in the last year, and it is a new and noisy drum, a kind of smooth and then tormented engine. It startled me that I had new parts of myself, real sections, now. I hadn't had compartments as a kid.

My hands and wrists were new and big, my mouth was like a small salmon on my face, in looks and in how it felt to me: it leaped and spawned—words sometimes, sometimes expressions, in its excitements, in compulsions; a lot of my time lately, I lived in a chemical high, drugged, intent, and in chemical lows, furtive paranoias.

On a steep section, where the road lay as if sunken while it climbed between steep, shading rises of broken rock, with bushes and a lot of very skinny, very tall trees rising up on arched trunks well above me, here in the shady underworld, long after Jimmy starts angling on long diagonals while he pedals aloft, I continue straight to see if I am, as I half-believe and would like to show, much stronger than he is and latently better at sports. The bike slows and goes yet slower. The bike locks onto the smudged rhythmlessness of making no headway. It's a little as if the front wheel is rotting or as if the bike was plowing into an airy hedge. I persist. Breathless, then, partly defeated, I give in only in the airy half-lurch before keeling (a fall), but I give in actively, heroically, more as if fighting back, me now, the underdog—but mighty nonetheless. I right it, the bike; I grab the bike upright with my arms; I am leveraged on the straining arch of my body, my legs: calfless legs, handsome in their way, fairly strong but clumsy at the moment (my arms haven't much shape, either, but they're good-looking anyway—also—and strong), and I curse to mobilize myself. I threaten the hill with hell and God's wrath; the bike—its frame, an edited, two-dimensional diagram, lime green—is lifted (the front wheel comes off the ground); I aim it diagonally, on the lesser slope, and then the galvanized half-leap and semi-glide forward means what I did was O.K. I am decently, skeletally athletic.

I then embark on the irresolute, crooked stitching back and forth, a tactic to get uphill further; the bicycle occasionally lurches in a deadened, nerveless way.

Now, the morning swimmingly, sweatily jerks around in zigzags in front of my eyes, and I get postcardlike rectangles, road, roadside, ditch, fences, lawns, houses, window sashes, carriage lanterns, façades. The postcard rectangles, the pictured morning is not looked at but indirectly seen and instantly remembered while I pedal and sweatily blink. It cuts and slaps paperishly at me. Behind my forehead, in my buzzing skull, my mind winces in steady, little slips. My legs do not pulse and bulge, though, and my eyes do not protrude, and my lips don't hang open as they did when I was small and went uphill on my bike, this bike; its seat is raised now.

I resented it that I had to remember in order to know what I saw, I have to put a step, a jackleg, a distance in, if I want to *know* what is in front of me. If I see alively, I sort of know, but I can't be sure.

The morning's crimped edges slap my inward eyes, which are less shy because they see only when I blink or when the jackleg is in operation, when the corridors are patrolled and speed is regulated—they are more elegantly mindful than my outward eyes.

I use my weight to force down the obstinate pedals, this one, that one, and they jerk up oppositely. The powering, or enabling, motto—the motto motor—is, *Get your ass up the hill.*

The light, the rays of the sun at a morning angle strike my eyes and then my wheeling ears and side of my neck as the bicycle slowly, heavily advances on an erratic line and switches directions again and then again. Flowers of glare flourish on my handlebars and on the spokes of Jimmy's bike. Jimmy is maybe sixteen yards ahead of me. I slouch more and more, becoming miniature in admission that I am clumsy, that I have certain deficiencies in my body and mind, omissions of experience and some muscular training and knowledge because of my father's having been ill and what was asked of me and that I am not gaining on Jimmy and am not a better athlete than he is—at this moment.

Everything in the world measures me and other men, and me against other men. I try to follow my duty. I try, also, as a mindly kid, to "know" what happens. That means to keep track, with a continuing sense, of what is done in the movement of time—that is, of what is actual. After a while, I remember too much and seem strange and bullying to some people—seem and am. Sometimes the abundance itself weighs me down, and this stuff crumbles into a pile, a single point or two, or indicators: *Here I am—sort of—sorry—this is a lousy hill.* At this time in my life, I haven't the ability to phrase this and so it slides around like something unfastened in the trunk of a car, but I live it with an odd stubbornness.

Let me get up this goddamn hill.

I do the nut thing of *maybe it's not true that I'm here.* This shreds the brute intoxication of *irrevocability.* This destroys the fabric of the real—I mean, for me as audience of my own doings on this slope. My identity as an adolescent male, the space around my senses, titters now, and scowls in opposition to The Real: I'm a man, sort of, and I can do and think what I want: I'm not dependent like a woman or a child: I am and I'm not.

I start being in a school-y state, an agony, a restlessness, a reckless boredom: I am persecuted, deftly oppressed: *What kind of person AM I, why am I doing this, God . . .*

I seek asylum as a brainy kid, I flee the country of such matters as maleness, and I think about books and soak myself in a pretense of rationality and escape the strain of bicycling.

At school, in order to pass as correct, since I won't risk being eccentric or having doctrines, I lie *always* and don't tell the teacher or the class when I make a book report or answer a question that a book or sentence or line in a poem is not the same for me on two successive readings, ever, the same sentence, the same *word—Don't be a philosopher; you tire everyone out, Wiley* (Wiley Silenowicz, Ulysses Silenus in a Jew-American version, since my adoption when I was two, when my real mother died). The second reading, which is meant to check the first, always so alters the snowy reaches of the first reading and my notes or impressions that it silences me: it's as if I was always wrong if I am right now. I hate myself because I lie about this and pretend I think it is mad stuff when I really think it is obvious and true, and basically useful. But I try to fit in even if at the expense of truth. *Don't tell people what you think; that's crazy.* So I don't. And I have daydreams of confessing someday to what I see. But I'm only a kid.

I am not A Good Kid with a single spine of doctrine and character. As I said, I have become *restless*; other people might say I started to get nervous—or they'd say Wiley's about to act up—AGAIN; he's mischievous, he likes to make trouble, he overreacts. When I feel good, I don't judge things much except to say things like *These are people's lives, Let's be kind*, but when I'm bothered, like now, the neatened houses, wood and half-size brick, medium-strength dilutions of ideas of *farmhouses*, a prairie turned into cozy and self-conscious nooks makes me embarrassed for everyone's life and for the sorrow in their lives and for the Middle West; and I know that would irritate a lot of people—I mean if they knew.

I don't understand, but I'm really unhappy suddenly, so I call out to amuse and interest myself and to be a sport and to get back in touch with reality while I sweat and pump in the crisscross pattern upward, "Hey, Juh—(breath)IMMY."

My mood is uncured, and maybe worsened. This isn't felt as a smooth thing but lurchingly, among breaths and gasps. Anyway, the enlarged trees and shrubs of the lawns seem out of place in the Middle Western light, which is, after all, illumination for a prairie, for a vegetable sea, rising week by week in the summer, all summer long, a rippling broth of weeds and high grass and tall flowers, elbowing each other and leaning and bowing, culminating in sunflowers, farfetched and gargantuan, giraffelike maybe, August steeples, giant disks, solar, coarse, and yellow, nature's pragmatic and almost farcical climax before the collapse in autumn in a brown rush of cold.

The hill was once a burial mound. Now it's got these houses. The burial mound was once filthy, stinking—savages are no better than we are. Savages and everyone and everything else—each thing in the universe, with or without consciousness, has intent, a limitless will is a bloody tyrant emperor—I mean, each thing tries to run everything, to have its way. Everything is imperial—without exception. Everything drags at you. This is a universe of trash tyrants. You have to sacrifice your life to prove goodness exists. *Do you think doing your duty sweetens things?* I sort of asked Jimmy in my head. Here's a secret: we are not entirely subject to laws. Everything can be cheated on for a while; you can put "an alternate irrevocability" into the system; you can *quickly* give something away, for instance, against your self-interest.

"Hey-ay, JUH-immy—YOU THINK GOODNESS eggzIsss(T)s?"

"Hunh?"

"YOU THUH-INK WE'RE IMPROOVING THE GAL-AX-EE?"

"WHA(T) DYou WUHNNN(T) TO KNOW FORR?"

"I DON'T KNOW, I FORGOT, I'M OUT OF BREATH."

This is what I shouted, with various long pauses, or holes in the sound. But I wasn't exactly talking to him, and I wasn't quite talking to myself: it was an early-adolescent version of weeping and sweating and being red-faced.

"WE'RE ALL TIE-RUNTTS—" I know he won't get that: no one understands, no one listens through the technical haze of problems that inhere in speech.

As I pump, I feel an immoderate extent of will. I also get an erection, as I often do when I am in despair: this is a source of further despair. I go mad with sensual *restlessness*—a mode of despair; but even if I am to be a bad person in my life, I want to be it clearly and as *a disappointed good man,* do you know what I mean? When I feel the bike pedal scrape the macadam on one of my wobbly turns, I dismount. Good or bad, I am a free man.

[*In the course of what happens, for one reason and another, Wiley lies down shirtless on the sticky macadam of the road.*]

TWO

I did not want to lie in the road. It's corny, it's dirty. I am fastidious and have intellectual pretensions (Middle Western, middle-class).

I reach over and undo my T-shirt from the bar.

Jimmy is a horrible person in a lot of ways—*a lot of ways*. Notice that he doesn't come rushing to see if I'm O.K.; he suspects a trap. He is buried in his own life; he has a lot of rebellious self-love. He sees my lying down and having a death stroke or recovering or having a nervous breakdown; but he waits to see if it's safe to feel concern or even curiosity—will he be a fool if he offers to help, if he shows solicitude—am I ribbing him?

I mind that, because it interrupts the nobility of my effort to enact freedom and heartfeltness or something. Also *worship* of something— goodness, probably. Part of my purpose was that, and also to belong to the devil rather than to hypocritical pieties on this suburban road, et cetera. I think about Jimmy in a spasm of irritation and sadness: Why are middle-class kids so *canny?* The road stink rises around me; the tar gulpingly pushes against my knobby back. He doesn't trust me—my moods, my ideas and logics, arguments and beliefs. He lives with safe statements. He has only so many acceptable signals of peace and aid in his data bank. He is about as much a romantic adventurer in thoughts and words about love and help as your average Boy Scout troopmaster.

I loathe lying in the road. I loathe most of the would-be *important* acts and big-time gestures I make. I loathe being imprisoned in things I start. So, I sit up and put on my shirt and I fold my legs in a lotus posture: but then I unfold them and sit like that on the tarry surface.

A maybe nine-year-old girl and her shrewd and good-looking and slim-titted and cretinously sweet and suspicious mother are holding each other's hands and watching *me*.

Maybe they're worried about me, both ways, as a possible menace and as someone who is to be worried about because he has to be helped soon if you want to be a *nice* person about it.

Jimmy coasts crossways across the road and down a little ways on a diagonal.

My mood is severe and defended like an encampment of an army. He's a mere Carthaginian—no: Gaul.

"Jimmy, where are we headed?" I say. "What does my life mean?" He ignores that, or I say it too blurredly and he can't figure out; it's too unfocused.

He is nearer but still cautiously yards away. He glides on his bike, mostly backwards, brakes with his feet, looks at me, looks at the sky, hesitates. How does someone who is not a truth teller recognize a truth? He never knows why I'm irritable. He thinks I'm strange.

My sense of action, me being a man(ettino) of action, that fades, and my mind resumes its privacy because Jimmy is so suspicious of me. My images are resummoned; they return mostly as fumes of will, they never stay the same for long; but outdoors that changeability is worse, is even foul, although beautiful. To claim otherwise is to lie. To be an invalid and kept indoors is intellectually more honorable. For example, the reasons and mood I had are gone, and I don't any longer know why I'm sitting on this macadam in humid, smoggy sunlight, in my shorts and T-shirt. I am now martyred by carrying on an act of will that once had a warbonneted ferocity (and freshness) to it; I have compromised it a dozen times by now; the whole thing is dull and stinking; it's time to give up, stand up, but that idea (of standing up) becomes sad, an infliction. The macadam stinks and sticks; pebbles gnaw into my thin-muscled butt and the skimpy calves of my legs; the idea of freedom has turned into an outline, penciled and geometrical, which may be colored in, or painted and then seen as containing *life*—that's a symbol. Mostly. My existence plunges and filters and buzzes along *meanwhile*; but I am a prisoner of the drawing, and my life is, too. I mean I believe in freedom even if it's only the postures one takes for the fall.

He's looking at me: I have the sense, maybe wrong, that he's *amused*. *Charmed*, in a way. That's not O.K. It's distracting. The landscape, the slope, the wall and tree, the staring women. James, my companion, up to a point, everything is sun-caped above abysses of the hardly seen *truth* of a gesture, let alone of my works and days. This matches, or simulates, the visual truth, which is that what I see flimmers over or at the rim of abysses: the *hardly seen by me*—literally *half*-seen. I see in fits and starts, with emphasis here and there—near abysses of shadows and subsidiary glimmers. *The periphery.* The at-the-moment Minor Stuff—in which truth might be found. It is the case that I see one thing—Jimmy's mouth, let's say—and I hope the rest is there.

I now rise and am half on one knee, undecided about everything, one hand is on the tarmac.

My mouth feels like a salmon, muscular, tugged; Jimmy's mouth, now seen in this light and at a distance when he turns his head to me. I see as a large dot, or maybe big dash on his face, but it is remembered, imagined as a mouth, with shapes and colors seen in another light and at different angles; it is as free as a particle in the wind, it seems.

I lay my bike on the macadam: it had no kickstand, and I still held its handlebars. I ganglingly collapse backward, because freedom also means not caring if I break my back or my neck, sort of. I lie panting. Jimmy is now nearer, near enough that I am released from the Roman camp of solitude; I am unlocked from my head and am aware of, or even oppressed by him, his presence; I can see that he glimpses me and disbelieves; that is, he only partly believes I am doing what I am doing. He now coasts backward some more, on the diagonal, back down the slope, toward me, to the body of glimmer and shadows and odd behavior which is me. Who is me. Whatever. He halts, his legs spread, the bike heroically between his thighs. On my shirted back, the tar is a bed of cupping, sucking, semi-melted octopus tentacles, fatally attached.

I am in a sort of rage of thwarted gesture and I want him to "love" and admire me. To love and to admire are so overlapping, they are just about the same emotion in me, separated by one or two seconds of mental time, seconds in which I blink and compete and do my best with the pain of admiration and try to fit it. I am heartsick but stubborn inside my lying here, and I am lonely because this thing I'm doing seems like metaphysical brattishness pretty much—not entirely—but I want him somehow to help this stuff along until it's O.K. It occurs to me that one has to devote almost a lifetime to this kind of act (and thought) to make it grown-up and really good (valid). I ought to go limp now and be married to this and really suffer. Only pain can validate this, can validate me, and this is hell to know, to guess at, I mean, and to live out. It is bratty, therefore, even if it's honest of me, to want Jimmy to help—but I insist on being *happy sometimes*. And Jimmy can make me happy(er). But it is facile and glib not to suffer in one's truths, they are real acts, and strain the shit out of you in your real moments, and it's dumb not to recognize that they are true. But it's facile and glib to suffer all the time; things can turn good without warning, without any warning at all.

I said, moist-eyed, "I am a free man—boy—man." Then I said, in a very well-educated way but mumbling and local, "It is one of my privileges not to have to be careful to make sense by your standards when I speak."

I want him to remember that I'm a smart kid and can be—well, *trusted*, you know. So, I had spoken in a really careful sentence. To show I could be trusted—this was out of loneliness, and folly, a cheating on myself, to explain myself as if in a footnote in school. I mean, I heard dialogue in my head—him saying, *Wiley, what are you doing? What are you saying? Why are you showing off? Are you being a jackass?* I saw this on his face—in his eyes, outlined and bowed and pointy, and in the set of his mouth, and I answered it in the long and careful sentence which he hardly heard. He thought about it and then dropped the effort of remembering and figuring out so many words.

"Wiley, what is it?" he said—as if I'd groaned and not spoken.

It was much more tender than I had expected.

I'd finessed him into it, I'd willed it, but part of the point was also what he decided on when he came near me.

Then he said, "Are you all right?"

"I am—a—free—man."

"Did you have an asthma attack?"

He wasn't being pleasant. I mean, who wants *medical* attention?

He wasn't being derisive—just bored and standoffish and self-enraptured in his concern.

"Listen, jackass. I don't believe in manliness," I said.

Of course, he didn't know *the context*, so that didn't make too much sense.

Jimmy blinked: "Why are you attacking me—now?"

"Oh cut the innocent-bystander crap." Then I said. "*You* exist, you do things for people, jackass—my feelings about *human* freedom don't make *me* a jackass, Setchell, whatever you want to think—for your own purposes."

I add metaphysical overtones to his sense of his own day while he gets along in his canny goings-on.

When I talk, the stuff I'm saying grinds into me as failure and loneliness.

I am falling, in a state of off-again, on-again, blurred, low-key rage for freedom, or whatever it is; and his looking at me in whatever degree of affection or mix-up or incuriosity or desire or whatever state and mixtures of things he's in doesn't help—the light is behind him, the pale sky; and he's like the dark nucleus at the center.

He is shirtless, and bare-legged, bare-ankled: I'm in running shoes; he has bicycle shoes.

I can understand his not understanding me when I talk. I'm not a clear person.

He twitches; he isn't calm, and, so, when I see that, I get ashamed, in case I've been a show-off and have upset him; but, really, you know, I don't know why he twitches, and, in a way, I am too cowardly to ask, but his life is attached to mine today, for these hours: I'm immune to nothing.

I am not tough—merely mean at times. I stand up in quick stages, *segments*. I haul my bike upright.

Then he reached over, and I was careful not to stiffen, and he touched me with two fingers on the back of my neck where my hair started and he picked off a piece of tar. The tar was stuck to me, and then it whistled free; and behind it, on my skin, was a burning sensation insecurely placed; but it did abut on an emotion.

His fingers moved in what I considered to be a Jimmylike way, like the words in a First Grade Reader, careful and clear, so that you don't get startled by meanings.

But I get startled by them anyway. I am a glorious mirror for other people in some ways, unfortunately—for their heroisms of existing in the real world. I often feel I don't exist physically, in the inherited world of parents and the like. Sometimes it's O.K. I stood still, and he went after some of the pebbles that were stuck to my back under the loose T-shirt; I have a skinny back. It's odd not to be someone worthless. I grew stilled inwardly, pondlike, *girlish*—I mean with guilt and responsiveness. I really mean with greed and also with a kind of suspicion, and then with stiff gratitude, stiff with resistance because of the suspicion, and then not, but kind of wildly generous, like a kid, but one my size—me, I guess. His fingers are *small*, considering his size. I'm six two and he's six three. His fingers taper down and are kidlike in the last joints. "You're being so goddamm tender, I can't stand it," I said, and he gasped, or groaned, like my Dad—as my Dad used to, wanting me not to talk. I would guess the tenderness was real, but it's his and I don't know what it means in relation to who I am and what I do and what I have just done. I was overborne by the mysterious chemical fires he lit with his acting like this and his continuing to act—with tenderness—while currying me of dirt after my dumb gesture, or whatever I should call it. What I'm trying to get to is to say that this stuff with the fingers, the tender-fingers business, occurs along the lines of the irrevocable, too—the masculine irrevocable.

If he likes me this much, why didn't he lie down beside me?

Why didn't he say, *Jesus, God, Jesus, God*?

How come he's so stubbornly set on doing things his way, inside his own way, inside his own life?

Why didn't he give up his own will and his own speech? Look, he's being so—*nice*. Medically generous. In each touch, in each movement of his fingers are inspired little puffs of soul-deeps and absentmindedness, like birds in dust or leaves, forgetting themselves and leaning or fluffing and being almost still: stilled birds in very early morning sunlight. Something like that.

How can I live up to his silly goddamn fingers?

How do you live up to anything halfway decent?

How do you live with anything that's really just about entirely decent?

People don't stay decent. This is a trap, what he's doing.

It's so terrible to be irritated by people. How do you live with people?

The tenderness was already turning nasty. His fingers were getting sharp and quick and gouge-y. Of course, it wouldn't stay like that, either, but now his touches were rough and rebuking.

Then he began doing it as if I were inanimate, and my back was his teddy bear or his bike tire; that was O.K., but then it's not O.K. Frankly, I am not usually in love with him—only a few moments here and there—but I had been for a few seconds: paralyzed, frozen, stilled, or whatever, for a moment there.

If he'd been knowingly *physical*, limitlessly sexual by a sort of nostalgic implication back toward childhood but with self-conscious purposes and within virginal limits and virginal and whore-y knowledges, like a smart kid, it would have been easier. Different. Well, to tell the truth, he was like that, too, but slyly, and with more vanity than confidence. Second by second, he changed, or I saw or imagined a change. Some of what he did was derisory. Also, I hate being touched.

Finally, I pulled away from him, glanced at him. I suppose he thought it was all nuts, but I kept thinking I was being obvious and that he understood everything—*every single thing*. And he did, in his way. After all, I am obvious in what I do, and very, very *logical*.

THREE

In boyish shame at the imperfections of my speeches and my affections, my mind opens onto the morning: I am looking down over my arms, my hands, the handlebars of the bike, past the racer's wheel in motion, to the road spinning or pulling, or being pulled backwards under the wheel.

After a second or two, the slope picks up steepness going down.

I enter what is like a tunnel, windy and speedy, going downhill in an accelerating swoop and with half-circles of rush pulling at my hair. The increment of speed and the steadiness of balance formed transparent tents and invisible hallways and domes with echoes in them.

And something like the hands, fingers, tongues, and feet and toes of the wind push and prod me in an airy but semi-breathless tumble, a giddy free-for-all, a seduction in the key of free fall, and weirdly roofed and walled, I guess, in the concentration or seduction of the senses or whatever it is, in staying alive and whizzing dangerously down and down and down . . .

I am startled by how pretty sometimes the musics of movement are.

Jimmy idly—or as if idly—passes me.

He can't see me anymore: he is ahead of me.

The animal sense of the moment tickles, it startles in a blood way—I glance up with a fox's heat of dreadful attention, a predator's study in the wanton speed, the early feverishness, the being out for the day with James Setchell (Jimmy), the irregular heat of the morning, aliveness, the downhill, the riding free-handed, the idle whooping under my breath, air on my bare chest, skinny ribs, and with my face upturned I catch sight of a wide-winged hawk; it swings hangingly in the air not far past some trees, not far, not high, in an oval of open sky: it is uncandled but alight, whitened by glare. I glance down the road ahead of me and then back up, and I locate again the patient, blood-hungry, peculiar chandelier in the pallid air. On its stringed circuit, on its heaven-descended chain, it marks in its circles the inclination of the lurching earth. I look down again and locate potholes and I steer some on the descending road and its shadows, and then I look back up again and to the side and I locate the hawk but with more difficulty: it has shifted eastward. I try but I can't make out its markings; it is mostly a white blur, plus a spikily black line swaying: the feathered edge of an airy paddle, mostly motionless on its own; but it moves anyway. The hawk. I hardly know how to look at it: man oh man oh man: the black, splayed back pinions of the wings are like a fat boy's fingers gripping a windowsill of air. His head is hidden in blur; I am moving and can't see anyway—the pressure of wind is on my eyes. The road has its magical tunnel *descent*. When I look up again, the hawk is entirely gone, the sky is empty, the hawk's swing and my movements have covered more territory than time permits to be inside a single moment. So, it is another moment and a new territory. And there are more blocks to sight than I had thought to associate with the sky here, roofs, roadside clifflets and trees taller on this slope than on the other one, on the ascent. So, the sky is not wide here, it is not a great field in many dimensions but is a bunch of falling and rising glades or clearing or depth-y, height-y air, leaf-trimmed and almost exploding and zooming screens, here and there above me, through the failures of the trees along here to be fat and wild.

This slope of the ridge is more wooded and stylish than the ascent. The houses have more expensive yards among the trees; it is really mostly a woods here.

Again and again, my sight, diving upward, is a quick ballooning rush into blue particles, into stuff that has no resemblances but only a dissolving beauty—the planelessness—and the illuminated blue aerial substance of the day. My eyes are then lowered and fixed again on the striped and confettied road, and I squint ably in the wind and the downward rush.

And then a sexual rush buzzes along my ribs, and then a memory of white light, breathlessness: a flick, a flicker, which is a pinpoint of the vaster drowning, the convulsion of coming when I masturbate.

It's gone. I have an erection that hurts. I'm me, a bicyclist, and there is Jimmy: I have a maybe brutal sense of romance.

FOUR

We move along on our slender machines among the conditions of travel: the potholes, the crookedly and swoopingly, centrally humped road, macadam, and pebbled; we bounce and sway in the air currents and rush of nerves when a brushing, racing, wind-loaded and wind-spilling, bristling, and snuffling boar-machine, an automobile goes by, then another: Christ, the weird hissing and, neurally, the staggering hesitation of their passing; then their dusty and advantaged, motor-steadied, keeled diminishing into the glimmering and dusty glow of distance with their amazing speed . . . Distance is golden this time of day, in this part of the country, this part of the world . . .

The sun, at moments when it is sunny, heats the air, which then rises like a ghost of a huge dairywoman, gray and yellow, and of another century, and in the immense fluster of her clothes, sounds are lost.

I am testing him, in part. If he makes a real attempt to hear now, it will mean he is in a state of affection, even infatuation. This test is and isn't purposeful, on my part. I want to talk to him: I am used to being with him, I mean, since we started out: I am young and flexible in my habits: it's something I've gotten into over the years, doing this, testing people but a little dishonestly (as in act of intimacy of a kind, as I'm doing with Jimmy) but I really want to see if he is A Good Person. He's An All-Right Person (in some ways), but he is not good. But I am so far out of control, so overfitted with energies and blustering restlessness at this hour—this vacationer's day in my life—that I am almost as pleased by his not listening, by some blindness in his friendship as by the other. I'm almost as pleased as if it were a sign of goodness, his being wicked or whatever. Anyway, the goodness probably is not there. And while I really can't live (or love) without it, I can't want it to happen now. I'm probably safe. He's leaning back and just pedaling, which indicates his vanity and my unimportance. If he felt a lot of affection, he might listen and feel still more affection, and common sense might leave him, and he might come to me and cuddle and nurture me, here on these backward and decaying slopes of childhood, and I know pretty goddamn fucking well I would never be able to bear that.

Rosellen Brown

A GOOD DEAL

My father does not live in what I would call a "home." We'd never have considered anything that even resembled the word, with its hypocrisy built right into its name (home cooking, comforts of home). I like to think he is in a sort of benign arm of the Catskills out on Long Island, a brightly decorated and well-kept hotel complete with live entertainment and a built-in a synagogue a few blocks from the ocean. The air outside his hotel has that sharp salty extra dimension that makes you realize you are standing in something nourishing, almost tangible, not transparent, nonexistent, like most air. He won't go out in it because for him the extra dimension he anticipates (besides mugging or murder) is germs—a cold, bronchitis, pneumonia: who wants to smell *air*? Not at his age.

When we visit, we take him walking once around the building as if "outside" were a destination in itself. He's got his hat—a pale yellow golf hat for our summer visit, a formal fedora for the winter, the kind the FBI used to wear before they started passing as hippies and stoned collegians. "Come on, let's go for a walk," I suggest as soon as I see my wife and the kids sinking into torpor on his room-mate's bed in the room on the fourth floor.

This time we have brought him a little radio with earphones because the room-mate complains about noise, any and all, after 8:30 and the management will not "mix in," either out of scrupulous fairness or their (correct) suspicion that reason is destined for defeat here among the elderly with their habits that have turned to stone.

Jane has correctly predicted his reaction again—she maintains that my father is the only person she knows who has never said an unexpected thing. He is, for some reason I can't fathom, bewildered by the radio dials and I can see that it will go unused, he will leave it in its little blue box on his half of the closet shelf, another failed toy alongside the hearing aid and the electric razor. Inertia overpowers energy, impossible as it sounds. Entropy makes promises; someday I suppose I'll know what it is saying.

He has embraced his grandsons, offered them small dusty-looking cookies that he's saved from lunch in a napkin. They are touched, Timmy especially (he is the little one), at a sign of awareness that they were coming, that they might have needs or pleasures he could gratify. They don't ask or expect much—some rudimentary consciousness, a sign. They take one cookie apiece and chew it carefully, as if they are thinking hard. I ask more, although I don't get it. Well, I am his son, the remoteness of the third generation has not made me forgiving.

So we troop downstairs, Jane ahead of us, wearing her glorious red hair that made my father, when he first saw her, call her a Yankee; the two boys trying ceremoniously not to step on each other's heels, giving off, though, with every gesture the suppressed air of kittens in a sack, all frisky irresistible quenched movement. The elevator is one machine Pop seems to have mastered; not only does he hold the door, assured, while we file in, but he smiles and keeps his hand on the OPEN button for another tenant of his floor, a short, vividly-muumuued woman who hobbles on slowly inside a walker. As we move down the floors, sinking so hard our stomachs rise up into our chests and Josh says "Gulp" out loud, she looks at us, smiling, and then, apologetically at her aluminum contraption and shakes her head. "Don't get old, *kinder*, that's all I can say."

After she's gone—we politely wait for her to drag herself out and disappear around the elevators toward the gift shop—my father says "So who asked her? We need her opinion on anything, we'll remember to ask her."

Jane opens her mouth and closes it; so do I. We are going to berate him for his lack of generosity but instead we berate ourselves: the same impatience that bit her into speech bit him into anger. The hotel is fine, we assure ourselves, it is age that's depressing.

But no. I watch my father walk toward the door slowly but securely. It is mostly women who are seated, watching, in the purple and yellow leather chairs on both sides of the aisle, because life seems for the most part to be a widowing. He has very few real complaints, considering what a man his age can expect—even the Bible would agree. It is all that has never changed that rankles: he is the same father I've always had, lacking a few appurtenances (teeth, hearing, hair, a wife) but otherwise stock still the same. "Kill me!" he pleaded after my mother died. "It's a mistake, how could such a mistake happen! I was always going to go first." I don't know how much losing her cost him. But he was terrified to face his life alone without a mother, that I know. He was bewildered, and he's still bewildered—how could it be that he has come through eighty-two years intact when strong men, men twice his size and a hundred times more vigorous and full of will, have died and left these women?

Timmy pushes on the hotel door with all his weight and the live air opens to us, edgy with salt, the sky bright blue as pure deep water. "Oy," my father says, turning his face back toward the building. "I'm climbing into my grave out here. What are you doing, Joey, punishing me with this cold?"

I wish I could find a sin in my father's past. I thought this once when I was embroiled in an episode of, what shall I call it, a brief unsanctioned lust—Janie never did find out, no harm was done—because I was caught in a paradox. My father didn't drink (a litle schnapps on *shabbos*, gone in a blink) and neither did I; he was a dutiful breadwinner, earnest in his work, and so was I, give or take the moments of insolvency any writer is heir to. His shortcomings were all of omission, never of commission. He and my mother, however they had begun, had endured a marriage of convention and dependency. They mocked and quibbled, demanded and berated, my father thrust his neck out to be shamed and my mother enthusiastically did her best to shame him, and how they had me is hard to envision. As a teen-ager (like all teen-agers who have everyone experimentally in bed with everyone else, their teachers, their friends' mothers, the President!) I could never manage to imagine them so much as acknowledging each other in the Murphy bed they pulled down from the living room closet. (It was a tiny apartment; their son got the bedroom for his more hallowed activities.) But just as people unquestioningly needed marriages in those days, so did those marriages need children. I suppose I was a duty and they did me.

But then, as I said, the moment presented itself when I was less than dutiful and I found myself gathering up the odd ingredients for a great stew of justifications. I found myself thinking, I am not my father repeated once down the line. Even though you could confuse us in the dark by the shape of our bodies, the nap of our hair, he is a man in whom the blood beats weakly, whom the traces bind. Admirable and not admirable, those things. I didn't know just where I stood on virtue just then. It seemed to me, but only in flashes, as if there were a blinking sign at the corner of my vision, that virtue was only safety and safety was timidity. Cowering. Then that sign would blink again and I wasn't so sure. I saw Janie's face, innocent of worry (though I tried to see it anywhere but in the bedroom) and I saw the blond, thoroughly gentile, slim-hipped woman (a student of mine, not, to be honest, as innocent as my wife) who wanted me enough to put a lot of foregone conclusions in danger, hers and mine; and it was my father who seemed, or at least ought, I thought, to be begging me to *do* it, leave the straight and narrow, seize the hour and be bad.

I was bad; I could achieve badness with the best of them (only perhaps not as a recidivist). As it happened, I didn't enjoy it much, either in anticipation or in retrospect, only in the single blinding instant, gone as quickly as that ritual fire-in-the-throat whiskey after *kiddush*, that drives all of us every time, in the dark, on the sly, the animal instant that slaughters reason. And perhaps I enjoyed this colloquy too: Pop, I thought, a man has to dare to dare. Then I would ask myself why. To be able to say he dared? Say it to whom? I wasn't telling *him*. If my father, who was too simple and decent to lie or even give short-weight, wasn't good, only frightened, what was a good man? Sometimes he seemed to me, all of a sudden, not so naive as I had thought: telling me about a gangster neighbor, a philandering cousin, his aunt who took in boarders and then took off with one. He had noticed there was a world out there. But his own record, I thought, that was clean enough to be an incitement. In retrospect I see I was averaging my guilt over two generations. In my own way I was a coward too.

A few months ago, the night before we were to make our biennial trip to the city to see him, he called me. A call up here to Providence—"the country," he calls it—is a long-distance affair, very daunting. He hazards it rarely and only in emergencies. His voice had broken through distance to me, quavering, when he went into the hospital with pneumonia a few years ago, and once when his brother Abie died in Miami, to weep for twenty minutes while he cursed himself for the bill he was running up. This time, hearing his voice saying "Joey?" as if he doubted it was really me, I was alarmed.

"What's the matter, Pop? Are you okay?" Our suitcases were already out on the bed waiting for our New York City clothes.

"I'm okay, a little cold, I cough, but I'm okay," he told me and his equivocal voice seemed to wait there for me to tell him why he had called.

"Listen, sonny," he said finally, "I got to ask you something."

"Couldn't it wait? We're—"

"I wouldn't bother you without a reason. I don't need a phone call on my bill, you know."

"Well—" I hadn't intended to be so uninviting. It was all to the good when he made himself push against the world; using the telephone was the challenge to him that climbing up a sheer rockface would be to me. I could see him pacing while he held the phone; I do that too.

"Listen. What do you think if—I want you should tell me if you think this is such a good idea."

"Right. Okay." I imagined he was going to ask to change rooms and be done with his room-mate's *mishugas* once and for all. Play the tv till midnight. Sing in the shower.

"What?" he asked.

"All right, go ahead."

"What head?"

"Nothing. Tell me what you want to tell me." Janie and the kids sometimes come running when they don't know I'm on the phone with him. "Who are you shouting at?" they ask. He must hear me if we had one of those ancient undersea connections. "Pop. What idea?"

"I'm thinking I might get married, Joey. But I'm not so sure."

I bit my lips closed to keep from laughing. Then, guilty, I made my voice approximate simple interest and possibly even approval. "Married," I yelled. "Married?" The world was an astounding place; maybe if I leaped out the bedroom window I could fly.

"I don't want you should think this has to do with Mommy," he began, and I listened speechless while he explained. Then I went downstairs and told Jane he had finally said something surprising.

And so we were ready to meet Frieda the next day. "Is Frieda grandpa's fiancée?" Timmy asked, saying the words as if he were holding a fishbone by its repulsive tip. I said I didn't know. My father had asked my advice but I hadn't given any.

Usually he was seated just inside the front door of the hotel so that he could jump up anxiously at the sight of every clump of people who approached. This time, confirming my understanding that all his routines had changed, there was no one waiting for us.

The woman at the desk rang his room; no one answered. (His room-mate, he had told me incidentally, was in the hospital for tests—"He was falling down"—and, although such an intimation of mortality had always frightened and depressed him before, not for the room-mate's sake but for his own, this time he was too distracted by his own changing fortunes to take much notice.)

The receptionist suggested we try the card room where they were having their daily bingo. "He's in there a lot," she told us amiably. "And *she's* a hot one at games," she added indiscreetly. "Let me tell you, she wins real money!" We were dealing with common knowledge, then. The boys giggled and Jane looked grim.

We walked down the long hall that had the mildly antiseptic, beige, asensual ambience of a Holiday Inn. The door to the card room was open and I could see him from the hall, seated next to the cage in which the bingo pieces flopped and fluttered like lottery tickets, so that he could hear the caller with his better ear. Which one was Frieda, then?

On one side of him sat a dishevelled woman with hair twice as red as Jane's but slightly purple at the roots, as if it were emerging from a wound. She had the look of someone on loan from a back ward. On his other side sat a *ketselah,* a little cat, smaller, under what looked like a real lace shawl: my mother would have called her quality. She had a good hairdresser for her dry sherry curls (or was it a wig?) and a vaguely European tinge of irony, or tolerance, to her smile. Everyone here was European, of course, but I don't mean Poland, I don't mean Odessa, I mean, say, middle-class Prague or Vienna. *Café mit Schlag.*

And she was raking in the chips. "Good Lord," Janie breathed at my side. She was thinking, I know it, of my mother's orthopedic shoes, the plastic flounce and flowers that spread like a rash to cover every undefended piece in the now-dispersed apartment, the Decline of Rome wall decorations, all pillars and crumbling temples, or Gainsborough ladies in gilt frames. She was thinking of the little piece of paper we had found in my mother's coat pocket when we were going through her "effects," the rain check from Waldbaum's for a 39¢ cauliflower. This Frieda, you could tell from a hundred yards, knew her antiques, her armoires, her netsukes; a hundred to one she kept sachet in her bureau drawers.

Pop introduced us but not until he had pulled everybody into the hall so that we wouldn't impede the next bingo round. "You look as if you've won enough for one day," I said to Frieda as pleasantly as I could. "You must have talent."

She laughed and shrugged self-deprecatingly. Even her teeth were a cut above the hotel average. Her winnings had gone into a delicate purse that closed with a businesslike snap of finality.

What had they agreed to? I couldn't tell—on the phone my father had simply said she had "asked him" and he was "thinking about it." She had been widowed fairly recently and was lonely living alone, and so she had (admirably? shamelessly?) come to see whom she could meet here. To make a deal. She had her own money and apartment and didn't need his, her own children and grandchildren ditto. On the phone that had made sense: a frightened little woman, permanent immigrant-class like Pop, toward whom, not on purpose, I had been—I and my generation, I mean—condescending since we were children.

But this Frieda was something else again. She entertained us. I had suggested we do something besides the usual tour around the shabby block and she suggested a nice little restaurant, "strictly Kosher"— with a calculating smile at Pop that would have passed, in his book, for "consideration." It was nearby, her daughter had found it and they'd gone there for brunch just last week. "It has privacy," she promised. "Booths. Nice. Upholstered."

The boys were ostentatiously enjoying all this. I could see they liked this new wrinkle in the dull fabric of their grandfather's life. She looked like the kind of grandmother who could reach into her purse or her pockets—not that she'd done so yet—and produce charming surprises, more interesting than plain butter cookies. At very least she was an impressive gambler. Or maybe it was relief at the chance to do something besides sit in the blank air of a dozen old people with their canes and cataracts and forced cheerful Happy-to-meet-yous and their self-absorption.

As I say, she knew she was charming and so she entertained us. She told stories, in a firm quiet voice, about her father who had been a scholar in Cracow (therefore a pauper here, untrained to do a day's work). Her husband, continuing the tradition of useless luxury—a philistine she was, but honest—had been a violist. Whatever are you doing *here,* I wanted to ask her. What do you want of my poor father? He will make a woman like you more lonely still.

Well, the violist had dreamed of music, as it happened, but worked in "clucks"—that's cloaks and suits—like the rest of his *landsmen.* A cutter, then a presser at Waranow Togs on 35th Street. An unhappy man, unreconciled. For forty years, music on the side.

And that was how she had met my father, all those years ago. Some kind of garment workers' union picnic, wives invited. A rare Sunday in a park on Staten Island. An unforgettable day.

"How you met my father?" I echoed stupidly. Pop was eating a bagel, trying to negotiate it in spite of his insecure teeth. He looked at me shyly, blinking.

"He din't tell you? Sam—" She lay one wrinkled but manicured hand on his bare arm. She was a woman who made disappointment into a charming pretext for flirtation. How my mother would have laughed. "Sam! A *tschotskele!*" she'd have said. A little trinket. But Frieda turned her widened eyes on all of us with innocent enthusiasm. "Yes—he didn't tell you we knew each other in the old days? So when I met him here, what a surprise. A shock! Children—" and she fixed them, unfairly I thought, in her softening gaze and put one hand helpless on her chest as if to still her heart's persistent amazement. "Can you imagine, this old tired lonely lady comes out here to a strange place, she doesn't know a single soul—but, you know, my daughter, my son thought it would be good for me to get out from my apartment, they said it wasn't healthy to be all the time alone. And they were right, now I can see that!" The boys were attentive to her gaiety even if it was the kind of love story that only brought forth from them retching noises when it concerned the young and the beautiful. "And who do I meet the very first day, I'm sitting next to him at supper, they put me there, you know, just like that, and they bring the soup and I look at him—"

My father is embarrassed. He struggles with the cream cheese, which will not spread evenly on his bagel. Timmy reaches across unsmiling and does it for him. "Thanks, sonny," Pop says, shame-faced. Do you know you will be a nursemaid? I want to ask this stranger. Do you know he gets lost on his way to the bathroom? He lived with us for a year after my mother died, and there wasn't a day I came home not expecting the house to have burned down because he'd left the gas on again, long after the kettle had gone dry.

I wasn't used to complex and contradictory feelings in my father's presence, I have to admit that—except for the contradiction of loving someone you don't respect. About myself and the way I live my life, he is impossibly ignorant, try as I might to enlighten him: beginning back when I first refused to put on my galoshes for the rain, that old story, I have been a confusing rebellious undutiful son whom he has loved, as I love him, in spite of all. (Had I been lovable on his terms I'd have killed myself long ago.) That I should have become (happy or not) an impecunious writer instead of a doctor or, at worst, a businessman, has been an unforgivable affront to his dreams for me. My working wife, the dishevelment of our house—no bedroom set, no wall-to-wall—have only been corroborations. He is a straightforward little man desperate for solvency, invisibility, silence. Tit for tat, I failed him, he failed me.

Now what am I to think?

Why does this woman want him? He is a live male, in better shape than most—two eyes, however cloudy; two ears, however shot; vestiges of a sense of humor, though that was better when he could hear.

No stick to lean on, no apparent illnesses. Perhaps that makes him a prize. Is he flattered? Does he want to get out of this hotel because, comfortable as it is, you live in public here? Does he see her as a woman? What would he *do* with a woman besides hand her his dirty socks, his underwear?

We do not talk marriage; or, that is, we talk around it by admiring her preferred proofs of ownership: pictures of her Sheryl, a teacher; her Arthur, a podiatrist with blow-dried hair and stunning practice; their children; a polaroid of her living room, which is not so different, actually, from my mother's: Italian Renaissance chairs, pseudo, only no plastic to protect them from the depredations of use. It is not so much her dowry as the bride-price, I am thinking, studying the stubborn hairs that sprout like weeds from my father's nearest ear.

Later, when we'd left her—awkwardly—in the lobby of the hotel where she claimed she had some business with a friend but hoped she'd see us again soon (were we off to Providence immediately or would we take advantage of the wonderful city, the shops, the shows?) I went up to my father's room alone with him. He looked deflated, though for a man who hasn't much wind in his small sails to begin with, that's a matter of conjecture. "You like her, Joe?" he asked me, afraid to meet my eyes.

"She's—fine, Pop. A lovely woman. Very well-preserved." I hated to say that, it always made me think of embalming, on the one hand, and a feat against great odds on the other. But I sometimes found myself purposely blunt with him, if not downright cruel. Partly it was to fulfill his disappointment in me, to rub his nose in it since he'd think it anyway. But also I think I did it out of disrespect, as if I knew his hide was so thick nothing I said could penetrate to sting him. How could I ask what she saw in him? I made it a question about calculation which he, ever the paranoid, could appreciate.

"What she wants? I don't know, Joey, but it's true. Living alone is no way. Especially a woman, all the way out there on Ocean Parkway by herself. . . ." He left the meaningful details to my imagination. "She's a good woman. Not selfish. Anyway, she's got her own."

"A little—fancy, maybe—in her habits? Do you think?"

He shrugged. "You know, I told her she wouldn't get much from me in the—you know—that department." He raised his eyebrows on "that," which made it sound like what my mother had darkly referred to as "dorten"—"down *there*," that island that was to be isolated from thought, speech, and, most important, touch. "Not like before."

I assumed the "before" was his marriage."Well, there are lots of ways men and women can be friends," I said, and wondered if that sounded as pious as it felt. "She's probably not interested in—she just sounds lonely."

"Before she was always very—she's a modest woman, considering she's what you would call attractive."

The conversation was getting deeper than I tended to expect with my father. "Before she was modest? Pop, what do you mean, before?"

"*Before.*"

"When you met her on that picnic, you mean?"

His eyes lit for just an instant with a warmth I had myself seen often before I was, say, twelve.

"You met her—more than at that picnic? You got to know her?"

He shrugged again, this time not for vagueness but for its opposite: detailed memory he did not care to discuss. I sat down gingerly on his room-mate's bright blue bedspread and clasped my hands between my knees. "A lot of things I wouldn't tell you, sonny. A father wouldn't tell his son certain things. You shouldn't be mad—"

"You knew her—well? For very long?"

He was looking out the window, though the blinds were three-quarters closed. "Oy, sonny," he said the way he did when something hurt him. "What can I say? Not long enough."

"Did—" I couldn't ask if my mother knew about it. "It" was not so very horrible, considering the facts of their marriage, or not even considering: my marriage is perfectly fine. But I had no memory in forty years of having addressed a single sentence to my father's back.

"Nobody knew it, Mommy never, you never. Not even Harry either."

"Harry."

"Her husband, Harry Abrahams. He was a nice man. He had some temper but when he wasn't mad. . . . Not what you call a hard worker but a nice man." He twirled the string of the blinds in his hand. "We only wanted nobody should get hurt." He looked at me briefly, to check my face. All I knew about my face was that it felt very red, hot, inflamed with confusion.

"What happened, then?" I managed to ask. I think I was stuck somewhere between laughter and a huge chest-clearing shout, a massive bleating beyond good or bad taste, beyond a son's discretion. "What?!" I wanted to yell. "What?!" like Archie's father in the comic strip.

"Once we almost—people were asking a lot of questions. So we couldn't take no more chances."

"Pop," I said from where I sat. I wanted to touch him, comfort both of us, but he was very calm, very distant from this tumult in my chest. "Were you glad? Did it—" I looked down, embarrassed. "Were you happy?"

"Happy? With her?" He hadn't mentioned her name once. He laughed. "I was all the time looking over my shoulder Mommy shouldn't find out. I don't know if that was so happy." He ran his hands hard along the sides of his head, where the remaining fringes of his grey stubble grew; it was not a gesture I recognized, probably something he did when he had a full head of hair. "So anyway, Joey, you children with your happy, all the time happy this and not-so-happy that—how do you know what this happy feels like?"

It was the thing that had separated us, really: my choice to be happy in my life, not simply "comfortable." "You'd have known," I said with a bitterness I thought nervy but couldn't take back. "Well, then, why did you do it? Why would you take such a chance?" If it wasn't for joy, I meant, if it wasn't for ecstasy. I saw him trudging up from the subway with the Journal-American under his arm, and sometimes the Daily News or the Post if he had found one abandoned on the train, summer, winter, all the time except the slack season when there was no work. I couldn't imagine the mechanics of an affair in the life of a man of such regular habits. Did he really go to union meetings when he said he did? Or to play pinochle?

"Why?" he echoed. He had sat down facing me, in his familiar defeated slouch. All his life my father has looked as if the chairs and mattresses he sat on were too soft. "Why?" He shook his head. "She was a nice woman, I told you. Very lively. A good talker. She dressed good, it was a pleasure to sit by her." He looked to see if I understood. "And miserable, all the time he made her sad. I don't know about his problem, what it was. Maybe the music. He thought he was a genius, a Heifetz, the world should see it, so all the time he was taking it out on her. How she suffered by him! I don't know what it was."

No matter what kind of English a man spoke he could be an adulterer, I thought. The word seemed hollow, as if its meaning had spilled out of it, leaving a dry pod with no mischief in it. I still felt as if I'd fallen hard on my stomach, though, the way I used to when I was a kid. And he was not apologizing. I was impressed.

"So are you going to marry her? Have you been dreaming of this ever since you were—"

He shrugged and looked into his baggy lap. "I don't know, sonny, it's not the same thing now. After all. Then I was, you know. . . . A man. Now." My father pulling his clothes off in a frenzy, not taking the bills and coins out of his pockets, his glasses, his comb, not laying his slacks scrupulously over the back of the fat brown armchair with the clawfoot legs to keep the crease, not putting on the pajamas my mother had ironed, striped or figured with one of those aimless silly patterns, green or gray. I used to run the drawstring through with a pin when it came out in the wash. No, my father locking the door, approaching her, this Frieda, slowly, to draw out the pleasure a little longer. I knew the dream ritual too in which everything moves incredibly fast and incredibly slowly, both. It is forbidden pleasure that leaves a scar. Memory heals ragged when it isn't repeated a thousand times. He would know, if I said that, he would recognize the crater where the shame and jeopardy lay, and the sharp ridge of healing. Everything in me heaved once, the feeling in the elevator that had made my son say "Gulp" and press his palm to his stomach.

"Well, think about it, then. You don't have to decide right now." I stood up as if this had been a routine conversation. I was glad to find my knees steady. "See how it feels to think about it. Waking up with somebody there besides old Morris." I hit Morris's bedspread with my hand.

"I don't know, Joe. Ocean Parkway, what am I going to do all the way out there?" Being with Frieda didn't seem to loom large in this proposal.

"What do you do here?" You can sit in a chair anywhere, I thought. You can wrap your *tfillin*, eat your poached egg, huddle out of the wind.

"If she could drive a car. I got my doctors' appointments, and the *shul* maybe isn't so close. Here it's convenient under one roof." He was teetering. A shove either way could do it. I embraced him, showed him how to work the radio one more time, went down to the lobby by the stairs two at a time, agitated, while he stood bewildered beside the elevator whose button he had pushed for me hospitably, the way a host watches till the car departs, taking you with it.

We began the drive toward the city in silence. Jane asked me what was wrong and I snapped at her. "Why are you angry?" she said, though I swore I wasn't angry. My father rising from the warm rumpled bed and pulling on his rough layers of clothing, shrugging on his coat, his muffler, his gloves, and coming home to the Bronx, to me and to my mother standing over the endlessly steaming *tup* of soup. Steam coming out of his mouth as he turned the corner from the hilly avenue and headed toward me where I sat in front of the apartment house, on its two wide brick steps, in exactly the same place every day, even, preposterously (and to my mother's irritation) in the dead heart of winter. It was my challenge to myself, my hardship, my fifty-pound weights, my four-minute mile, my swan dive, to sit with my corduroy knees drawn up in the three-quarter dark, tears of cold in my eyes, my gloveless hands jammed in my pockets, waiting for him, knowing it was only my secret endurance that made him come.

BOXES

My mother is packed and ready to move. But Sunday afternoon, at the last minute, she calls and says for us to come eat with her. "My icebox is defrosting," she tells me. "I have to fry up this chicken before it rots." She says we should bring our own plates and some knives and forks. She's packed most of her dishes and kitchen things. "Come on and eat with me one last time," she says, "You and Jill."

I hang up the phone and stand at the window for a minute longer, wishing I could figure this thing out. But I can't. So finally I turn to Jill and say, "Let's go to my mother's for a goodbye meal."

Jill is at the table with a Sears catalogue in front of her, trying to find us some curtains. But she's been listening. She makes a face. "Do we have to?" she says. She bends down the corner of a page and closes the catalogue. She sighs. "God, we been over there to eat two or three times in this last month alone. Is she ever actually going to leave?"

Jill always say what's on her mind. She's thirty-five years old, wears her hair short, and grooms dogs for a living. Before she became a groomer, something she likes, she used to be a housewife and mother. Then all hell broke loose. Her two children were kidnapped by her first husband and taken to live in Australia. Her second husband, who drank, left her with a broken eardrum before he drove their car through a bridge into the Elwha River. He didn't have life insurance, not to mention property-damage insurance. Jill had to borrow money to bury him, and then—can you beat it?—she was presented with a bill for the bridge repair. Plus, she had her own medical bills. She can tell this story now. She's bounced back. But she has run out of patience with my mother. I've run out of patience, too. But I don't see my options.

"She's leaving day after tomorrow," I say. "Hey, Jill, don't do any favors. Do you want to come with me or not?" I tell her it doesn't matter to me one way or the other. I'll say she has a migraine. It's not like I've never told a lie before.

"I'm coming," she says. And like that she gets up and goes into the bathroom, where she likes to pout.

We've been together since last August, about the time my mother picked to move up here to Longview from California. Jill tried to make the best of it. But my mother pulling into town just when we were trying to get our act together was nothing either of us had bargained for. Jill said it reminded her of the situation with her first husband's mother. "She was a clinger," Jill said. "You know what I mean? I thought I was going to suffocate."

It's fair to say that my mother sees Jill as an intruder. As far as she's concerned, Jill is just another girl in a series of girls who have appeared in my life since my wife left me. Someone, to her mind, likely to take away affection, attention, maybe even some money that might otherwise come to her. But someone deserving of respect? No way. I remember—how can I forget it?—she called my wife a whore before we were married, and then called her a whore fifteen years later, after she left me for someone else.

Jill and my mother act friendly enough when they find themselves together. They hug each other when they say hello or goodbye. They talk about shopping specials. But Jill dreads the time she has to spend in my mother's company. She claims my mother bums her out. She says my mother is negative about everything and everybody and ought to find an outlet, like other people in her age bracket. Crocheting, maybe, or card games at the Senior Citizens Center, or else going to church. Something, anyway, so that she'll leave us in peace. But my mother had her own way of solving things. She announced she was moving back to California. The hell with everything and everybody in this town. What a place to live! She wouldn't continue to live in this town if they gave her the place and six more like it.

Within a day or two of deciding to move, she'd packed her things into boxes. That was last January. Or maybe it was February. Anyway, last winter sometime. Now it's the end of June. Boxes have been sitting around inside her house for months. You have to walk around them or step over them to get from one room to another. This is no way for anyone's mother to live.

After a while, ten minutes or so, Jill comes out of the bathroom. I've found a roach and am trying to smoke that and drink a bottle of ginger ale while I watch one of the neighbors change the oil in his car. Jill doesn't look at me. Instead, she goes into the kitchen and puts some plates and utensils into a paper sack. But when she comes back through the living room I stand up, and we hug each other. Jill says, "It's O.K." What's O.K., I wonder. As far as I can see, nothing's O.K. But she holds me and keeps patting my shoulder. I can smell the pet shampoo on her. She comes home from work wearing the stuff. It's everywhere. Even when we're in bed together. She gives me a final pat. Then we go out to the car and drive across town to my mother's.

I like where I live. I didn't when I first moved here. There was nothing to do at night, and I was lonely. Then I met Jill. Pretty soon, after a few weeks, she brought her things over and started living with me. We didn't set any long-term goals. We were happy and we had a life together. We told each other we'd finally got lucky. But my mother didn't have anything going in her life. So she wrote me and said she'd decided on moving here. I wrote her back and said I didn't think it was such a good idea. The weather's terrible in the winter, I said. They're building a prison a few miles from town, I told her. The place is bumper-to-bumper tourists all summer, I said. But she acted as if she never got my letters, and came anyway. Then, after she'd been in town a little less than a month, she told me she hated the place. She acted as if it were my fault she'd moved here and my fault she found everything so disagreeable. She started calling me up and telling me how crummy the place was. "Laying guilt trips," Jill called it. She told me the bus service was terrible and the drivers unfriendly. As for the people at the Senior Citizens—well, she didn't want to play casino. "They can go to hell," she said, "and take their card games with them." The clerks at the supermarket were surly, the guys in the service station didn't give a damn about her or her car. And she'd made up her mind about the man she rented from, Larry Hadlock. King Larry, she called him. "He thinks he's *superior* to everyone because he has some shacks for rent and a few dollars. I wish to God I'd never laid eyes on him."

It was too hot for her when she arrived, in August, and in September it started to rain. It rained almost every day for weeks. In October it turned cold. There was snow in November and December. But long before that she began to put the bad mouth on the place and the people to the extent that I didn't want to hear about it anymore, and I told her so finally. She cried, and I hugged her and thought that was the end of it. But a few days later she started in again, same stuff. Just before Christmas she called to see when I was coming by with her presents. She hadn't put up a tree and didn't intend to, she said. Then she said something else. She said if this weather didn't improve she was going to kill herself.

"Don't talk crazy," I said.

She said, "I mean it, honey. I don't want to see this place again except from my coffin. I hate this g.d. place. I don't know why I moved here. I wish I could just die and get it over with."

I remember hanging on to the phone and watching a man high up on a pole doing something to a power line. Snow whirled around his head. As I watched, he leaned out from the pole, supported only by his safety belt. Suppose he falls, I thought. I didn't have any idea what I was going to say next. I had to say something. But I was filled with unworthy feelings, thoughts no son should admit to. "You're my mother," I said finally. "What can I do to help?"

"Honey, you can't do anything," she said. "The time for doing anything has come and gone. It's too late to do anything. I wanted to like it here. I thought we'd go on picnics and take drives together. But none of that happened. You're always busy. You're off working, you and Jill. You're never at home. Or else if you are at home you have the phone off the hook all day. Anyway, I never see you," she said.

"That's not true," I said. And it wasn't. But she went on as if she hadn't heard me. Maybe she hadn't.

"Besides," she said, "this weather's killing me. It's too damned cold here. Why didn't you tell me this was the North Pole? If you had, I'd never have come. I want to go back to California, honey. I can get out and go places there. I don't know anywhere to go here. There are people back in California. I've got friends there who care what happens to me. Nobody gives a damn here. Well, I just pray I can get through to June. If I can make it that long, if I can make it that long, if I can last to June, I'm leaving this place forever. This is the worst place I've ever lived in."

What could I say? I didn't know what to say. I couldn't even say anything about the weather. Weather was a real sore point. We said goodbye and hung up.

Other people take vacations in the summer, but my mother moves. She started moving years ago, after my dad lost his job. When that happened, when he was laid off, they sold their home, as if this were what they should do, and went to where they thought things would be better. But things weren't any better there, either. They moved again. They kept on moving. They lived in rented houses, apartments, mobile homes, and motel units even. They kept moving, lightening their load with each move they made. A couple of times they landed in a town where I lived. They'd move in with my wife and me for a while and then they'd move on again. They were like migrating animals in this regard, except there was no pattern to their movement. They moved around for years, sometimes even leaving the state for what they thought would be greener pastures. But mostly they stayed in Northern California and did their moving there. Then my dad died, and I thought my mother would stop moving and stay in one place for a while. But she didn't. She kept moving. I suggested once that she go to a psychiatrist. I even said I'd pay for it. But she wouldn't hear of it. She packed and moved out of town instead. I was desperate about things or I wouldn't have said that about the psychiatrist.

She was always in the process of packing or else unpacking. Sometimes she'd move two or three times in the same year. She talked bitterly about the place she was leaving and optimistically about the place she was going to. Her mail got fouled up, her benefit checks went off somewhere else, and she spent hours writing letters, trying to get it all straightened out. Sometimes she'd move out of an apartment house, move to another one a few blocks away, and then, a month later, move back to the place she'd left, only to a different floor or a different side of the building. That's why when she moved here I rented a house for her and saw to it that it was furnished to her liking. "Moving around keeps her alive," Jill said. "It gives her something to do. She must get some kind of weird enjoyment out of it, I guess." But enjoyment or not, Jill thinks my mother must be losing her mind. I think so, too. But how do you tell your mother this? How do you deal with her if this is the case? Crazy doesn't stop her from planning and getting on with her next move.

She is waiting at the back door for us when we pull in. She's seventy years old, has gray hair, wears glasses with rhinestone frames, and has never been sick a day in her life. She hugs Jill, and then she hugs me. Her eyes are bright, as if she's been drinking. But she doesn't drink. She quit years ago, after my dad went on the wagon. We finish hugging and go inside. It's around five in the afternoon. I smell whatever it is drifting out of her kitchen and remember I haven't eaten since breakfast. My buzz has worn off.

"I'm starved," I say.

"Something smells good," Jill says.

"I hope it tastes good," my mother says. "I hope this chicken's done." She raises the lid on a fry pan and pushes a fork into a chicken breast. "If there's anything I can't stand, it's raw chicken. I think it's done. Why don't you sit down? Sit anyplace. I still can't regulate my stove. The burners heat up too fast. I don't like electric stoves and never have. Move that junk off the chair, Jill. I'm living here like a damned gypsy. But not for much longer, I hope." She sees me looking around for the ashtray. "Behind you," she says. "On the windowsill, honey. Before you sit down, why don't you pour us some of that Pepsi? You'll have to use these paper cups. I should have told you to bring some glasses. Is the Pepsi cold? I don't have any ice. This icebox won't keep anything cold. It isn't worth a damn. My ice cream turns to soup. It's the worst icebox I've ever had."

She forks the chicken onto a plate and puts the plate on the table along with beans and coleslaw and white bread. Then she looks to see if there is anything she's forgetting. Salt and pepper! "Sit down," she says.

We draw our chairs up to the table, and Jill takes the plates out of the sack and hands them around the table to us. "Where are you going to live when you go back?" she says. "Do you have a place lined up?"

My mother passes the chicken to Jill and says, "I wrote that lady I rented from before. She wrote back and said she had a nice first-floor place I could have. It's close to the bus stop and there's lots of stores in the area. There's a bank and a Safeway. It's the nicest place. I don't know why I left there." She says that and helps herself to some coleslaw.

"Why'd you leave then?" Jill says. "If it was so nice and all." She picks up her drumstick, looks at it, and takes a bite of the meat.

"I'll tell you why. There was an old alcoholic woman who lived next door to me. She drank from morning to night. The walls were so thin I could hear her munching ice cubes all day. She had to use a walker to get around, but that still didn't stop her. I'd hear that walker *scrape, scrape* against the floor from morning to night. That and her icebox door closing." She shakes her head at all she had to put up with. "I had to get out of there. *Scrape, scrape* all day. I couldn't stand it. I just couldn't live like that. This time I told the manager I didn't want to be next to any alcoholics. And I didn't want anything on the second floor. The second floor looks out on the parking lot. Nothing to see from there." She waits for Jill to say something more. But Jill doesn't comment. My mother looks over at me.

I'm eating like a wolf and don't say anything, either. In any case, there's nothing more to say on the subject. I keep chewing and look over at the boxes stacked against the fridge. Then I help myself to more coleslaw.

Pretty soon I finish and push my chair back. Larry Hadlock pulls up in back of the house, next to my car, and takes a lawnmower out of his pickup. I watch him through the window behind the table. He doesn't look in our direction.

"What's he want?" my mother says and stops eating.

"He's going to cut your grass, it looks like," I say.

"It doesn't need cutting," she says. "He cut it last week. What's there for him to cut?"

"It's for the new tenant," Jill says. "Whoever that turns out to be."

My mother takes this in and then goes back to eating.

Larry Hadlock starts his mower and begins to cut the grass. I know him a little. He lowered the rent twenty-five a month when I told him it was my mother. He is a widower—a big fellow, mid-sixties. An unhappy man with a good sense of humor. His arms are covered with white hair, and white hair stands out from under his cap. He looks like a magazine illustration of a farmer. But he isn't a farmer. He is a retired construction worker who's saved a little money. For a while, in the beginning, I let myself imagine that he and my mother might take some meals together and become friends.

"There's the king," my mother says. "King Larry. Not everyone has as much money as he does and can live in a big house and charge other people high rents. Well, I hope I never see his cheap old face again once I leave here. Eat the rest of this chicken," she says to me. But I shake my head and light a cigarette. Larry pushes his mower past the window.

"You won't have to look at it much longer," Jill says.

"I'm sure glad of that, Jill. But I know he won't give me my deposit back."

"How do you know that?" I say.

"I just know," she says. "I've had dealings with his kind before. They're out for all they can get."

Jill says, "It won't be long now and you won't have to have anything more to do with him."

"I'll be so glad."

"But it'll be somebody just like him," Jill says.

"I don't want to think that, Jill," my mother says.

She makes coffee while Jill clears the table. I rinse the cups. Then I pour coffee, and we step around a box marked "Knickknacks" and take our cups into the living room.

Larry Hadlock is at the side of the house. Traffic moves slowly on the street out in front, and the sun has started down over the trees. I can hear the commotion the mower makes. Some crows leave the phone line and settle onto the newly cut grass in the front yard.

"I'm going to miss you, honey," my mother says. Then she says, "I'll miss you, too, Jill. I'm going to miss both of you."

Jill sips from her coffee and nods. Then she says, "I hope you have a safe trip back and find the place you're looking for at the end of the road."

When I get settled—and this is my last move, so help me—I hope you'll come and visit," my mother says. She looks at me and waits to be reassured.

"We will," I say. But even as I say it I know it isn't true. My life caved in on me down there, and I won't be going back.

"I wish you could have been happier here," Jill says. "I wish you'd been able to stick it out or something. You know what? Your son is worried sick about you."

"Jill," I say.

But she gives her head a little shake and goes on. "Sometimes he can't sleep over it. He wakes up sometimes in the night and says, 'I can't sleep. I'm thinking about my mother.' There," she says and looks at me. "I've said it. But it was on my mind."

"How do you think I must feel?" my mother says. Then she says, "Other women my age can be happy. Why can't I be like other women? All I want is a house and a town to live in that will make me happy. That isn't a crime, is it? I hope not. I hope I'm not asking too much out of life." She puts her cup on the floor next to her chair and waits for Jill to tell her she isn't asking for too much. But Jill doesn't say anything, and in a minute my mother begins to outline her plans to be happy.

After a time Jill lowers her eyes to her cup and has some more coffee. I can tell she's stopped listening. But my mother keeps talking anyway. The crows work their way through the grass in the front yard. I hear the mower howl and then thud as it picks up a clump of grass in the blade and comes to a stop. In a minute, after several tries, Larry gets it going again. The crows fly off, back to their wire. Jill picks at a fingernail. My mother is saying that the secondhand-furniture dealer is coming around the next morning to collect the things she isn't going to send on the bus or carry with her in the car. The table and chairs, TV, sofa, and bed are going with the dealer. But he's told her he doesn't have any use for the card table, so my mother is going to throw it out unless we want it.

"We'll take it," I say. Jill looks over. She starts to say something but changes her mind.

I will drive the boxes to the Greyhound station the next afternoon and start them on the way to California. My mother will spend the last night with us, as arranged. And then, early the next morning, two days from now, she'll be on her way.

She continues to talk. She talks on and on as she describes the trip she is about to make. She'll drive until four o'clock in the afternoon and then take a motel room for the night. She figures to make Eugene by dark. Eugene is a nice town—she stayed there once before, on the way up here. When she leaves the motel, she'll leave at sunrise and should, if God is looking out for her, be in California that afternoon. And God *is* looking out for her, she knows he is. How else explain her being kept around on the face of the earth? He has a plan for her. She's been praying a lot lately. She's been praying for me, too.

"Why are you praying for him?" Jill wants to know.

"Because I feel like it. Because he's my son," my mother says. "Is there anything the matter with that? Don't we all need praying for sometimes? Maybe some people don't. I don't know. What do I know anymore?" She brings a hand to her forehead and rearranges some hair that's come loose from a pin.

The mower sputters off, and pretty soon we see Larry go around the house pulling the hose. He sets the hose out and then goes slowly back around the house to turn the water on. The sprinkler begins to turn.

My mother starts listing the ways she imagines Larry has wronged her since she's been in the house. But now I'm not listening, either. I am thinking how she is about to go down the highway again, and nobody can reason with her or do anything to stop her. What can I do? I can't tie her up, or commit her, though it may come to that eventually. I worry for her, and she is a heartache to me. She is all the family I have left. I'm sorry she didn't like it here and wants to leave. But I'm never going back to California. And when that's clear to me I understand something else, too. I understand that after she leaves I'm probably never going to see her again.

I look over at my mother. She stops talking. Jill raises her eyes. Both of them look at me.

"What is it, honey?" my mother says.

"What's wrong?" Jill says.

I lean forward in the chair and cover my face with my hands. I sit like that for a minute, feeling bad and stupid for doing it. But I can't help it. And the woman who brought me into this life, and this other woman I picked up with less than a year ago, they exclaim together and rise and come over to where I sit with my head in my hands like a fool. I don't open my eyes. I listen to the sprinkler whipping the grass.

"What's wrong? What's the matter?" they say.

"It's O.K.," I say. And in a minute it is. I open my eyes and bring my head up. I reach for a cigarette.

"See what I mean?" Jill says. "You're driving him crazy. He's going crazy with worry over you." She is on one side of my chair, and my mother is on the other side. They could tear me apart in no time at all.

"I wish I could die and get out of everyone's way," my mother says quietly. "So help me Hannah, I can't take much more of this."

"How about some more coffee?" I say. "Maybe we ought to catch the news," I say. "Then I guess Jill and I better head for home."

Two days later, early in the morning, I say goodbye to my mother for what may be the last time. I've let Jill sleep. It won't hurt if she's late to work for a change. The dogs can wait for their baths and trimmings and such. My mother holds my arm as I walk her down the steps to the driveway and open the car door for her. She is wearing white slacks and a white blouse and white sandals. Her hair is pulled back and tied with a scarf. That's white, too. It's going to be a nice day, and the sky is clear and already blue.

On the front seat of the car I see maps and a thermos of coffee. My mother looks at these things as if she can't recall having come outside with them just a few minutes ago. She turns to me then and says, "Let me hug you once more. Let me love your neck. I know I won't see you for a long time." She puts an arm around my neck, draws me to her, and then begins to cry. But she stops almost at once and steps back, pushing the heel of her hand against her eyes. "I said I wouldn't do that, and I won't. But let me get a last look at you anyway. I'll miss you, honey," she says. "I'm just going to have to live through this. I've already lived through things I didn't think were possible. But I'll live through this, too, I guess." She gets into the car, starts it, and runs the engine for a minute. She rolls her window down.

"I'm going to miss you," I say. And I *am* going to miss her. She's my mother, after all, and why shouldn't I miss her? But, God forgive me, I'm glad, too, that it's finally time and that she is leaving.

"Goodbye," she says. "Tell Jill thanks for supper last night. Tell her I said goodbye."

"I will," I say. I stand there wanting to say something else. But I don't know what. We keep looking at each other, trying to smile and reassure each other. Then something comes into her eyes, and I believe she is thinking about the highway and how far she is going to have to drive that day. She takes her eyes off me and looks down the road. Then she rolls her window up, puts the car into gear, and drives to the intersection, where she has to wait for the light to change. When I see she's made it into traffic and headed toward the highway, I go back in the house and drink some coffee. I feel sad for a while, and then the sadness goes away and I start thinking about other things.

A few nights later my mother calls to say she is in her new place. She is busy fixing it up, the way she does when she has a new place. She tells me I'll be happy to know she likes it just fine to be back in sunny California. But she says there's something in the air where she is living, maybe it's pollen, that is causing her to sneeze a lot. And the traffic is heavier than she remembers from before. She doesn't recall there being so much traffic in her neighborhood. Naturally, everyone still drives like crazy down there. "California drivers," she says. "What else can you expect?" She says it's hot for this time of the year. She doesn't think the air-conditioning unit in her apartment is working right. I tell her she should talk to the manager. "She's never around when you need her," my mother says. She hopes she hasn't made a mistake in moving back to California. She waits before she says anything else.

I'm standing at the window with the phone pressed to my ear, looking out at the lights from town and at the lighted houses closer by. Jill is at the table with the catalogue, listening.

"Are you still there?" my mother asks. "I wish you'd say something."

I don't know why, but it's then I recall the affectionate name my dad used sometimes when he was talking nice to my mother—those times, that is, when he wasn't drunk. It was a long time ago, and I was a kid, but always, hearing it, I felt better, less afraid, more hopeful about the future. "*Dear*," he'd say. He called her "dear" sometimes—a sweet name. "Dear," he'd say, "if you're going to the store, will you bring me some cigarettes?" Or "Dear, is your cold any better?" "Dear, where is my coffee cup?"

The word issues from my lips before I can think what else I want to say to go along with it. "Dear." I say it again. I call her "dear." "Dear, try not to be afraid," I say. I tell my mother I love her and I'll write to her, yes. Then I say goodbye, and I hang up.

For a while I don't move from the window. I keep standing there, looking out at the lighted houses in our neighborhood. As I watch, a car turns off the road and pulls into a driveway. The porch light goes on. The door to the house opens and someone comes out on the porch and stands there waiting.

Jill turns the pages of her catalogue, and then she stops turning them. "This is what we want," she says. "This is more like what I had in mind. Look at this, will you." But I don't look. I don't care five cents for curtains. "What is it you see out there, honey?" Jill says. "Tell me."

What's there to tell? The people over there embrace for a minute, and then they go inside the house together. They leave the light burning. Then they remember, and it goes out.

/

AT THE PRADO:

A SHORT STORY

His father went to Cuba, then Newark, New Jersey, then finally White Plains. He did not live to see the Socialists' rise to power, but he extracted a deathbed promise that Thomas would return when Spain was free. Thirty-eight years old, an Assistant Program Manager in a Public Television Station, Thomas went to Europe with some frequency. Once he spent two weeks on a piece about the Basques near Narbonne and Perpignan. He respected his father's injunction, however, and did not cross the border into Spain. He saw the movie *To Die in Madrid* and admired Yves Montand. He did not encounter but claimed he could nonetheless see the shadowy continual presence of the Guardia Civil.

Claudia, their five year old, slept on the ride into town; she had covered her head with her blanket during the fight scenes in flight. Her elder sisters, the twins, said Sly Stallone was cool; he could be a real boxer, they said. When Felipe Gonzalez became Prime Minister of Spain, Thomas took four-thousand dollars from the scrimped and set-by legacy his father had bequeathed, and bought five round-trip tickets to Madrid. Gonzalez, he had read, celebrated the Socialist victory in the Palace Hotel; he therefore booked rooms at the Palace.

The day was cool and clear. Elsie needed a shower, she said. While she unpacked and the twins wrangled over who got the roll-bed and examined the bidet, he stood at the window, watching the street. He had gone through the procedures of bereavement four months earlier, dutiful at the funeral home and at the reception and then at the burial grounds. He had known few people at the service; he was an only son.

At ten they assembled downstairs. The rotunda of the Palace was a domed vault, with a suspended chandelier, and sofas and tables arranged in a circle for tea. A waiter approached. He wore a white jacket and carried a tray; he offered them napkins and menus. Thomas deciphered the text; the children wanted cocoa. Claudia had her blanket—a woven blue square with frayed silk edging, and a corner which she sucked to the correct consistency and shape. The twins, eleven, were missing the first week of school. This pleased them. They asked repeatedly, "What time is it in Lexington?" and when he translated the time they argued as to what everyone was doing in class, which homework assignments were easy, and if they had new seats. He placed his order, pointing to the hot chocolate and coffee—"*con leche*," Elsie said, "that much I know"—and croissants and brioches on the list. The waiter bowed and withdrew.

"Did you see his buttons?" Betsy asked. "They look like gold."

"Real gold," said Susan. "I bet they're doubloons."

"What?" asked Claudia.

"Doubloons. The ancient Spanish treasure horde that sank to the sea in gallons."

"Galleons," Thomas said.

"What time is it?" Betsy asked, and then she said, "It's time to go home on the bus."

The hot chocolate was not to their taste. "It's bitter," they chorussed. "It's awful." They wrinkled up their noses at the sight of the steamed milk. Elsie lit a cigarette. "We'll go to the museum first," he said. "The Prado. And then we'll find a wonderful place to eat lunch."

He tipped the waiter lavishly; light streamed through the glass dome. He piloted his daughters through the lobby, then out into the street. Traffic was thick. They crossed an avenue—the Gran Villa—in front of the hotel; vendors sold postcards and paintings and lace. The

Prado rose in front of them; they paid and entered. Claudia had a stomachache, she said. He promised her a piggy-back on the way to the restaurant. "No, now," she said, and he swung her onto his shoulders. "For just a few minutes, OK?" She positioned herself on his neck.

Elsie had heard of a way to interest children in museums. Her friend claimed it worked like a charm. You buy some postcards at the entrance lobby and the children each get a postcard and have to find the original in the museum. This provides them with a sense of purpose, a mission, she said; it forces them to look. It turns the history of art into a treasure hunt. "Let's try it," Thomas said.

He told the girls there were three great Spanish painters. There were more than three, of course, but the most famous were El Greco, Goya and Velázquez. El Greco means "the Greek." The twins had seen a movie called *The Toy*. In the movie there was an oil portrait of a rich man's wife, and when someone pressed a button her clothes fell away. This was based on two paintings by Goya, Thomas explained, and the museum had both. In one portrait Goya showed a woman— Maja—completely naked; this portrait he kept for himself. The other was for sale. Susan found the postcard of the *Maja Desnuda*, and she said, "My dibs." Betsy took riding lessons at home. She chose a Velázquez portrait of a princess on a horse. "That leaves El Greco," he told Claudia. "Which picture do you choose?"

She bent across him, pondering. At length she picked a Crucifixion scene. "Domenico Theotocopoulos," Thomas said to Elsie. "That was his real name. They think he was an astigmatic; that's why his people are twisted."

The museum was cold. The strategy worked. The twins were delighted, tearing through the halls and rooms and paying no attention to a painting if they did not hold it in their hands. They would enter a gallery, glance at its display and leave. "Not here," they said. "Nothing here."

The Goya collection was large. There were portraits of courtiers in lace, panels representing bucolic and pastoral pleasures. There was an oil painting of a firing squad. A man in a white shirt, hands raised in surrender, not two feet from the rifle that would murder him, his brother at his feet—Thomas tried to show this to the twins. They would not pause. There were nightmare visions as Goya drew deaf and old: the bleak staring shapes of disaster, the processionals of death. A giant chewed a boy's head. The head itself was swallowed and the upper part of the body mere meat; the torso became more human, descending, and resolved itself down into legs. His daughters danced through the room.

When she found the naked *Maja*, Susan held up her postcard, triumphant. They ascended to the second floor and Betsy discovered her Velázquez; they admired the horse's mane and how carefully Velázquez painted flesh. Claudia ran ahead of them. "That's motivation," Elsie said. She was wearing her red jacket and blue dress and yellow boots; she leaped at the *Crucifixion*, shouting, "Daddy, this is it!" She thrust the postcard up against the surface of the oil, saying, "Look, this man is lying down both places; look, it's blue exactly there, it's blue!"

The guard, alarmed, advanced on her. The room was full. "Don't touch it," Thomas said. For some minutes they studied the composition, its elongated shapes. Thomas showed them what little he knew: the disproportion in El Greco between body length and the size of the head, the twisted intensity of Christ's features, the fierce white glow of flesh. It was quarter to twelve. "The place of the Muses," he said. "That's what Museum means."

"I'm hungry," said the twins in unison. They agreed to leave.

Crossing the Gran Villa, he again bore Claudia piggyback. She kicked him when the green man in the traffic light began to walk; he wondered if the vendors recognized them now. They looked at newsstands and garages, the facades of government buildings, the January sales. "We could do a story," he told Elsie, "on Madrid. The cultural bias here maybe. Did you hear that the King wrecked his pelvis?"

"Where?"

"Skiing. In Gstaad, I think, or maybe Saint Moritz. So he failed to appear in the Plaza Mayor in order to distribute gifts. That's what I mean by the cultural bias; how different is it now from when Franco was in power?"

They found a restaurant. As of twelve o'clock, there were no other customers; the headwaiter commended shrimp. "I need a drink," Elsie said. He ordered wine. Claudia asked for her blanket, and they could not find it; there was panic at the table. They searched in the cloakroom and in their pockets and in the sleeves of their coats. They looked on the floor and in Elsie's handbag repeatedly; the blanket was not there. They asked if she was certain she had carried it to the museum, or if she left it in the hotel; they remembered having seen the blanket in the lounge.

"I'll go back and look," Thomas said. He left in irritation; Claudia had lost her blanket several times before. There were always obstacles: a stomachache, a bloody nose, a sleepless child who needed sleep, a gallery transformed into an amusement park. He started for the Prado, scanning the pavement; they had not walked far. The blanket had been made for Claudia by a friend of his father's in Rye. He did not know if she—he hunted her name: Mrs. Rachel Colombi—were still alive. A blanket appeared in the mail, but there were other blankets and they had had no way of knowing which one Claudia would choose. She slept with this one and sucked at its edging until it acquired the smell and particular texture and shape that made it indispensable; these things happen, Elsie said, and who knows what makes it happen, no one knows.

Claudia took the blanket everywhere. He had had a teddy bear but could not remember having been so needy; she carried the blanket to play group and friends' houses and restaurants and in the car. It was not on the street. It was not on the bench where they had paused nor in the lobby of the Prado where they purchased cards. His Spanish faltering, he asked the guards if they had found a blanket and if there was such a location, in the museum, as a Lost and Found. After much discussion, they pointed him upstairs. Two old men shared a newspaper by a turnstile; they sat on folding chairs. They had not shaved. He asked them if a blanket had been found. Aggrieved, they shook their heads. One of them spoke English and penned, laboriously, a message saying, "Have you found a baby's blanket. Blue?" He wrote it in large upper-case letters, underlining MANTA and AZUL? Thomas received this with thanks.

Next he returned to the Palace and inquired at the desk; they had found nothing. He took his keys and searched their rooms, entertaining for the first time the reality of loss. He retraced his steps and looked inside the wastepaper containers on the Gran Villa, in the gutters and construction bins. He approached policemen with the printed message, holding it out for inspection as if mute. At length he returned to the restaurant and entered empty-handed; Claudia looked up at him, tearful. "You didn't find it," she said.

"No."

"Where *is* it, Mommy?"

"Darling, I don't know," said Elsie. "I haven't any idea."

They asked him if he asked at the museum; he said yes. He detailed his route: he had searched the lobby of the Palace, and their suite. The table had been set for five, and the children had been eating breadsticks and carrots; the twins liked olives, and there were many olive pits. Elsie poured wine. "She's been very brave so far. We've been hoping that you'd find it. She hasn't yet lost hope."

"Blanket's lonely," Claudia said.

"Yes."

"I miss my blanket." Sobbing, she put her head on the table.

"Maybe it's not lost," he said.

"It *is*."

"I'll look again."

She lifted her pale face. "It's in the street."

"Maybe it's in blanket heaven," Susan said. He could not tell if she were being sympathetic. Then she added, "You can sleep with my rabbit tonight."

"I want *blanket*."

"We'll get you another," he said.

"It's not the same."

"Of course not. But I'll ask that very nice lady—the lady who made it, the one who loved you so much before you were born that she made you a blanket—I'll ask her to get us another."

She was not mollified. She sat cradled in the crook of Elsie's arm. "I miss it too." said Elsie. "I'm really really sorry it's not here."

The waiter brought shrimp. The twins shared chicken; Claudia did not eat. They spent the afternoon consoling her; it did not work. She was being brave, they said, being hopeful and grown-up. He looked beneath the taxis in the taxi stand.

Late that night in the Palace, Claudia could not sleep. Elsie lay with her and stroked her head; he leaned, in the next room, against the dark blue drapery and watched the lights of Madrid. His father used to say the town lived only after midnight: the Madrileno embraces politics and women and religion in the dark. Elsie appeared at his side. "I feel terrible," she said. "It took her all that time to fall asleep."

"She'll get over it."

"I won't. Twenty years from now I'll still think of this city as the place she lost her blanket. Tomorrow let's go back again. Back to the Prado, I mean."

What goes is irrecoverable; what is lost stays lost. "My father was born here," he said.

Richard Ford

FIREWORKS

Eddie Starling sat at the kitchen table at noon reading the newspaper. Outside in the street some neighborhood kids were shooting firecrackers. The Fourth of July was a day away, and every few minutes there was a lot of noisy popping followed by a hiss then a huge boom loud enough to bring down an airplane. It was giving him the jitters, and he wished some parent would go out and haul the kids inside.

Starling had been out of work six months—one entire selling season and part of the next. He had sold real estate, and he had never been off work any length of time in his life. Though he had begun to wonder, after a certain period of time not working, if you couldn't simply forget *how* to work, forget the particulars, lose the reasons for it. And once that happened, he worried, it could become possible never to hold another job as long as you lived. To become a statistic: the chronically unemployed. The thought worried him.

Outside in the street he heard what sounded like kids' noises again. They were up to something suspicious, and he stood up to look out, just when the phone rang.

"What's new on the home front?" Lois's voice said. Lois had gone back to work tending bar near the airport and always tried to call up in good spirits.

"Status quo. Hot." Starling walked to the window, holding the receiver, and peered out. In the middle of the street some kids he'd never seen before were getting ready to blow up a tin can using an enormous firecracker. "Some kids are outside blowing up something."

"Anything good in the paper?"

"Nothing promising."

"Well," Lois said. "Just be patient, hon. I know it's hot. Listen, Eddie, do you remember those priests who were always setting fire to themselves on TV? Exactly when were they? We were trying to remember here. Was it '68 or '72? Nobody could remember to save their life."

"Sixty-eight was Kennedy," Starling said. "They weren't just setting themselves on fire for TV, though. They were in Asia."

"Okay. But when was Vietnam exactly?"

The kids lit the firecracker under the can and went running away down the street, laughing. For a moment Starling stared directly at the can, but just then a young woman came out of the house across the street. As she stepped into her yard the can went boom, and the woman leaped back and put her hands into her hair.

"Christ, what was that!" Lois said. "It sounded like a bomb."

"It was those kids," Starling said.

"The scamps," Lois said. "I guess they're hot, too, though."

The woman was very thin—too thin to be healthy, Starling thought. She was in her twenties and had on dull yellow shorts and no shoes. She walked out into the street and yelled something vicious at the kids, who were far down the street now. Starling knew nothing more about her than he did about anybody else in the neighborhood. The name on the mailbox had been taped over before he and Lois had moved in. A man lived with the woman and worked on his car in the garage late at night.

The woman walked slowly back across her little yard to her house. At the top step she turned and looked at Starling's house. He stared at her, and the woman went inside and closed the door.

"Eddie, take a guess who's here," Lois said.

"Who's where?"

"In the bar. One wild guess."

"Arthur Godfrey," Starling said.

"Arthur Godfrey. That's great," Lois said. "No, it's Louie. He just waltzed in the door. Isn't that amazing?"

Louie Reiner was Lois's previous husband. Starling and Reiner had been business acquaintances of a sort before Lois came along, and had co-brokered some office property at the tail end of the boom. Reiner had been in real estate then, along with everybody else. Reiner and Lois had stayed married six weeks, then they had gone over to Reno and gotten an annulment. A year later Lois married Starling. That had all been in '76, and Lois didn't talk about it or about Reiner anymore. Louis had disappeared somewhere—he'd heard Europe. He didn't feel like he had anything against Louie now, though he wasn't particularly happy he was around.

"Just take a guess what Louie's doing?" Lois said. Water had started to run where Lois was.

"Who knows. Washing dishes. How should I know?"

Lois repeated what Starling said and some people laughed. He heard Louie's voice saying, "Well, *excuuuse* me."

"Seriously, Ed. Louie's an extraditer." Lois laughed. Hah.

"What's that mean?" Starling said.

"It means he travels the breadth of the country bringing people back here so they can go to jail. He just brought a man back from Montana who'd done nothing more than pass a forty-seven-dollar bad check, which doesn't seem worth it to me. Louie isn't in uniform, but he's got a gun and a little beeper."

"What's he doing there?" Starling said.

"His girlfriend's coming in at the airport from Florida," Lois said. "He's a lot fatter than he used to be, too, though he wouldn't like me to say that, would you, Louie?" Starling heard Reiner say "*Excuuuse* me" again. "Do you want to talk to him?"

"I'm busy right now."

"Busy doing what, eating lunch? You're not busy."

"I'm fixing dinner," Starling lied.

"Talk to Louie, Eddie."

Starling wanted to hang up. He wished Reiner would go back to wherever he came from.

"Helloooo dere," Reiner said.

"Who left your cage open, Reiner?"

"Come on down here and have a drink, Starling, and I'll tell you all about it. I've seen the world since I saw you. Italy, France, the islands. You know what an Italian girl puts behind her ears to make herself more attractive?"

"I don't want to know," Starling said.

"That's not what Lois says." Reiner laughed a horselaugh.

"I'm busy. Some other time, maybe."

"Sure you are," Reiner said. "Listen, Eddie, get off your face and come down here. I'll tell you how we can both retire in six months. Honest to God. This is not real estate.

"I already retired," Starling said. "Didn't Lois tell you?"

"Yeah, she told me a lot of things," Reiner said.

He could hear Lois say, "Please don't be a nerd, Eddie. Who needs nerds?" Some people laughed again.

"I shouldn't even be talking about this on the phone. It's that hot." Reiner's voice fell to a whisper. He was covering the mouthpiece of the receiver, Starling thought. "These are Italian rugs, Starling. I swear to God. From the neck of the sheep, the neck only. You only get tips on things like this in law enforcement."

"I told you. I'm retired. I retired early," Starling said.

"Eddie, am I going to have to come out there and arrest you?"

"Try it," Starling said. "I'll beat the shit out of you, then laugh about it."

He heard Reiner put the phone down and say something he couldn't make out. Then he heard Reiner shout out, "Stay on your face then, cluck!"

Lois came on the line again. "Baby, why don't you come down here?" A blender started in the background, and a big cheer went up. "We're all adults. Have a Tanqueray on Louie. He's on all-expenses. There might be something to this. Louie's always got ideas."

"Reiner's just got ideas about you. Not me." He heard Reiner say to Lois to tell him—Starling—to forget it. "Tell Reiner to piss up a rope."

"Try to be nice," Lois said. "Louie's being nice. Eddie—"

Starling hung up.

When he worked, Starling had sold business properties—commercial lots and office buildings. He had studied that in college, and when he got out he was offered a good job. People would always need a place to go to work, was his thinking. He liked the professional environment, the atmosphere of money being made, and for a while he had done very well. He and Lois had rented a nice, sunny apartment in an older part of town by a park. They bought furniture and didn't save money. While Starling worked, Lois kept house, took care of plants and fish, and attended a night class for her degree in history. They had no children, and didn't expect any. They liked the size of the town and the stores, knew shopkeepers' names and where the streets led. It was a life they could like, and better than they could both have guessed would come their way.

Then interest rates had gone sky-high, and suddenly no one wanted commercial property. Everything was rent. Starling rented space in malls and in professional buildings and in empty shops downtown where older businesses had moved out and leather stores, health food, and copy shops moved in. It was a holding action, Starling thought, until people wanted to spend again.

Then he had lost his job. One morning, his boss at the agency asked him back to his private office along with a fat woman named Beverley, who'd been there longer than Starling had. His boss told them he was closing down and wanted to tell them first because they'd been there longest, and he wanted them to have a chance for the other jobs. Starling remembered feeling like he was in a daze when he heard the bad news, but he remembered thanking the boss, wishing him luck, then comforting Beverley, who went to pieces in the outer office. He had gone home and told Lois, and they had gone out to dinner at a Greek restaurant that night, and gotten good and drunk.

As it turned out, though, there weren't any other jobs to get. He visited the other agencies and talked to salesmen he knew, but all of his friends were terrified of being laid off themselves and wouldn't say much. After a month, he heard that his boss hadn't closed the agency down, but had simply hired two new people to take his and Beverley's places. When he called to ask about it the boss apologized, then claimed to have an important call on another line.

In six weeks Starling had still not found a job, and when the money ran out and they could not pay the rent, he and Lois sublet the apartment to two nurses who worked at a hospital, and got out. Lois found an ad in the *Pennysaver* that said, "No Rent for Responsible Couple—House Sit Opportunity." And they had moved in that day.

The house was a ranchette in a tract of small insignificant houses on fenced-in postage-stamp lots down on the plain of the Sacramento River, out from town. The owner was an Air Force sergeant who had been stationed in Japan, and the house was decorated with Oriental tastes: wind chimes and fat, naked women stitched over silk, a red enamel couch in the living room, rice-paper lanterns on the patio. There was an old pony in the back, from when the owner had been married with kids, and a couple of wrecked cars in the carport. All the people who lived on the street, Starling noticed, were younger than the two of them. More than a few were in the Air Force and fought loud, regular arguments, and came and went at all hours. There was always a door slamming after midnight then a car starting up and racing away into the night. Starling never thought he'd find himself living in such a place.

He stacked the dishes, put the grounds in the newspaper, and emptied all the wastebaskets into a plastic bag. He intended to take the garbage for a ride. Everybody in the subdivision either drove their garbage to a dump several miles away, or toured the convenience stores and shopping malls until they found a Dumpster no one was watching. Once a Negro woman had run out of a convenience store and cursed at him for ditching his garbage in her Dumpster, and since then he'd waited till dark. This afternoon, though, he needed to get out of the house, as though with the heat and talking to Reiner there wasn't enough air inside to breathe.

He had the garbage set out the back door when the phone rang again. Sometimes car dealers called during lunch, wanting to talk to the Air Force sergeant, and Starling had learned not to answer until after one, when car salesmen all left for lunch. This time it might be Lois again, wanting him to come by the bar to see Reiner, and he didn't want to answer. Only he didn't want Lois going off some- where, and he didn't want Reiner coming over. Reiner would think the house with the pony was a comedy act.

Starling picked up the phone. "All right, what is it?"

An unfamiliar voice said, "Dad? Is that you?"

"No dads here, Reiner," Starling said.

"Dad," the voice said again, "it's Jeff."

A woman's voice came on the line. "I have a collect call to anyone from a Jeff. Will you pay for the call?"

"Wrong number," Starling said. He couldn't be sure it wasn't Reiner still.

"Dad," the voice said. It was a teenager's voice, a worried voice. "We're in awful trouble here, Dad. They've got Margie in jail."

"No, I can't help." Starling said. "I'm sorry. I can't help you."

"This party says you've got the wrong number, Jeff," the operator said.

"I know my own father's voice, don't I? Dad, for God's sake. This is serious. We're in trouble."

"I don't know any Jeffs," Starling said. "It's just the wrong num- ber."

Starling could hear whoever was on the line hit something against the phone very hard, then say, "Shit! This isn't happening, I can't believe this is happening." The voice said something to someone else who was wherever he was. Possibly a policeman.

"It's the wrong number," the operator said. "I'm very sorry."

"Me too," Starling said. "I'm sorry."

"Would you like to try another number now, Jeff?" The operator asked.

"Dad, *please* accept. Please, my God. *Please.*"

"Excuse the ring, sir," the operator said, and the line was disconnected.

Starling put down the phone and stared out the window. The three boys who had blown up the tin can were walking past, eyeing his house. They were going for more fireworks. The torn can lay in the street, and the woman across the way was watching them from her picture window, pointing them out to a man in an undershirt who did not look like the man who worked on his car at night. He wondered if the woman was married or divorced. If she had children, where were they? He wondered who it was who had called; the sergeant's kids were all too young. He wondered what kind of trouble Jeff was in, and where was he? He should've accepted the charges, said a word of consolation, or given some advice, since the kid had seemed at wit's end. He'd been in trouble in his life. He was in trouble now, in fact, but he hadn't been any help.

He drove toward town and cruised the lot at the King's Hat Drive-Inn, took a look in at the Super-Duper, then drove around behind a truck stop. The garbage was with him in the hot front seat and already smelled bad despite the plastic. It was at the Super-Duper that the Negro woman had yelled at him and threatened to turn his garbage over to the police. Starling stopped back at the Super-Duper, parked at the side of the lot by the Dumpster, and went inside, leaving the garbage in the driver's seat. A different Negro woman was inside. He bought some breakfast cereal, a bag of frozen macaroni, and a bottle of hot sauce, then went back out to the car. Another car had driven in and parked beside his, and the driver, a woman, was sitting in view of the Dumpster, waiting for someone who had gone inside. The woman might be another Super-Duper employee, Starling thought, or possibly the wife of someone in the back he hadn't noticed.

He got in his car and drove straight out to a campground beside the river, less than a mile from the house. He had come here and picnicked once with Lois, though the campground was empty now, all the loops and tables deserted. He pulled up beside a big green campground Dumpster and heaved his garbage in without getting out of the car. Beyond the Dumpster, through some eucalyptus, he could see the big brown river sliding swiftly by, pieces of yellow foam swirling in and out of the dark eddies. It was a treacherous river, he thought, full of perils. Each year someone drowned, and there were currents running deep beneath the surface. No one in his right mind would think of swimming in it, no matter how hot it got.

As he drove out he passed two motorcycles with Oregon plates, parked at the far end of the campground, and two hippies with long hair sitting on a rock, smoking. The hippies watched him when he drove by and didn't bother hiding their dope. Two young women were coming out of the bushes nearby, wearing bathing suits, and one of the hippies gave Starling the black power salute and grinned. Starling drove back out to the highway.

The hippies reminded him of San Francisco. His mother, Irma, had lived there with her last husband, Rex, who'd had money. When he was in community college Starling had lived there with them for six months, before moving with his first wife across the bay to Alameda near the airport. They had been hippies of a certain kind themselves then and had smoked dope occasionally. Jan, his first wife, had had an abortion in a student apartment right on the campus. Abortions were not easy to get then, and they'd had to call Honolulu to get a name out in Castroville. They had been married six months, and Starling's mother had had to lend them money she'd gotten from Rex.

When the man came, he brought a little metal box with him, like a fishing-tackle box. They sat in the living room of the student apartment and talked about this and that, and drank beer. The man was named Dr. Carson. He told them he was being prosecuted at that very moment and was losing his license for doing this very thing, performing abortions. But people needed help. He had three children of his own, he said, and Starling wondered if he performed abortions on his own wife. Dr. Carson said it would cost $400, and he could do it the next night, but needed all cash. Before he left he opened his metal box. There was nothing in it but fishing gear: a Pflueger reel, some monofilament line, several red-and-white Jitterbug lures. They had all three laughed. You couldn't be too cautious, Dr. Carson said. They had all liked each other and acted like they could be friends in happier days.

The next night Dr. Carson came with a metal box that looked exactly the same as the one before, green with a silver handle. He went into the bedroom with Jan and closed the door while Starling sat in the living room, watched TV, and drank beer. It was Christmastime, and Andy Williams was on, singing carols with a man in a bear suit. After a while a loud whirring noise like an expensive blender's, came out of the bedroom. It continued for a while, then stopped, then started. Starling became nervous. Dr. Carson, he knew, was mixing up his little baby, and Jan was feeling excruciating pain but wasn't making noise. Starling felt sick then with fear and guilt and helplessness. And with love. It was the first time he knew he knew what real love was, his love for his wife and for all the things he valued in his life but could so easily lose.

Later, Dr. Carson came out and said everything would be fine. He smiled and shook Starling's hand and called him Ted, which was the phony name Starling had given him. Starling paid him the money in hundreds, and when Dr. Carson drove off, Starling stood out on the tiny balcony and waved. The doctor binked his headlights, and in the distance Starling could see a small private plane settling down to the airport in the dark, its red taillight blinking like a wishing star.

Starling wondered where the hell Jan was now, or Dr. Carson, fifteen years later. Jan had gotten peritonitis and almost died after that, and when she got well she wasn't interested in being married to Eddie Starling anymore. She seemed very disappointed. Three months later she had gone to Japan, where she'd had a pen pal since high school, someone named Haruki. For a while she wrote Starling letters, then stopped. Maybe, Starling thought, she had moved back down to L.A. with her mother. He wished his own mother was alive still, and he could call her up. He was thirty-nine years old, though, and he knew it wouldn't help.

Starling drove along the river for a few miles until the wide vegetable and cantaloupe fields opened out, and the horizon extended a long way in the heat to the hazy wind line of Lombardy poplars. High, slatsided trucks sat stationed against the white skyline, and men were picking there and beyond in long, dense crews. Mexicans, Starling thought, transients who worked for nothing. It was a depressing thought. There was nothing they could do to help themselves, but it was still depressing, and Starling pulled across the road and turned back toward town.

He drove out toward the airport, along the strip where it was mostly franchises and consignment lots and little shopping plazas, some of which he had once found the tenants for. All along the way, people had put up fireworks stands for the Fourth of July, red-white-and-blue banners fluttering on the hot breeze. Some of these people undoubtedly lived out where he and Lois lived now, in the same subdivision. That would mean something, he thought, if one day you found yourself looking out at the world going past from inside a fireworks stand. Things would've gotten far out of hand when that time came, there was no arguing it.

He thought about driving past the apartment to see if the nurses who sublet it were keeping up the little yard. The nurses, Jeri and Madeline, were two big dykes with men's haircuts and baggy clothes. They were friendly types, and in the real estate business dykes were considered A-1s—good tenants. They paid their rent, kept quiet, maintained property in good order, held a firm stake in the status quo.

They were like a married couple, was the business thinking. Thinking about Jeri and Madeline, he drove past the light where their turn was, then just decided to keep driving.

There was nothing to do now, Starling thought, but drive out to the bar. The afternoon shift meant no one came in until Lois was almost ready to leave, and sometimes they could have the bar to themselves. Reiner would be gone by now and it would be cool inside, and he and Lois could have a quiet drink together, toast better cards on the next deal. They had had some good times doing nothing but sitting talking.

Lois was leaning over the jukebox across from the bar when Starling came in. Mel, the owner, took afternoons off, and the place was empty. A dark-green bar light shone over everything, and the room felt cool.

He was glad to see Lois. She had on tight black slacks and a frilly white top and looked jaunty. Lois was a jaunty woman to begin with, and he was happy he'd come.

He had met Lois in a bar called the Am-Vets down in Rio Vista. It was before she and Louie Reiner became a twosome, and when he saw her in a bar now it always made him think of things then. That had been a high time, and when they talked about it Lois liked to say, "Some people are just meant to experience the highest moments of their lives talking in bars."

Starling sat on a barstool.

"I hope you came down here to dance with your wife," Lois said, still leaning over the jukebox. She punched a selection and turned around smiling. "I figured you'd waltz in here pretty soon." Lois came by and patted him on the cheek. "I went ahead and punched in all your favorites."

"Let's have a drink first," Starling said. "I've got an edge on that needs a drink."

"Drink first, dance second," Lois said and went behind the bar and got down the bottle of Tanqueray.

"Mel wouldn't mind," Starling said.

"Mary-had-a-little-lamb," she said while she poured a glassful. She looked up at Starling and smiled. "It's five o'clock someplace on the planet. Here's to old Mel."

"And some better luck," Starling said, taking a big first drink of the gin and letting it trickle down his throat as slowly as he could.

Lois had been drinking already, he was sure, with Reiner. That wasn't the best he could have hoped for, but it could be worse. She and Reiner could be shacked up in a motel, or on their way to Reno or the Bahamas. Reiner was gone, and that was a blessing, and he wasn't going to let Reiner cast a shadow on things.

"Poor old Lou," Lois said and came around the bar with a pink drink she'd poured out of the blender.

"Poor Lou what?" Starling said.

Lois sat down beside him on a barstool and lit a cigarette. "Oh, his stomach's all shot and he's got an ulcer. He said he worries too much." She blew out the match and stared at it. "You want to hear what he drinks?"

"Who cares what a dope like Louie drinks out of a glass," Starling said.

Lois looked at him, then stared at the mirror behind the bar. The smoky mirror showed two people sitting at a bar alone. A slow country tune started to play, a tune Starling liked, and he liked the way—with the gin around it—it seemed to ease him away from his own troubles. "So tell me what Reiner drinks," he said.

"Wodka," Lois said matter-of-factly. "That's the way he says it. Wodka. Like Russian. Wodka with coconut milk—a Hawaiian Russian. He says it's for his stomach, which he says is better though it's still a wreck. He's a walking pharmacy. And he's gotten a lot fatter, too, and his eyes bulge and he wears a full Cleveland now. I don't know." Lois shook her head and smoked her cigarette. "He's got a cute girlfriend though, this Jackie, from Del Rio Beach, Florida. She looks like Little Bo Peep."

Starling tried to picture Reiner. Louie Reiner had been a large, handsome man at one time, with thick eyebrows and penetrating black eyes. A sharp dresser. He was sorry to hear Reiner was fat and bug-eyed and wore a leisure suit. It was bad luck if that was the way you looked to the world.

"How was it, seeing Louie, was it nice?" He stared at himself in the smoky mirror. He hadn't gotten fat, thank God.

"No," Lois said and dragged on her cigarette. "*He* was nice. Grown-up and what have you. But *it* wasn't nice. He didn't look healthy, and he still talked the same baloney, which was all before Jackie arrived, naturally."

"All what baloney?"

"You know that stuff, Eddie. Everybody makes *themselves* happy or unhappy. You don't leave one woman for another woman, you do it for yourself. If you can't make it with one, make it with all of them. That baloney he was always full of. Take the tour. Go big casino. That stuff. Reiner stuff."

"Reiner's big casino, all right," Starling said. "I guess he wanted you to go off with him.

"Oh sure. He said he was off to Miami next week to arrest some poor soul. He said I ought to go, and we could stay at the Fontaine-bleau or the Eden Roc or one of those sharp places."

"What about me?" Starling said. "Did I come? Or did I stay here? What about little Jackie?"

"Louie didn't mention either one of you, isn't that funny? I guess it slipped his mind." Lois smiled and put her arm on Starling's arm. "It's just baloney, Eddie. Trashy talk."

"I wish he was here now," Starling said. "I'd use a beer bottle on him."

"I know it, hon. But you should've heard what his little girlfriend said. It was a riot. She's a real Ripley's."

"She'd need to be," Starling said.

"Really. She said if Louie ran around on her she was going to sleep with a black man. She said she already had him picked out. She really knew how to work Louie. She said Louie had a house full of these cheap Italian carpets, and nobody to sell them to. That was his big deal he needed a partner for, by the way—not a very big market over here, I guess. She said Louie was thinking of selling them in Idaho. She said—and this would've made you laugh, Eddie, it would've truly— she said it's a doggy-dog world out there. Doggy-dog. She was real cute. When she said that, Louie got down on the floor and barked like a dog. He dropped his pistol out of his what-ever-you-call-it, his scabbard, and his beeper"—Lois was laughing—"he was like a big animal down on the floor of the bar."

"I'm sorry I missed it."

"Louie can be funny," Lois said.

"Maybe you should've married him, then."

"I *did* marry him."

"Too bad you didn't stay married to him instead of me. I don't have a beeper."

"I like what you have got, though, sweetheart." She squeezed his arm. "Nobody would love me like you do, you know I think that. Reiner was just my mistake, but I can laugh at him today because I don't have to live with him. You're such a big mama's boy, you don't want anybody to have any fun."

"I'd like to have a little fun," Starling said. "Let's go where there's some fun."

Lois leaned and kissed him on the cheek. "You smell awfully nice." She smiled at him. "Come on and dance with me, Ed. Justice demands that you dance with me. You have that light step. It's nice when you do."

Lois walked out onto the little dance floor and took Starling's hand. He stood close to her and they danced to the slow music on the jukebox, holding together the way they had when he'd first known her. He felt a little drunk. A buzz improved a thing, he thought, made a good moment out of nothing.

"You're a natural dancer, Eddie," Lois said softly. "Remember us dancing at Powell's on the beach, with everybody watching us?"

"You like having men think about you?" Starling said.

"Oh, sure. I guess." Lois's cheek was against his cheek. "It makes me feel like I'm in a movie, sometimes, you know? Everybody does that, don't they?"

"I never do."

"Don't you ever wonder what your ex thinks about you? Old Jan. That was a long time ago, I guess."

"Bygones are bygones to me," Starling said. "I don't think about it."

"You're such a literal, Eddie. You get lost in the lonely crowd, I think sometimes. That's why I want to be nice and make you happy." She held him close to her so her hard, flat hips were next to his. "Isn't this nice? It's nice to dance with you."

Starling saw now that the bar was decorated with red, white, and blue crepe paper—features he'd missed. Little curlicues and ribbons and stars hung from the dark rafters and down off the shaded green bar lights and the beer signs and the framed pictures behind the back bar. This was festive, he thought. Lois had fixed it, it showed her hand. Before long a crowd would be in, the lights would go up and shine out, the music would be turned up loud. It would be a good time. "That's nice," Starling said.

"I just love this," Lois said. Her head was on his shoulder. "I just love this so much."

On the highway toward home, Starling passed the hippies he had seen at the campground. They were heading in now, the women on the backseats, the men driving fast, leaning as if the wind blew them.

In town, a big fireworks display staged by a shopping mall was beginning. Catherine wheels and starbursts and blue and pink sprays were going off in the twilight. Cars were stopping along the road, and people with children sat on their car hoods, drinking beer and watching the sky. It was nearly dark and rain had begun to threaten.

"Everything's moved out to the malls now," Lois said, "including the fireworks." She had been dozing and now she leaned against her door, staring back toward the lights.

"I wouldn't care to work in one," Starling said, driving.

Lois said nothing.

"You know what I was just thinking about?" she said after a while.

"Tell me," Starling said.

"Your mother," Lois said. "Your mother was a sweet old lady, you know that? I liked her very much. I remember she and I would go to the mall and buy her a blouse. Just some blouse she could've bought in Bullock's in San Francisco, but she wanted to buy it here to be sweet and special." Lois smiled about it. "Remember when we bought fireworks?"

Starling's mother had little fireworks. She liked to hear them pop so she could laugh. Starling remembered having fireworks one year in the time since he'd been married to Lois. When was that, he thought. A time lost now.

"Remember she held the little teenies right in her fingers and let them go pop? That seemed to tickle her so much."

"That was her trick." Eddie said. "Rex taught her that."

"I guess he did," Lois said. "But you know, I don't blame you, really, for being such a mama's boy, Eddie. Not with *your* mama—unlike mine, for instance. She's why you're as nice as you are."

"I'm selfish," Starling said. "I always have been. I'm capable of lying, stealing, cheating."

Lois patted him on the shoulder. "You're generous, though, too."

Rain was starting in big drops that looked like snow on the windshield. It was almost dark. Lights from their subdivision glowed out under the lowered sky ahead.

"This weird thing happened today," Starling said. "I can't quit thinking about it."

Lois slid over by him. She put her head on his shoulder and her hand inside his thigh. "I knew something had happened, Eddie. You can't hide anything. The truth is just on you."

"There's no truth to this," Starling said. "The phone just rang when I was leaving, and it was this kid, Jeff. He was in some kind of mess. I didn't know who he was, but he thought I was his father. He wanted me to accept charges."

"You didn't, did you?"

Starling looked toward the subdivision. "No. I should have, though. It's on my mind now that I should've helped him. I'd just finished talking to Reiner."

"He might've been in Rangoon, for Christ's sake." Lois said. "Or Helsinki. You don't know where he was. It could've cost you $500, then you couldn't have helped him anyway. You were smart, is exactly what I think."

"It wouldn't matter though. I could've given him some advice. He said somebody was in jail. It's just on my mind now, it'll go away."

"Get a good job and then accept charges from Istanbul," Lois said and smiled.

"I just wonder who he was," Starling said. "For some reason I thought he was over in Reno, isn't that odd? Just a voice."

"It'd be worse if he *was* in Reno," Lois said. "Are you sorry you don't have one of your own?" Lois looked over at him strangely.

"One what?"

"A son. Or, you know. Didn't you tell me you almost had one? There was something about that, with Jan."

"That was a long time ago," Starling said. "We were idiots."

"Some people claim they make your life hold together better, though," Lois said. "You know?"

"Not if you're broke they don't," Starling said. "All they do is make you sorry, then."

"Well, we'll just float on through life together, then, how's that?" Lois put her hand high on his leg. "No blues today, hon, okay?"

They were at the little dirt street where the ranchette was, at the far end. A fireworks hut had been built in the front yard of the first small house, a chain of bright-yellow bulbs strung across the front. An elderly woman was standing in the hut, her face expressionless. She had on a sweater and was holding a little black poodle. All the fireworks but a few Roman candles had been sold off the shelves.

"I never thought I'd live where people sold fireworks right in their front yards," Lois said and faced the front. Starling peered into the lighted hut. The rain was coming down in a slow drizzle, and water shone off the oiled street. He felt the urge to gesture to the woman, but didn't. "You could just about say that we lived in a place you wouldn't want to live in if you could help it. It's funny, isn't it? That just happens to you." Lois laughed.

"I guess it's funny," Starling said. "It's true."

"What'd you dream up for dinner, Eddie? I've built up hunger all of a sudden."

"I forgot about it," Starling said. "There's some macaroni."

"Whatever," Lois said. "It's fine." Starling pulled into the gravel driveway. He could see the pony standing out in the dark where the fenced weed lot extended to the side of the house. The pony looked like a ghost, its cold, white eyes unmoving in the rain.

"Tell me something," Starling said. "If I ask you something, will you tell me?"

"If there's something to tell," Lois said. "Sometimes there isn't anything, you know. But go ahead."

"What happened with you and Reiner?" he said. "All that Reno stuff. I never asked you about that. But I want to know."

"That's easy," Lois said and smiled at him in the dark car. "I just realized I didn't love Reiner, that's all. Period. I realized I loved you, and I didn't want to be married to somebody I didn't love. I wanted to be married to you. It isn't all that complicated or important." Lois put her arms around his neck and hugged him hard. "Don't be cloudy now, sweet. You've just had some odd luck is all. Things'll get better. You'll get back. Let me make you happy, baby doll." Lois slid across the seat against the door and went down into her purse. Starling could hear wind chimes in the rain. "Let me just show you," Lois said.

Starling couldn't see. Lois opened the door out into the drizzle, turned her back to him and struck a match. Starling could see it brighten. And then there was a sparkling and hissing, and then a brighter one, and Starling smelled the harsh burning and the smell of the rain together. Then Lois closed the door and danced out before the car into the rain with the sparklers, waving her arms round in the air, smiling widely and making swirls and patterns and star falls for him that were brilliant and illuminated the night and the bright rain and the little dark house behind her and, for a moment, caught the world and stopped it, as though something sudden and perfect had come to earth in a furious glowing for him and for him alone—Eddie Starling—and only he could watch and listen. And only he would be there, waiting, when the light was finally gone.

Gail Godwin

OVER THE MOUNTAIN

If you have grown to love your life, it seems ungrateful to belabor old injustices, especially those that happened in childhood, that place of sheltered perspectives where you were likely to wake up and go to bed without anyone ever disabusing you of your certainty that all days were planned around you. After all, isn't it possible that the very betrayal that flags your memory and constricts your heart led to a development in character that enabled you to forge your present life?

This is not a belaboring. I know by now that behind every story that begins "When I was a child" there exists another story in which adults are fighting for their lives. It is because I accept this that I am ready to go back and fill in some of the blank spaces in the world of a ten-year-old girl whose mother takes her on an overnight train journey. The train carries them out of their sheltered mountains to a town some thousand feet below. The mother and daughter walk around this town, whose main attraction is that the mother spent her happy girlhood years there. The mother and her little girl stay the night in a respectable boarding house. The next day, they get on the north-bound version of yesterday's train and go back to the mountains.

Why do I remember nothing particular about that journey? I, with my usually prodigious memory for details? Except for a quality of light and atmosphere—the lowland town throbbed with a sociable, golden-yellow heat that made people seem closer, whereas our mountain town had a cool, separating blue air that magnified distances—I have no personal images of this important twenty-four hours. I say important because it was a landmark in my life: it was the first time I had gone away alone with my mother.

Despite the fact that I believe I now know why that excursion lies blank among my memory cells, there is something worth exploring here. The feeling attached to that event, even today, signals the kind of buried affect that shapes a life.

We were not, our little unit of three, your ordinary "nuclear" family, but, as I had known nothing else, we seemed normal enough to me. Our living arrangements were somewhat strange for a trio of females with high conceptions of their privileges in society, but, as my grand-mother hastened to tell people, it was because of the war. And when the war ended, and all the military personnel who had preempted the desirable dwellings had departed from town, and we continued to stay where we were, I accepted my mother's and grandmother's continual reminders that "it was only a matter of time now until the right place could be found."

The three of us slept in one gigantic room, vast enough to swallow the two full-sized Persian carpets that had once covered my grand-mother's former living room and dining room and still reproach us with its lonely space, even when we filled it with all the furniture from the two bedrooms of her previous home. The rest of her furniture crowded our tiny living room and dark, windowless kitchen and then spilled out into the shabby public entrance hall of our building, euphemistically called "the lobby" by our landlord and my grand-mother. My grandmother spent a lot of time trying to pounce on a tenant in the act of sitting on "our" sofa in the lobby, or winding up "our" old Victrola. She would rush out of our apartment like a fury and explain haughtily that this furniture did not belong to the lobby, it was our furniture, only biding its time in this limbo until it could be resettled into the sort of room to which it was accustomed. She actually told one woman, whom she caught smoking while sitting on "our" sofa, to please "consider this furniture invisible in the future." The woman ground out her cigarette on the floor, told my grandmother she was crazy, and went upstairs.

Our building was still known in town by its old name: The Piping Hot. During the twenties, when Asheville overflowed with landboom speculators and relatives visiting TB patients, this brownshingled monstrosity had been thrown up on a lot much too small for it. It had come into existence as a commercial establishment whose purpose was to make money on not-too-elegant people willing to settle for a so-so room and a hot "home-cooked" meal. Therefore it had none of those quaint redeeming features of former private residences fallen on hard times. The reason our bedroom was so huge was simple: it had been the dining room.

It was a pure and simple eyesore, our building: coarse, square, and mud-colored, it hulked miserably on its half-acre with the truculent insecurity of a social interloper. It was a building you might feel sorry for if you were not so busy feeling sorrier for yourself for living in it. Probably the reason its construction had been tolerated at all on that leafy, genteel block was because its lot faced the unsightly physical plant of the proud and stately Manor Hotel which rambled atop its generous acreage on the hill across the street; moreover, the guests at the Manor were prevented by their elevation from seeing even the roof of the lowlier establishment. Our landlord had bought Piping Hot when it went out of business just before the war, chopped it up into as many "apartments" as he could get away with legally, and now collected the rents. Whenever he was forced to drop by, breathless and red-faced, a wet cigar clamped in one corner of his mouth, he would assure my grandmother he had every intention of sowing grass in the bare front yard, of having someone come and wash the filthy windows of the lobby, of cutting down the thorny bushes with their suspicious red berries that grew on either side of the squatty, brown-shingled "shelter" at the sidewalk's edge, where Negro maids often sat down to rest on their way to the bus stop from the big houses at the upper end of the street.

The most "respectable" tenants lived on the ground floor, which must have been some consolation to my grandmother. The Catholic widow, Mrs. Gannon, and her two marriageable daughters lived behind us in a rear apartment which had been made over from pantries and half of the old kitchen. (Our kitchen had been carved out of the other half.) When my grandmother or Mrs. Gannon felt like chatting, either had only to tap lightly on the painted-over window above her sink; they would gossip about the upstairs tenants while snapping beans or peeling potatoes at their facing sinks. The apartment across the lobby was inhabited by another widow, the cheerful Mrs. Rhinehart, who went limping off to work in a china shop every day; her numerous windowsills (her apartment was the Piping Hot's ex-sunporch) were crowded with delicate painted figurines. She suffered from a disease that made one leg twice the width of the other. Among the three windows existed a forebearing camaraderie. Mrs. Rhinehart did not like to gossip, but she always stopped and listened pleasantly if my grandmother waylaid her in the lobby; and, though both my grandmother and Mrs. Gannon thought Mrs. Rhinehart had too many little objects in her windows for good taste, they always amended that, at any rate, she was a brave lady for standing in a shop all day on that leg; and when sailors trekked regularly past our side windows on the way to call on the Gannon girls, my grandmother did not allow her imagination to run as wild as she would have if those same sailors had been on their way to one of the apartments upstairs.

Except for the policeman and his wife, whose stormy marital life thudded and crashed directly above our bedroom, the other upstairs apartments were filled with people my grandmother referred to simply as "the transients." They didn't stay long. You would have to be pretty desperate to stay long in those rear upstairs apartments, which were weird amalgams of former guestrooms, opening into hallways or one another in inconvenient, embarrassing ways, their afterthought bathrooms and kitchens rammed into ex-closets and storage rooms. We didn't even bother to learn their names, those constantly changing combinations of women, of women and children and the occasional rare man, who occupied those awkward upper quarters. They were identified merely by their affronts: the two working girls who clopped around most of the night in their high heels; the woman with the little boy who had written the dirty word in chalk on the sidewalk shelter; the woman who sat down on "our" sofa and stomped out her cigarette on the floor.

Those were the politics of our building. There were also, within our family unit, the politics of my mother's job, the politics of my school, and the subtler triangular dynamics that underpinned life in our apartment.

"Today has been too much for my nerves," my grandmother would say as we huddled over her supper at one end of our giant mahogany dining table which, even with its center leaf removed, took up most of the kitchen. "I was out in the lobby trying to wipe some of the layers of dust off those windows when I happened to look out and there was that little boy about to eat some of the berries on those poison bushes. I rushed out to warn him, only to have his mother tell me she didn't want him frightened. Would she rather have him frightened or dead? Then, not five minutes later, the LaFarges' Negro maid came along and sat down in our shelter and I happened to see her hike her dress up and her stockings were crammed with eggs. I had to debate with myself whether I shouldn't let the LaFarges know . . ."

"I hope you didn't," said my mother, rolling her eyes at me in that special way which my grandmother was not meant to see.

"No. You have to let them get away with murder if you're going to keep them. I remembered that. Do you Remember Willy Mae, when we lived in Greenville?"

My mother laughed. Her voice was suddenly younger and she looked less tired. Greenville was the town on the other side of the mountain where, in a former incarnation, she had lived as a happy, protected young girl. But then a thought pinched her forehead, crimping the smoothness between her deep blue eyes. "I do wish that ass Dr. Busey could see through that snake Lu Ann Leach," she said.

"Kathleen. Lower your voice."

My mother gave an exasperated sigh and sent me a signal: We've got to get out of here. After supper we'll go to the drugstore.

"He hasn't said anything about her staying on at the college, has he?" asked my grandmother *sotto voce*, casting her eyes balefully towards the painted-over window above our sink behind which even a good friend like Mrs. Gannon might be straining to hear how other people's daughters were faring in this uncertain world without a man.

"No, but he hasn't said anything about her leaving, and now she's taken over the literary magazine. She was only supposed to fill in for Miss Pennell's operation and Miss Pennell has been back three weeks. The college can't afford to keep all three of us. There aren't that many students taking English. All the GI's want their math and science so they can go out and make *money*."

"Well, they have to keep you," declared my grandmother, drawing herself up regally.

"They don't have to do anything, Mother." My mother was losing her temper.

"What I mean is," murmured my grandmother in a conciliatory manner to ward off a "scene" which might be overheard, "they will naturally want to keep you, because you're the only one with your MA. I'm so thankful that Poppy lived long enough so we could see you through your good education."

"You should see the way she plays up to him," my mother went on, as if she hadn't heard. "She has that plummy, little-girl way of talking, and she asks his *advice* before she'll even go to the bathroom. If she weren't a Leach, people couldn't possibly take her seriously; she couldn't get a job in a kindergarten."

"If only Poppy had lived," moaned my grandmother, "you would never have had to work."

"My work is all I've *got*," blurted my mother passionately. "I mean, besides you two, of course."

"Of course," agreed my grandmother. "I only meant if he had lived.

Then we could have had a nice house, and you could have worked if you wanted."

My mother's eyes got round, the way they did when someone had overlooked an important fact. She was on the verge of saying more, but then with an effort of her shoulders harnessed her outburst. She sat with her eyes still rounded, but cast down, breathing rapidly through her nostrils. I thought she looked lovely at such times.

"Can we walk to the drugstore and look at the magazines?" I asked.

"If you like," she said neutrally. But, as soon as my grandmother rose to clear the dishes, she sneaked me a smile.

"The thing is, no matter how much I wipe at those lobby windows from the inside," my grandmother said, as much to herself as to us, "they can never been clean. They need to be washed from the outside by a man. Until they are, we will be forced to look through dirt."

"It was on the tip of my tongue to say, 'If you stay *out* of the lobby you won't have to worry about the dirt,'" my mother told me as we walked to the drugstore a block away.

"That would have been perfect!" I cried, swinging her hand. "Oh, why *didn't* you?" I was a little overexcited, as I always was when the two of us finally made it off by ourselves. Here we were, escaped together at last, like two sisters from an overprotective mother. Yet even as the spring dusk purpled about our retreating figures, we both knew she was watching us from the window: she would be kneeling in the armchair, her left hand balancing her on the windowsill, her right hand discreetly parting the white curtains; she could see us all the way to our destination. She had left the lights off in the apartment, to follow us better.

"It would have been cruel," my mother said. "That lobby is her outside world."

Though complaining about my grandmother often drew us closer, I could see my mother's point, it was not that we didn't love her; it was that the heaviness of her love confined us. She worried constantly that something would happen to us. She thought up things, described them aloud in detail, which sometimes ended up scaring us all. (The mother of the little boy about to eat the berry had been right.)

We had reached the corner of our block. As we waited for a turning car to go by, we looked up and saw the dining-room lights of the Manor Hotel twinkling at us. The handful of early spring guests would just be sitting down to eat.

I looked up at one of the timbered gables. "There's nobody in Naomi Benjamin's room yet," I said.

"The season will be starting soon. All the rooms will be filled. But never again will I ever write *anybody's* autobiography. Unless I write my own someday."

My mother and grandmother had been so excited last summer when Naomi Benjamin, an older woman from New York who had come to our mountains for her health, offered my mother $500 to "work with her on her autobiography." Someone at the Manor had told Naomi that my mother was a published writer, and she had come down from the hill to call on us at The Piping Hot and make her offer. We were impressed by her stylish clothes and her slow, gloomy way of expressing herself, as if the weight of the world lay behind her carefully chosen words. But, before the end of the summer, my mother was in a rage. Sometimes, after having "worked with" Naomi Benjamin all afternoon, and after typing up the results at night, my mother would lie back and rant while my grandmother applied a cold washcloth to her head and told her she was not too young to get a stroke. "A stroke would be something *happening*," snarled my mother, "whereas not a damn thing has happened to that woman; how dare she aspire to autobiography!" "Well, she is Jewish," reflected my grandmother. "They never have an easy time." "Ha!" spat my mother. "That's what I thought. I thought I'd learn something interesting about other ways of suffering, but there's not even that. I'd like to tell her to take her five hundred dollars and buy herself some excitement. That's what she really needs." "Kathleen, tension can burst a blood vessel . . ." "I wish to God I could make it up," my mother ranted on, growing more excited, "at least I wouldn't be dying of boredom!" "I'm going to phone her right now," announced my grandmother, taking a new tack; "I'm going to tell her you're too sick to go on." "No, no, no!" My mother sprang up, waving the cold cloth aside. "It's all right. I'm almost finished. Just let me go walk up and down the street for a while and clear my head."

We had reached the drugstore in the middle of the next block, our oasis of freedom. We passed into its brightly lit interior, safe for a time behind brick walls that even my grandmother's ardent vision could not penetrate. Barbara, the pharmacist, was doing double duty behind the soda fountain, but when she looked up and saw it was us she went on wiping the counter; she knew that, despite her sign (THESE MAGAZINES ARE FOR *BUYING*, NOT FOR BROWSING), we would first go and look through the pulp magazines to see if there was any new story by Charlotte Ashe. But we always conducted our business as quickly and unobtrusively as possible, so as not to set a bad example for other customers; we knew it pained Barbara to see her merchandise sinking in value with each browser's fingerprints, even though she admired my mother and was in on the secret that Charlotte Ashe's name had been created from the name of this street and the first half of the name of our town.

There was no new story by Charlotte Ashe. It was quite possible all of them had appeared by now, but my mother did not want to spoil our game. It had been a while since Charlotte Ashe had mailed off a story. During the war, when my mother worked on the newspaper, it had been easier to slip a paragraph or two of fiction into the typewriter on a slow-breaking news day. But now the men had come home, to reclaim their jobs at the newspaper, and fill up the seats in the classroom where my mother taught; there was less time and opportunity to find an hour alone with a typewriter and let one's romantic imagination soar—within the bounds of propriety, of course.

We sat down at the counter. It would not do to make Barbara wait on us in a booth. She was, for all her gruff tones, the way she pounced on children who tried to read the comic books, the pharmacist. As if to emphasize this to customers who might confuse her with a mere female employee, Barbara wore trousers and neckties and took deep, swinging strides around her store; she even wore men's shoes.

"Kathleen, what'll you have?"

"A Coke, please, Barbara, for each of us. Oh, and would you put a tiny squirt of ammonia in mine? I've got a headache coming on?"

"How tiny?" Barbara's large hand with its close-clipped nails hovered over the counter pump that discharged ammonia.

"Well, not too tiny."

Both women laughed. Barbara made our Cokes, giving my mother an indulgent look as she squirted the pump twice over one of the paper cups. All the other customers got glasses if they drank their beverages in the store, but my grandmother had made us promise never to drink from a drugstore glass after she saw an ex-patient of the TB sanatorium drink from one. "Your cups, ladies," said Barbara ironically, setting them ceremoniously before us. She and my mother rolled their eyes at each other. Barbara knew all about the promise; my mother had been forced to tell her after Barbara had once demanded gruffly, "Why can't you all drink out of glasses like everybody else?" But Barbara did not charge us the extra penny for the cups.

We excused ourselves and took our Cokes and adjourned to a booth, where we could have privacy. As there were no other customers, Barbara loped happily back into her rear sanctum of bottles and pills.

At last I had my mother all to myself.

"How was school today?"

"We had field day practice," I said. "Mother Donovan was showing us how to run the three-legged race and she pulled up her habit and she has really nice legs."

"That doesn't surprise me, somehow. She must have had a real vocation, because she's certainly pretty enough to have gotten married. How are you and Lisa getting along?"

"We're friends, but I hate her. I hate her and she fascinates me at the same time. What has she *got* that makes everybody do what she wants?"

"I've told you what she's got, but you always forget."

"Tell me again. I won't forget."

My mother swung her smooth pageboy forward until it half-curtained her face. She peered into the syrupy depths of her spiked Coke and rattled its crushed ice, as if summoning the noisy fragments to speak the secret of Lisa Gudger's popularity. Then, slowly, she raised her face and her beautiful dark blue eyes met mine. I waited, transfixed by our powerful intimacy.

"You are smarter than Lisa Gudger," she began, saying her words slowly. "You have more imagination than Lisa Gudger. And, feature by feature, you are prettier than Lisa Gudger . . ."

I drank in this litany, which I did remember from before.

"But Lisa likes herself better than you like yourself. Whatever Lisa has, she thinks it's best. And this communicates itself to others, and they follow her."

This was the part I always forgot. I was forgetting it again already. I stared hard at my mother's face, I could see myself reflected in the small pupils, contracted from the bright drugstore lights; I watched the movement of her lips, the way one front tooth crossed slightly over the other. The syllables trying to contain the truth about a girl named Lisa Gudger broke into smaller and smaller particles and escaped into the air as I focused on my mother, trying to show her how well I was listening.

I partially covered up by asking, after it was over, "Do you hate Lu Ann Leach the way I hate Lisa?"

"Now that's an interesting question. Now, Lisa Gudger would not have had the imagination to ask that question. I do hate Lu Ann, because she's a real threat; she can steal my job. I hate her because she's

safe and smug and has a rich father to take care of her if everything else
falls through. But Lu Ann Leach does not fascinate me. If I could
afford it, I would feel pity for her. See, I've figured her out. When
you've figured someone out, they don't fascinate you anymore. Or at
least they don't when you've figured out the kind of thing I figured out
about her."

"Oh, what? What have you figured out?"

"Shh." My mother looked around towards Barbara's whereabouts.
She leaned forward across our table. "Lu Ann hates men, but she
knows how to use them. Her hatred gives her a power over them,
because she just doesn't care. But I'd rather be myself, without that
power, if it means the only way I can have it is to become like Lu Ann
Leach. She's thirty, for God's sake, and she still lives with her parents."

"But you live with your mother."

"That's different."

"How is it different?"

My mother got her evasive look. This dialogue had strayed into
channels where she hadn't meant it to. "It's a matter of choice versus
necessity," she said, going abstract on me.

"You don't hate men, then?" I could swear I'd heard her say she
had: the day she got fired from the newspaper, for instance.

"Of course I don't. They're the other half of the world. *You* don't
hate men, do you?" She gave me a concerned look.

I thought of Men. There was the priest at school, Father Lilley,
whose black skirts whispered upon the gravel; there was Jovan, our
black bus driver; there was Hal the handyman who lived in a basement
apartment under the fifth-grade classroom with his old father, who
drove the bus on Jovan's day off. There was Don Olson, the sailor I
had selected as my favorite out of all those who passed our window on
their way to see the Gannon girls; I would lie in wait for him at our
middle-bedroom window, by the sewing machine, and he would look
in and say, "Hi there, beautiful. I might as well just stop here." Which
always made me laugh. One day my grandmother caught me in the act

of giving him a long list of things I wanted him to buy me in town. "She's just playing, she doesn't mean it," she cried, rushing forward to the window. But he brought me back every item on the list. And there was my father, who had paid us one surprise visit from Florida. His body shook the floor as he strode through our bedroom to wash his hands in the bathroom. He closed the bathroom door behind him and locked it. My mother made me tell everybody he was my uncle, because she had already told people he had been killed in the war: a lie she justified because, long ago, he had stopped sending money, and because people would hire a war widow before they would a divorced woman. Still, I was rather sorry not to be able to claim him; with his good-looking face and sunburnt ankles (he wore no socks, even with his suit), he was much more glamorous than my friends' dull business fathers.

"Sure. I like men," I told my mother in the booth. I was thinking particularly of Don Olson. The Gannon girls were fools to let him get away.

"Well, good," said my mother wryly, shaking her ice in the paper cup. "I wouldn't want *that* on my conscience. That I'd brought you up to hate men."

As if we had conjured him up by our tolerant allowance of his species, a Man materialized in front of our booth.

"Well looky here what I found," he said, his dark brown eyes dancing familiarly at us.

My mother's face went through an interesting series of changes. "Why, what are *you* doing home?" she asked him.

It was Frank, one of her GI students from the year before, who was always coming by our apartment to get extra help on a term paper, or asking her to read a poem aloud so he could understand it better. Once last year, out of politeness, I had asked him to sign my autograph book; but whereas her other GIs had signed things like "Best of luck from your friend Charles," or "To a sweet girl," Frank had written in a feisty slant: "To the best daughter of my best teacher." His page troubled me, with its insinuating inclusion of himself between my mother and me; also, his handwriting made "daughter" look like "daughtlet." It was like glimpsing myself from a sudden unflattering angle: a "daughtlet." And what did he mean *best* daughter? I was my mother's only daughter. At the end of last spring, when I knew he would be transferring to Georgia Tech, I took a razor and carefully excised his page.

"I can't stay out of these mountains," said Frank, reaching for a chair from a nearby table and fitting it backwards between his legs. Barbara looked out from the window of her pharmacy, but when she saw who it was did not bother to come out.

"I should think it would be nice to get out of them for a change," said my mother.

"Well, what's stopping you?" asked Frank, teetering forward dangerously on two legs of his chair. He rested his chin on the dainty wrought-iron back of the chair and assessed us, like a playful animal looking over a fence.

My mother rolled her eyes, gave her crushed ice a fierce shake, and emptied the last shards into her mouth. They talked on for a few more minutes, my mother asking him neutral questions about his engineering courses, and then she stood up. "We've got to be getting back or Mother will start worrying that we've been kidnapped."

He stood up, too, and walked us to the door with his hands in his pockets. "Want a ride?"

"One block? Don't be silly," said my mother.

He got into a little gray coupe and raced the motor unnecessarily, I thought, and then spoiled half of our walk home by driving slowly along beside us with his lights on.

"I wish we could go off sometime, just by ourselves," I said in the few remaining steps of cool darkness. My grandmother had pulled down the shades and turned on the lamp, and we could see the shadow of the top of her head as she sat listening to the radio in her wing chair.

"Well, maybe we can," said my mother. "Let me think about it some."

We went inside and the three of us scrubbed for bed and the women creamed their faces. I got in bed with my mother, and, across the room, my grandmother put on her chin strap and got into her bed. We heard the policeman coming home; his heavy shoes shook the whole house as he took the stairs two at a time. "He has no consideration," came my grandmother's reproachful voice from the dark. There soon followed their colorful exchange of abuses, the wife's shrieks and the policeman's blows. "It's going too far this time," said my grandmother, "he's going to kill her, I'm going to call the police." "You can't call the police on the police, Mother. Just wait, it'll soon be over." And my mother was right; about this time the sound effects subsided into the steady, accelerated knocking against our ceiling which would soon lead to silence. "If Poppy had lived, we would not be subjected to this," moaned my grandmother. "Even he couldn't keep life out," sighed my mother, and turned her back to me for sleep.

Our trip alone together came to pass. I don't know how my mother talked my grandmother out of going with us. She was a respectful daughter, if often impatient, and would not have hurt my grandmother's feelings for the world. And it would have been so natural for my grandmother to come: she was the only one of us who could ride free. The widow of a railroad man, she could go anywhere she wanted on Southern Railways until the end of her life.

But, at any rate, after what I am sure were exhaustive preparations sprinkled with my grandmother's imaginative warnings of all the mishaps that might befall us, we embarked—my mother and I—from Biltmore Train Station south of Asheville. My grandmother surely drove us there in our ten-year-old Oldsmobile, our last relic of prosperity from the days when Poppy lived. I am sure we arrived at the station much too early, and that my grandmother probably cried. Poppy had been working at Biltmore Station when my grandmother

met him. His promotions had taken them out of her girlhood mountains to a series of dusty piedmont towns which she had never liked;
and now here she was back in the home mountains, in the altitude she
loved—but old and without him. My mother and I were going to the
first of the towns to which he had been transferred when my mother
had been about the age I was now.

I do not remember our leaving from Biltmore Station or our returning to it the next afternoon. That is the strange thing about those
twenty-four hours: I have no mental pictures that I can truly claim I
inhabited during that timespan. Except for that palpable recollection
of the golden heat which I have already described, there are no details.
No vivid scenes. No dialogues. I know we stayed in a boarding house,
which my grandmother, I am sure, checked out in advance. It is
possible that the owner might have been an old acquaintance, some
lady fallen on harder times, like ourselves. Was this boarding house in
the same neighborhood as the house where my mother had lived? I'm
sure we must have walked by that house. After all, wasn't the purpose
of our trip—other than going somewhere by ourselves—to pay a
pilgrimage to the scene of my mother's happy youth? Did we, then,
also walk past her school? It seems likely, but I don't remember. I do
have a vague remembrance of "downtown," where, I am sure, we
must have walked up and down streets, in and out of stores, perhaps
buying something, some small thing that I wanted; I am sure we
must have stopped in some drugstore and bought two Cokes in paper
cups.

Did the town still have streetcars running on tracks, jangling their
bells; or was it that my mother described them so well, the streetcars
that she used to ride when she lived there as a girl?

I do not know.

We must have eaten at least three meals, perhaps four, but I don't
remember eating them.

We must have slept in the same bed. Even if there had been two beds in the room, I would, sooner or later, have crawled in with my mother. I always slept with her.

My amnesia comes to a stunning halt the moment the trip is over. My grandmother has picked us up from Biltmore Station and there I am, on Charlotte Street again, in the bedroom *née* dining room of the old Piping Hot.

It is late afternoon. The sun is still shining, but the blue atmosphere of our mountains has begun to gather. The predominant color of this memory is blue. I am alone in the bedroom, lying catty-cornered across the bed with my head at the foot; I am looking out the window next to the one where I always used to lie in wait for the sailor, Don Olson, on his way to call on the Gannon girls. The bedspread on which I am lying is blue, a light blue, with a raised circular pattern in white; it smells clean. Everything in this room, in this apartment, smells clean and womanly. There is the smell of linen which has lain in lavender-scented drawers; the smell of my mother's "Tweed" perfume, which she dabs on lightly before going to teach at the college; the acerbic, medicinal smell of my grandmother's spirits of ammonia, which she keeps in a small green cut-glass bottle and sniffs whenever she feels faint; the smell of a furniture polish, oil-based, which my grandmother rubs, twice a week, into our numerous pieces of furniture.

Where are they? Perhaps my grandmother is already in the kitchen, starting our early supper, hardly able to contain her relief that our trip without her is over. Perhaps my mother is out by herself in the late sunshine, taking one of her walks to clear her head; or maybe she is only in the next room, reading the Sunday paper, grading student themes for the following day, or simply gazing out at the same view I as gazing at, thinking her own thoughts.

I looked out at the end of that afternoon. The cars were turning from Charlotte Street into Kimberly, making a whishing sound. I could see the corner wall of the drugstore. But there was no chance of going there after supper, because we had already been away for more time than ever before.

An irremediable sadness gathered about me. *This time yesterday, we were there*, I thought; *and now we are here and it's all over*. How could that be? For the first time, I hovered, outside my own body, in that ghostly synapse between the anticipated event and its aftermath. I knew what all adults know: that "this time yesterday" and "this time tomorrow" are often more real than the protracted now.

It's over, I thought; and perhaps, at that blue hour, I abandoned childhood for the vaguely perceived kingdom of my future. But the knot in my chest that I felt then—its exact location and shape—I feel now, whenever I dredge up that memory.

A lot of things were over, a lot of things did come to an end that spring. My mother announced that she would not be going back to teach at the college. (Lu Ann Leach took her place, staying on into old age—until the college was incorporated into the state university.) And then, on an evening in which my grandmother rivaled the policeman's wife in her abandoned cries of protest, my mother went out for a walk and reappeared with Frank, and they announced to us that they were married. The three of us left that night, but now we are talking about a different three: my mother, Frank and me. All that summer we lived high on a mountain—a mountain that, ironically, overlooked the red-tiled roofs of the Manor Hotel. Our mountain was called Beaucatcher, and our address was the most romantic I've ever had: One Thousand Sunset Drive. Again we were in a house with others, but these others were a far cry from the panicked widows and lonely mothers of Charlotte Street. Downstairs lived a nightclub owner and his wife and her son (my age) from an earlier marriage; upstairs lived a gregarious woman of questionable virtue. One night, a man on the way upstairs blundered by accident into my room—I now had a room, almost as large as the one we three had shared in the life below—and Frank was so incensed that he rigged up a complicated buzzer system: if my door opened during the night, the buzzer-alarm would go off, even if it was I who opened it. That summer I made friends with the nightclub owner's stepson, learned to shoot out street lights with my own homemade slingshot, and, after seeing a stray dog dripping blood, was told about the realities of sex. First by the boy, the stepson, in his own words; then, in a cleaned-up version, by my mother. I invited Lisa Gudger up to play with me; we got into Frank's bottle of Kentucky Tavern and became roaring drunk; and I beat her up. My mother called Mrs. Gudger to come and get Lisa, and then hurriedly sewed onto Lisa's ripped blouse all the buttons I had torn off.

My grandmother, who had screamed she would die if we left her, lived on through the long summer. And through another summer, during which we were reconciled. Frank had quit Georgia Tech to marry my mother, and worked as a trainee in Kress's. Within a year, my mother and Frank had moved back to the old Piping Hot. They now had the former apartment of the policeman and his wife. My grandmother slept on in her bed downstairs, and I divided my time between them.

A few years later, we left my grandmother again. Frank was being transferred to a town on the other side of the mountain. One of those hot little towns a thousand feet below. After we had been away for some months, my grandmother shocked us all by getting her first job at the age most people were thinking about retiring. At the time most people were coming home from work, my grandmother pinned on her hat and put on her gloves and hid all of Poppy's gold pieces and his ring and his watch in a secret fold of her purse, and took the empty bus downtown to her job. She worked as night housemother at the YWCA residence for working girls. It was a job made in heaven for her: she sat up waiting for the girls. If they came in after midnight, they had to ring and she let them in with an admonition. After three admonitions she reported them to the directress, a woman she despised. We heard all about the posturings and deceptions of this directress, a Mrs. Malt, whenever we visited. My grandmother's politics had gone beyond the lobby into the working world; she was able to draw Social Security because of it.

When our brand new "nuclear family" arrived in the little lowland town where Frank was to be the assistant manager of Kress's, we moved into a housing development. Our yard had no grass, only an ugly red clay slope that bled into the walkway every time it rained. "I guess I'll never know what it's like to have grass in the front yard," I said, in the sorrowful, affronted, doom-laden voice of my grandmother. "Hell, honey," replied Frank with his mountain twang, "if you want grass in this world, you've got to plant it."

I forgive him for his treachery now, as I recall the thrill of those first tiny green spikes, poking up out of that raw, red soil.

Years and years passed. I was home on a visit to my mother and Frank and their little daughter and their two baby sons. "You know, it's awful," I told Mother, "but I can't remember a single thing about that trip you and I took that time on the train. You know, to Greenville. Do you remember it?"

"Of course I do," she said, her eyes going that distant blue. "Monie took us to the station and we had a lovely lunch in the dining car, and then we went to all my old haunts, and we stayed the night at Mrs. ———'s, and then we got back on the train and came home. It was a lovely time."

"Well, I wish I could remember more about it."

What else would you like to know?" asked Frank, who had been listening, his eyes as warm and eager to communicate as my mother's were cool and elegiac.

But she suddenly got an odd look on her face. "Frank," she said warningly.

"Well, hell, Kathleen." He hunched his shoulders like a rebuked child.

"Frank, please," my mother said.

"Well, I was there, too," he flared up.

"You were not! That was another time we met in Greenville." But her eyes were sending desperate signals and her mouth had twisted into a guilty smirk.

"The hell it was. The second time we went, it was to get married."

Then he looked at me, those brown eyes swimming with their eager truths. She had turned away, and I didn't want to hear. Fat chance. "I drove down," he said. "I followed your train. You were sick on the train and you had to have a nap when you got there. I waited till your mother met me on the corner after you fell asleep. And then after you fell asleep that night. Well, dammit, Kathleen," he said to the cool profile turned away from him, "it's the truth. Did the truth ever hurt anybody?"

He went on to me, almost pleading for me to see his side. "I don't know what we would have done without you," he said. "You were our little chaperon, in a way. Don't you *know* how impossible it was, in those days, ever to get her alone?"

NEBRASKA

The town is Americus, Covenant, Denmark, Grange, Hooray, Jerusalem, Sweetwater—one of the lesser-known moons of the Platte, conceived in sickness and misery by European pioneers who took the path of least resistance and put down roots in an emptiness like the one they kept secret in their youth. In Swedish and Danish and German and Polish, in anxiety and fury and God's providence, they chopped at the Great Plains with spades, creating green sodhouses that crumbled and collapsed in the rain and disappeared in the first persuasive snow and were so low the grown-ups stooped to go inside; and yet were places of ownership and a hard kind of happiness, the places their occupants gravely stood before on those plenary occasions when photographs were taken.

And then the Union Pacific stopped by, just a camp of white campaign tents and a boy playing his Harpoon at night, and then a supply store, a depot, a pine water tank, stockyards, and the mean prosperity of the twentieth century. The trains strolling into town to shed a boxcar in the depot side yard, or crying past at sixty miles per hour, possibly interrupting a girl in her high wire act, her arms looping up when she tips to one side, the railtop as slippery as a silver spoon. And then the yellow and red locomotive rises up from the heat shimmer over a mile away, the August noonday warping the sight of it, but cinders tapping away from the spikes and the iron rails already vibrating up inside the girl's shoes. She steps down to the roadbed and then into high weeds as the Union Pacific pulls Wyoming coal and Georgia-Pacific lumber and snowplow blades and aslant Japanese pickup trucks through the green, open countryside and on to Omaha. And when it passes by, a worker she knows is opposite her, like a pedestrian at a stoplight, the sun not letting up, the plainsong of grasshoppers going on and on between them until the worker says, "Hot."

Twice the Union Pacific tracks cross over the sidewinding Democrat, the water slow as an ox cart, green as silage, croplands to the east, yards and houses to the west, a green ceiling of leaves in some places, whirlpools showing up in it like spinning plates that lose speed and disappear. In winter and a week or more of just above zero, high school couples walk the gray ice, kicking up snow as quiet words are passed between them, opinions are mildly compromised, sorrows are apportioned. And Emil Jedlicka unslings his blue-stocked .22 and slogs through high brown weeds and snow, hunting ring-necked pheasant, sidelong rabbits, and—always suddenly—quail, as his little brother Orin springs across the Democrat in order to slide like an otter.

July in town is a gray highway and a Ford hay truck spraying by, the hay sailing like a yellow ribbon caught in the mouth of a prancing dog, and Billy Awalt up there on the camel's hump, eighteen years old and sweaty and dirty, peppered and dappled with hay dust, a lump of chew like an extra thumb under his lower lip, his blue eyes happening on a Dairy Queen and a pretty girl licking a pale trickle of ice cream from the cone. And Billy slaps his heart and cries, "O! I am pierced!"

And late October is orange on the ground and blue overhead and grain silos stacked up like white poker chips, and a high silver water tower belittled one night by the sloppy tattoo of one year's class at George W. Norris High. And below the silos and water tower are stripped treetops, their gray limbs still lifted up in alleluia, their yellow leaves crowding along yard fences and sheeping along the sidewalks and alleys under the shepherding wind.

Or January and a heavy snow partition the landscape, whiting out the highways and woods and cattle lots until there are only open spaces and steamed-up windowpanes, and a Nordstrom boy limping pitifully in the hard plaster of his clothes, in a small parka meant to be green and a snow cap meant to be purple, the snow as deep as his hips when the boy tips over and cannot get up until a little Schumacher girl sitting by the stoop window, a spoon in her mouth, a bowl of Cheerios in her lap, says in plain voice, "There's a boy," and her mother looks out to the sidewalk.

Houses are big and white and two stories high, each a cousin to the next, with pigeon roosts in the attic gables, green storm windows on the upper floor, and a green screened porch, some as pillowed and couched as parlors or made into sleeping rooms for the boy whose next step will be the Navy and days spent on a ship with his home-town's own population, on gray water that rises up and is allayed like a geography of cornfields, sugar beets, soybeans, wheat, that stays there and says, in its own way, "Stay." Houses are turned away from the land and toward whatever is not always, sitting across from each other like dressed-up children at a party in daylight, their parents looking on with hopes and fond expectations. Overgrown elm and sycamore trees poach the sunlight from the lawn and keep petticoats of snow around them into April. In the deep lots out back are wire clotheslines with flapping white sheets pinned to them, property lines are hedged with sour green and purple grapes, or with rabbit wire and gardens of peonies, roses, gladioli, irises, marigolds, pansies. Fruit trees are so closely planted that they cannot sway without knitting. The apples and cherries drop and sweetly decompose until they're only slight brown bumps in the yards, but the pears stay up in the wind, drooping under the pecks of birds, withering down like peppers until their passion and sorrow are justly noticed and they one day disappear.

Aligned against an alley of blue shale rock is a garage whose doors slash weeds and scrape up pebbles as an old man pokily swings them open, teetering with his last weak push. And then Victor Johnson rummages inside, being cautious about his gray sweater and high-topped shoes, looking over paint cans, junked electric motors, grass rakes and garden rakes and a pitchfork and sickles, gray doors and ladders piled overhead in the rafters, and an old wind-up Victrola and heavy platter records from the twenties, on one of them a soprano singing, "I'm a Lonesome Melody." Under a green tarpaulin is a wooden movie projector he painted silver and big cans of tan cellu-loid, much of it orange and green with age, but one strip of it preserved: of an Army pilot in jodhpurs hopping from one biplane and onto another's upper wing. Country people who'd paid to see the movie had been spellbound by the slight dip of the wings at the pilot's jump, the slap of his leather jacket, and how his hair strayed wild and was promptly sleeked back by the wind, but looking at the strip now, pulling a ribbon of it up to a windowpane and letting it unspool to the ground, Victor can make out only twenty frames of the leap and then snapshot after snapshot of an Army pilot clinging to the biplane's wing. And yet Victor stays with it, as though that scene of one man staying alive was what he'd paid his nickel for.

Main Street is just a block away. Pickup trucks stop in it so their drivers can angle out over their brown left arms and speak about crops or praise the weather or make up sentences whose only real point is their lack of complication. And then a cattle truck comes up and they mosey along with a touch of their cap bills or a slap of the door metal. High school girls in skintight jeans stay in one place on weekends and jacked-up cars cruise past, rowdy farmboys overlapping inside, pull-ing over now and then in order to give the girls cigarettes and sips of pop and grief about their lipstick. And when the cars peel out the girls say how a particular boy measured up or they swap gossip about Donna Moriarity and the scope she permitted Randy when he came back from boot camp.

Everyone is famous in this town. And everyone is necessary. Townspeople go to the Vaughn grocery store for the daily news, and to the Home restaurant for history class, especially at evensong when the old people eat gravied pot roast and lemon meringue pies and calmly sip coffee from cups they tip to their mouths with both hands. The Kiwanis Club meets here on Tuesday nights, and hopes are made public, petty sins are tidily dispatched, the proceeds from the gumball machines are talleyed up and poured into the upkeep of a playground. Yutesler's Hardware store has picnic items and kitchen appliances in its one window, in the manner of those prosperous men who would prefer to be known for their hobbies. And there is one crisp, white, Protestant church with a steeple, of the sort pictured on calendars; and the Immaculate Conception Catholic Church, grayly holding the town at bay like a Gothic wolfhound. And there is an insurance agency, a county coroner and justice of the peace, a secondhand shop, a handsome chiropractor named Koch who coaches the Pony League baseball team, a post office approached on unpainted wood steps outside of a cheap mobile home, the Nighthawk tavern where there's Falstaff tap beer, a green pool table, a poster recording the Cornhuskers scores, a crazy man patiently tolerated, a gray-haired woman with an unmoored eye, a boy in spectacles thick as paperweights, a carpenter missing one index finger, a plump waitress whose day job is in a basement beauty shop, an old woman who creeps up to the side door at eight in order to purchase one shotglass of whiskey.

And yet passing by, and paying attention, an outsider is only aware of what isn't, that there's no bookshop, no picture show, no pharmacy or dry cleaners, no cocktail parties, extreme opinions, jewelry or piano stores, motels, hotels, hospital, political headquarters, travel agencies, art galleries, European fashions, philosophical theories about Being and the soul.

High importance is only attached to practicalities, and so there is the Batchelor Funeral Home, where a proud old gentleman is on display in a dark brown suit, his yellow fingernails finally clean, his smeared eyeglasses in his coat pocket, a grandchild on tiptoes by the casket, peering at the lips that will not move, the sparrow chest that will not rise. And there's Tommy Seymour's for Sinclair gasoline and mechanical repairs, a green balloon dinosaur bobbing from a string over the cash register, old tires piled beneath the cottonwood, For Sale in the side yard a Case tractor, a John Deere reaper, a hay mower, a red manure spreader, and a rusty grain conveyor, green weeds overcoming them, standing up inside them, trying slyly and little-by-little to inherit machinery for the earth.

And beyond that are woods, a slope of pasture, six empty cattle pens, a driveway made of limestone pebbles, and a house where Alice Sorensen pages through a child's World Book encyclopedia, stopping at the descriptions of California, Capetown, Ceylon, Colorado, Copenhagen, Corpus Christi, Costa Rica, Cyprus.

Widow Dworak has been watering the lawn in an open raincoat and apron, but at nine she walks the green hose around to the spigot and screws down the nozzle so that the spray is a misty crystal bowl softly baptizing the ivy. She says, "How about some camomile tea?" And she says, "Yum. Oh boy. That hits the spot." And bends to shut the water off.

The Union Pacific night train rolls through town just after ten o'clock when a sixty-year-old man named Adolf Schooley is a boy again in bed, and when the huge weight of forty or fifty cars jostles his upstairs room like a motor he'd put a quarter in. And over the sighing industry of the train, he can hear the train saying Nebraska, Nebraska, Nebraska, Nebraska. And he cannot sleep.

Mrs. Antoinette Heft is at the Home restaurant, placing frozen meat patties on waxed paper, pausing at times to clamp her fingers under her arms and press the sting from them. She stops when the Union Pacific passes, then picks a cigarette out of a pack of Kools and smokes it on the back porch, smelling air as crisp as Oxydol, looking up at stars the Pawnee Indians looked at, hearing the low harmonica of big rigs on the highway, in the town she knows like the palm of her hand, in the country she knows by heart.

THE PACIFIC

This was probably the last place in the world for a factory. There were pine-covered hills and windy bluffs stopped still in a wavelike roll down to the Pacific, groves of fragrant trees with clay-red trunks and soft greenery that made a white sound in the wind, and a chain of boiling, fuming coves and bays in which the water—when it was not rocketing foam—was a miracle of glassy curves in cold blue or opalescent turquoise, depending upon the season, and depending upon the light.

A dirt road went through the town and followed the sea from point to point as if it had been made for the naturalists who had come before the war to watch the seals, sea otters, and fleets of whales passing offshore. It took three or four opportunities to travel into the hills and run through long valleys onto a series of flat mesas as large as battlefields, which for a hundred years had been a perfect place for raising horses. And horses still pressed up against the fences or stood in family groupings in golden pastures as if there were no such thing as time, and as if many of the boys who had ridden them had never grown up and had never left. At least a dozen fishing boats had once bobbed at the pier and ridden the horizon, but they had been turned into minesweepers and sent to Pearl Harbor, San Diego, and the Aleutians.

The factory itself, a long low building in which more than five hundred women and several hundred men made aircraft instruments, had been built in two months, along with a forty-mile railroad spur that had been laid down to connect it to the Union Pacific main line. In this part of the state the railroad had been used heavily only during the harvests and was usually rusty for the rest of the year. Now even the spur was gleaming and weedless, and small steam engines pulling several freight cars shuttled back and forth, their hammerlike exhalations silencing the cicadas, breaking up perfect afternoons, and shattering perfect nights.

The main halls and outbuildings were only a mile from the sea but were placed in such a way, taking up almost all of the level ground on the floor of a wide ravine, that they were out of the line of fire of naval guns. And because they were situated in a narrow trench between hills, they were protected from bombing.

"But what about landings?" a woman had asked an Army officer who had been brought very early one morning to urge the night shift to maintain the blackout and keep silent about their work. Just after dawn the entire shift had finished up and gathered on the railroad siding.

"Who's speaking, please?" the officer had asked, unable to see in the dim light who was putting the question.

"Do you want my name?" she asked back in surprise. She had not intended to say anything, and now everyone was listening to her.

Nor had the officer intended to ask her name. "Sure," he answered. "You're from the South."

"That's right," she said. "South Carolina. My name is Paulette Ferry."

"What do you do?"

"I'm a precision welder."

That she should have the word *precision* in her title seemed just. She was neat, handsome, and delicate. Every gesture seemed well considered. Her hands were small—hardly welder's hands, even those of a precision welder.

"You don't have to worry about troop landings," the officer said.

"It's too far for the Japanese to come in a ship small enough to slip through our seaward defenses, and it's too far for airplanes, too."

He put his hands up to shield his eyes. The sun was rising, and as its rays found bright paths between the firs, he was blinded. "The only danger here is sabotage. Three or four men could hike in with a few satchels of explosive and do a lot of damage. But the sea is clear. Japanese submarines just don't have the range, and the Navy's out there, though you seldom see it. If you lived in San Francisco or San Diego, believe me, you'd see it. The harbors are choked with warships."

Then the meeting dissolved, because the officer was eager to move on. He had to drive to Bakersfield and speak at two more factories, both of which were more vulnerable and more important than this one. And this place was so out of the way and so beautiful that it seemed to have nothing to do with the war.

Before her husband left for the South Pacific, he and Paulette had found a place for her to live, a small house above the ocean, on a cliff, looking out, where it seemed that nothing would be between them but the air over the water.

Though warships were not visible off the coast, she could see from her windows the freighters that moved silently within the naval cordon. Sometimes one of these ships would defy the blackout and become a castle of lights that glided on the horizon like a skater with a torch.

"Paulette," he had said, when he was still in training at Parris Island, "after the war's over, everything's going to be different. When I get back—if I get back," he added, because he knew that not all Marine lieutenants were going to make it home—"I want to go to California. The light there is supposed to be extraordinary. I've heard that because of the light, living there is like living in a dream. I want to be in a place like that—not so much as a reward for seeing it through, but because we will already have been so disconnected from everything we know. Do you understand?"

She had understood, and she had come quickly to a passionate agreement about California, swept into it not only by the logic and the hope but by the way he had looked at her when he had said "—if I get back." For he thought truly nothing was as beautiful as Paulette in a storm, riding above it smoothly, just about to break, quivering, but never breaking.

When he was shifted from South Carolina to the Marine base at Twentynine Palms, they had their chance to go to California, and she rode out with him on the train. Rather than have them suffer the whole trip in a Pullman with stiff green curtains, her parents had paid for a compartment. Ever since Lee had been inducted, both sets of parents had fallen into a steady devotion. It seemed as if they would not be satisfied until they had given all their attention and everything they had to their children. Packages arrived almost daily for Paulette. War bonds accumulated for the baby that did not yet exist. Paulette's father, a schoolteacher, was a good carpenter, and he had vowed that when Lee got back, if they wanted him to, he would come out to California to help with his own hands in building them a house. Their parents were getting old. They moved and talked slowly now, but they were ferociously determined to protect their children, and though they could do little more than book railway compartments and buy war bonds, they did whatever they could, hoping that it would somehow keep Lee alive and prevent Paulette from becoming a widow at the age of twenty-six.

For three nearly speechless days in early September, the Marine lieutenant and his young wife stared out the open window of their compartment as they crossed the country in perfect weather and north light. Magnificent thunderstorms would close on the train like Indian riders and then withdraw in favor of the clear. Oceans of wheat, the deserts, and the sky were gold, white, and infinitely blue, blue. And at night, as the train charged across the empty prairie, its spotlight flashing against the tracks that lay far ahead of it straight and true, the stars hung close and bright. Stunned by the beauty of all this, Paulette and Lee were intent upon remembering, because they wanted what they saw to give them strength, and because they knew that should things not turn out the way they wanted, this would have to have been enough.

Distant whirlwinds and dust storms, mountain rivers leaping coolly against the sides of their courses, four-hundred-mile straightaways, fifty-mile bends, massive canyons and defiles, still forests, and glowing lakes calmed them and set them up for their first view of the Pacific's easy waves rolling onto the deserted beaches south of Los Angeles.

Paulette lived in a small white cottage that was next to an orange grove, and worked for six months on instrumentation for P-38s. The factory was a mile away, and to get to it, she had to go through the ranks of trees. Lee thought that this might be dangerous, until one morning he accompanied her and was amazed to see several thousand women walking silently through the orange grove on their way to and from factories that worked around the clock.

Though Lee had more leave than he would have had as an enlisted man, he didn't have much, and the occasional weekends, odd days, and one or two weeks when he came home during the half year at Twentynine Palms were as tightly packed as stage plays. At the beginning of each furlough the many hours ahead (they always broke the time into hours) seemed like great riches. But as the hours passed and only a few remained, Lee no less than Paulette would feel that they would soon be parting as if never to be reunited. He was stationed only a few hours away and they knew that he would try to be back in two weeks, but they knew as well that someday he would leave for the Pacific.

When his orders finally came, he had ten days before he went overseas, and when Paulette came home from work the evening of the first day and saw him sitting on the porch, she was able to tell just by looking at him that he was going. She cried for half an hour, but then he was able to comfort her by saying that though it did not seem right or natural that they should be put to this kind of test in their middle twenties, everyone in the world had to face death and separation sometime, and it was finally what they would have to endure anyway.

On his last leave they took the train north and then hitchhiked forty miles to the coast to look at a town and at a new factory to which Lockheed was shifting employees from its plants in Los Angeles. At first Paulette had refused to move there, despite an offer of more money and a housing allowance, because it was too far from Twenty-nine Palms. But now that Lee was on his way overseas, it seemed perfect. Here she would wait, she would dream of his return, and she would work so hard that, indirectly, she might help to bring him back.

This town, isolated at the foot of hills that fronted the sea, this out-of-the-way group of houses with its factory that would vanish when the war was over, seemed like the proper place for her to hold her ground in full view of the abyss. After he had been gone for two or three weeks, she packed her belongings and moved up there, and though she was sad to give up her twice-daily walks through the orange groves with the thousands of other women, who appeared among the trees as if by magic, she wanted to be in the little house that overlooked the Pacific, so that nothing would be between them but the air over the water.

To withstand gravitational forces as fighter planes rose, banked, and dived, and to remain intact over the vibrations of 2,000-horsepower engines, buffeting crosswinds, rapid-fire cannon, and rough landings, aircraft instruments had spot welds wherever possible rather than screws or rivets. Each instrument might require as many as several hundred welds, and the factory was in full production of a dozen different mechanisms: altimeters, air-speed indicators, fuel gauges, attitude indicators, counters, timers, compasses, gyroscopes—all those things that would measure and confine objective forces and put them, like weapons, in the hands of the fighter pilots who attacked fortified islands and fought high over empty seas.

On fifteen production lines, depending upon the instrument in manufacture, the course of construction was interspersed with anywhere from twenty to forty welders. Amidst the welders were machine-tool operators, inspectors, assemblers, and supervisors. Because each man or woman had to have a lot of room in which to keep parts, tools, and the work itself as it came down the line, and because the ravine and, therefore, the building were narrow, the lines stretched for a quarter of a mile.

Welders' light is almost pure. Despite the spectral differences between the various techniques, the flash of any one of them gives rise to illusions of depth and dimension. No gaudy showers of dancing sparks fall as with a cutting torch, and no beams break through the darkness to carry the eye on a wave of blue. One sees only points of light so faithful and pure that they seem to race into themselves. The silvery whiteness is like the imagined birth of stars or souls. Though each flash is beautiful and stretches out time, it seldom lasts long. For despite the magnetizing brightness, or perhaps because of it, the flash is born to fade. Still, the sharp burst of light is a brave and wonderful thing that makes observers count the seconds and cheer it on.

From her station on the altimeter line, Paulette could see over gray steel tables down the length of the shed. Of the four hundred electric-arc or gas-welding torches in operation, the number lighted varied at any one time from twenty or thirty to almost all of them. As each welder pulled down her mask, bent over as if in a dive, and squeezed the lever on her torch, the pattern of the lights emerged, and it was never the same twice. Through the dark glass of the face plate the flames in the distance were like a spectacular convocation of fireflies on a hot, moonless night. With the mask up, the plane of the work table looked like the floor of the universe, the smoky place where stars were born. All the lights, even those that were distant, commanded attention and assaulted the senses—by the score, by the hundreds.

Directly across from Paulette was a woman whose job was to make oxyacetylene welds on the outer cases of the altimeters. The cases were finished, and then carried by trolley to the end of the line, where they would be hooded over the instruments themselves. Paulette, who worked with an electric arc, never tired of watching this woman adjust her torch. When she lit it, the flame was white inside but surrounded by a yellow envelope that sent up twisting columns of smoke. Then she changed the mixture and a plug of intense white appeared at the end of the torch, in the center of a small orange flare. When finally she got her neutral flame—with a tighter white plug, a colorless core, and a sapphire-blue casing—she lowered her mask and bent over the work.

Paulette had many things to do on one altimeter. She had to attach all the brass, copper, and aluminum alloy parts to the steel superstructure of the instrument. She had to use several kinds of flux; she had to assemble and brace the components; and she had to jump from one operation to the other in just the right order, because if she did not, pieces due for insertion would be blocked or bent.

She had such a complicated routine only because she was doing the work of two. The woman who had been next to her got sick one day, and Paulette had taken on her tasks. Everyone assumed that the line would slow down. But Paulette doubled her speed and kept up the pace.

"I don't know how you do it, Paulette," her supervisor had said, as she worked with seemingly effortless intensity.

"I'm going twice as fast, Mr. Hannon," she replied.

"Can you keep it up?"

"I sure can," she answered. "In fact, when Lindy comes back, you can put her down the line and give her work to me." Whereas Lindy always talked about clothes and shoes, Paulette preferred to concentrate on the instrument that she was fashioning. She was granted her wish. Among other things, Hannon and just about everyone else on the line wanted to see how long she could continue the pace before she broke. But she knew this, and she didn't break. She got better, and she got faster.

When Paulette got home in the morning, the sea was illuminated as the sun came up behind her. The open and fluid light of the Pacific was as entrancing as the light of the Carolinas in springtime. At times the sea looked just like the wind-blue mottled waters of the Albemarle, and the enormous clouds that rose in huge columns far out over the ocean were like the aromatic pine smoke that ascended undisturbed from a farmer's clearing fire toward a flawless blue sky.

She was elated in the morning. Joy and relief came not only from the light on the waves but also from having passed the great test of the day, which was to open the mailbox and check the area near the front door. The mailman, who served as the telegraph messenger, thought that he was obliged to wedge telegrams tightly in the doorway. One of the women, a lathe operator who had had to go back to her family in Chicago, had found her telegram actually nailed down. The mailman had feared that it might blow into the sea, and that then she would find out in some shocking, incidental manner that her husband had been killed. At the factory were fifty women whose husbands, like Lee, had passed through Twentynine Palms into the Second Marine Division. They had been deeply distressed when their men were thrown into the fighting on Guadalcanal, but, miraculously, of the fifty Marines whose wives were gathered in this one place only a few had been wounded and none had been killed.

When her work was done, knowing that she had made the best part of thirty altimeters that would go into thirty fighters, and that each of these fighters would do a great deal to protect the ships on which the Marines sailed, and pummel the beaches on which they had to fight, Paulette felt deserving of sleep. She would change into a nightgown, turn down the covers, and then sit in a chair next to the bed, staring at the Pacific as the light got stronger, trying to master the fatigue and stay awake. Sometimes she would listen to the wind for an hour, nod asleep, and force herself to open her eyes, until she fell into bed and slept until two in the afternoon.

Lee had returned from his training at Parris Island with little respect for what he once had thought were human limitations. His company had marched for three days, day and night, without stopping. Some recruits, young men, had died of heart attacks.

"How can you walk for three whole days without stopping?" she had asked. "It seems impossible."

"We had forty-pound packs, rifles, and ammunition," he answered. "We had to carry mortars, bazookas, stretchers, and other equipment, some of it very heavy, that was passed from shoulder to shoulder."

"For three days?"

"For three days. And when we finally stopped, I was picked as a sentinel. I had to stand guard for two hours while everyone else slept. And you know what happens if you fall asleep, God help you, on sentry duty?"

She shook her head, but did know.

"Article eighty-six of the Articles of War: 'Misbehavior of a sentinel.'" He recited it from memory. "'Any sentinel who is found drunk or sleeping upon his post, or leaves it before he is regularly relieved, shall, if the offense is committed in time of war, suffer death or such other punishment as a court-martial may direct.'

"I was so tired . . . My eyelids weighed ten thousand pounds apiece. But I stayed up, even though the only enemies we had were officers and mosquitoes. They were always coming around to check."

"Who?" she asked. "Mosquitoes?"

"Yeah," Lee replied. "And as you know, officers are hatched in stagnant pools."

So when Paulette returned from her ten-hour shifts, she sat in a chair and tried not to sleep, staring over the Pacific like a sentinel.

She had the privilege of awakening at two in the afternoon, when the day was strongest, and not having to be ashamed of having slept through the morning. In the six hours before the shift began, she would rise, bathe, eat lunch, and gather her garden tools. Then she walked a few miles down the winding coast road—the rake, hoe, and shovel resting painfully upon her shoulders—to her garden. No shed was anywhere near it, and had one been there she probably would have carried the tools anyway.

Because she shared the garden with an old man who came in the morning and two factory women who were on the second day shift, she was almost always alone there. Usually she worked in the strong sun until five-thirty. To allow herself this much hard labor she did her shopping and eating at a brisk pace. The hours in the garden made her strong and fit. She was perpetually sunburned, and her hair became lighter. She had never been so beautiful, and when people looked at her, they kept on looking. Seeing her speed through the various and difficult chores of cultivation, no one ever would have guessed that she might shoulder her tools, walk home as fast as she could, and then set off for ten hours on a production line.

"Don't write about the garden anymore," he had written from a place undisclosed. "Don't write about the goddamned altimeters. Don't write about what we're going to do when the war is over. Just tell me about you. They have altimeters here, they even have gardens. Tell me what you're thinking. Describe yourself as if we had never met. Tell me in detail exactly how you take your bath. Do you sing to yourself? What do the sheets on the bed look like—I mean do they have a pattern or are they a color? I never saw them. Take pictures, and send them. Send me your barrette. (I don't want to wear it myself, I want to keep it in my pocket.) I care so much about you, Paulette. I love you. And I'm doing my best to stay alive. You should see me when it gets tight. I don't throw myself up front, but I don't hold my breath either. I run around like hell, alert and listening every second. My aim is sure and I don't let off shots when I don't have to. You'd never know me, Paulette, and I don't know if there's anything left of me. But I'm going to come home."

Although she didn't write about the garden anymore, she tilled it deep. The rows were straight, and not a single weed was to be seen, and when she walked home with the tools on her shoulders, she welcomed their weight.

They exchanged postscripts for two months in letters that were late in coming and always crossed. "P.S. What do you eat?" he wrote.

"P.S. What do you mean, what do I eat? Why do you want to know? What do you eat?"

"P.S. I want to know because I'm hungry. I eat crud. It all comes from a can, it's very salty, and it has a lot of what seems to be pork fat. Some local vegetables haven't been bombed, or crushed by heavy vehicles, but if you eat them you can wave good-bye to your intestines. Sometimes we have cakes that are baked in pans four feet by five feet. The bottom is cinder and the top is raw dough. What happened to steak? No one has it here, and I haven't seen one in a year. Where are they keeping it? Is there going to be a big barbecue after the war?"

"P.S. You're right, we have no beef around here and practically no sugar or butter, either. I thought maybe you were getting it. I eat a lot of fresh vegetables, rice, fish that I get in exchange for the stuff in my garden, and chicken now and then. I've lost some weight, but I look real good. I drink my tea black, and I mean black, because at the plant they have a huge samovar thing where it boils for hours. What with your pay mounting up in one account, my pay mounting up in another, and what the parents have been sending us lately, when the war is over we're going to have a lot of money. We have almost four thousand dollars now. We'll have the biggest barbecue you've ever seen."

As long as she did her work and as long as he stayed alive, she sensed some sort of justice and equilibrium. She enjoyed the feminine triumph in the factory, where the women, doing men's work, sometimes broke into song that was as tentative and beautiful as only women's voices can be. They did not sing often. The beauty and the power embarrassed them, for they had their independence only because their men were at risk and the world was at war. But sometimes they couldn't help it, and a song would rise above the production lines, lighter than the ascending smoke, more luminous than the blue and white arcs.

The Pacific and California's golden hills caught the clear sunshine but made it seem like a dream in which sight was confused and the dreamer giddy. The sea, with its cold colors and foaming cauldrons in which seals were cradle-rocked, was the northern part of the same ocean that held ten thousand tropical islands. All these things, these reversals, paradoxes, and contradictions, were burned in day by day until they seemed to make sense, until it appeared as if some great thing were being accomplished, greater than perhaps they knew. For they felt tremendous velocity in the way they worked, the way they lived, and even in the way they sang.

On the twentieth of November, 1943, five thousand men of the Second Marine Division landed on the beaches of Tarawa. The action of war, the noise, smoke, and intense labor of battle, seemed frozen when it reached home, especially for those whose husbands or sons were engaged in the fighting. A battle from afar is only a thing of silence, of souls ascending as if drawn up in slow motion by malevolent angels floating above the fray. Tarawa, a battle afar, seemed no more real than a painting. Paulette and the others had no chance to act. They were forced to listen fitfully to the silence and stare faithfully into the dark.

Now, when the line broke into song, the women did not sing the energetic popular music that could stoke production until it glowed. Nor did they sing the graceful ballads that had kept them on the line when they would otherwise have faltered. Now the songs were from the hymnal, and they were sung not in a spirit of patriotism or of production but in prayer.

As the battle was fought on Tarawa, two women fell from the line. One had been called from her position and summoned to what they knew as the office, which was a maze of wavy-glass partitions beyond which other people did the paperwork, and she, like the lathe operator from Chicago, simply dropped away. Another had been given a telegram as she worked; no one really knew how to tell anyone such a thing. But with so many women working, the absence of two did not slow their industry. Two had been beaten. Five hundred were not, and the lights still flickered down the line.

Paulette had known from the first that Lee was on the beach. She wondered which was more difficult, being aware that he might be in any battle, or knowing for sure that he was in one. The first thing she did when she got the newspaper was to scan the casualty lists, dropping immediately to the *F*s. It did not matter that they sent telegrams, telegrams sometimes blew into the sea. Next she raced through reports of the fighting, tracing if she could the progress of his unit and looking for any mention of him. Only then would she read the narrative so as to judge the progress of the offensive and the chances of victory, though she cared not so much for victory as for what it meant to the men in the field who were still alive.

The line was hypnotic and it swallowed up time. If she wanted to do good work, she couldn't think about anything except what was directly in front of her, especially since she was doing the work of two. But when she was free she now dreamed almost continually of her young husband, as if the landings in Tarawa, across the Pacific, had been designed to make her imagine him.

During these days the garden needed little attention, so she did whatever she could and then went down to a sheltered cove by the sea, where she lay on the sand, in the sun, half asleep. For as long as her eyes were closed and the sea seemed to pound everything but dreams into meaningless foam and air, she lay with him, tightly, a slight smile on her face, listening to him breathe. She would awake from this half sleep to find that she was holding her hands and arms in such a way that had he been there she would have been embracing him.

She often spoke to him under her breath, informing him, as if he could hear her, of everything she thought and did—of the fact that she was turning off the flame under the kettle, of the sunrise and its golden-red light flooding against the pines, of how the ocean looked when it was joyously misbehaving.

These were the things she could do, the powers to which she was limited, in the town on the Pacific that was probably the last place in the world for a factory or the working of transcendent miracles too difficult to explain or name. But she felt that somehow her devotion and her sharp attention would have repercussions, that, just as in a concert hall, where music could only truly rise within the hearts of its listeners, she could forge a connection over the thin air. When a good wave rolled against the rocks of the cove, it sent up rockets of foam that hung in the sun, motionlessly and—if one could look at them hard enough to make them stand still—forever. To make them a target, to sight them with concentration as absolute as a burning weld, to draw a bead, to hold them in place with the eye, was to change the world.

The factory was her place for this, for precision, devotion, and concentration. Here the repercussions might begin. Here, in the darkness, the light that was so white it was almost blue—sapphire-colored—flashed continually, like muzzle bursts, and steel was set to steel as if swords were being made. Here she could push herself, drive herself, and work until she could hardly stand—all for him.

As the battle of Tarawa became more and more difficult, and men fell, Paulette doubled and redoubled her efforts. Every weld was true. She built the instruments with the disciplined ferocity that comes only from love. For the rhythm of the work seemed to signify something far greater than the work itself. The timing of her welds, the blinking of the arc, the light touch that held two parts together and was then withdrawn, the patience and the quickness, the generation of blinding flares and small pencil-shots of smoke—these acts, qualities, and their progress, like the repetitions in the hymns that the women sang on the line, made a kind of quiet thunder that rolled through all things, and that, in Paulette's deepest wishes, shot across the Pacific in performance of a miracle she dared not even name—though that miracle was not to be hers.

Robert Houston

LAWFULLY

After Violet's divorce happened to her, and she'd moved into the sagging white house with her mamma and daddy near Birmingham again, Wick Makewater, who looked like a frog and sold alphabetical Bibles, took to sleeping under her mamma's back porch. Violet found him there when she went to empty the morning's coffee grounds on the geraniums. Wick slept under the porch of most people who bought a Bible from him, as Violet had done the afternoon before; he figured that anybody who would spend fifty dollars on a Bible must understand Christian charity pretty well. He had the choice of seeing his commission go for a hotel room or for a fifth of Old Mr. Boston and he was a man who knew what was what.

Violet was her mamma and daddy's youngest, pretty in a not spectacular way, just beginning to wither a little, not frail but fragile. She believed in everything: love, propriety, charity and good works, her mamma's wisdom, her daddy's intellect, private property, happy and sanctified marriages, self-sacrifice, and most passionately in Salvation. Her first husband had believed exclusively in his red '48 Ford coupe. The divorce had happened to her at last when that husband sat up all night holding a deer rifle on her and making her pray out loud because, he said, he wanted to see just how long she could keep it up before her damn prayer juices dried up.

This was back in the fifties. Nobody in Alabama knew much about divorce then except that in Violet's case it seemed to help shove her deeper down into the black hole she had imagined herself sinking into all through the bad, childless marriage—the hole that kept filling up with tears and nearly drowning her as her grass-widowhood settled in. But without the divorce, how could she have discovered that she had been *sent* Wick Makewater to test her, to help her tread water in the black hole? She was almost forty. He was six years older and six inches shorter than she was. It took her just over a month after she discovered him among the coffee grounds under the rotting porch to decide she had to marry him.

Lord knew she tried everything else first before she finally understood she had to sacrifice herself and marry Wick to save them both. After she found him that first morning and got some coffee in him, and talked to him enough to understand just how abject he was, she decided he was a Sign, a miraculous Burden that would prove her life had some purpose after all. He was clearly one of the least of men. He could not help being from Yazoo, Mississippi, and not being related to anybody but sorry people nobody had ever heard of. She got him to put aside enough money from his commissions each week to set himself up in a truckers' motel on the edge of town, and she took him to tent meetings down in Rockett's Bottom at night. But he hid his Old Mr. Boston in the bushes outside the tent and went to sleep just after the Invocation hymn every time. She tried to get her mamma and daddy to talk to him but they wouldn't let him in the house. Finally, when he confessed the weakness of the flesh to her and asked her to come to his motel room, she went. For three nights running she sat up with him all night playing checkers until he'd slipped off into the bathroom to visit his Old Mr. Boston enough times that he fell asleep and she was safe.

It was an intolerable situation. She could neither abandon Wick nor, properly, keep staying in a motel room with him. The night would surely come when he *didn't* fall asleep. And after three nights without sleep herself the walls of the black hole had started rising up around her again as solid as the music of a pipe organ.

So on the morning of the fourth day, a wintery, soggy Friday with light like whey, she went to the bank, drew out her $137.00 in savings, and called a taxi. They would go the hundred miles to Georgia, since there was no waiting period before getting married there, and do the thing that very afternoon. When she woke Wick up to tell him what they were going to do, he said, "Damn straight!" and went into the bathroom a last time.

Violet got some lunch down him in Irondale, just out of town, but by the time they got fifteen miles to Grant's Mill he lost it all over the back seat of the cab. The only way she kept the cab driver from turning back was to get him to stop at a gas station so she could scrub his cab out for him.

In Anniston, halfway to the state line, she got Wick to eat a hot dog at a Dairy Queen, but by Tallapoosa, just inside Georgia, he spewed it on the back of the cab driver's neck. The cab driver swore that if they hadn't already been in Georgia he would have dumped them and gone back alone. But Violet scrubbed his car out again, and gave him a tract and two dollars to get his uniform cleaned. So he agreed to go through with the rest of the trip if she promised not to feed Wick again.

In Bremen they got their blood tests at a county health office just across the street from the Trojan prophylactic plant. The nurse had a bad time with Wick, who kept trying to scratch the ticks he said were crawling all over him. Violet sat and held both his hands and talked to him until he was able to sit still long enough for the needle to go in. They were compatible, the blood test showed, and the nurse gave them a souvenir card that said, "Get married in Buchanan County, Georgia. No Waiting."

From Bremen it was nine miles to the county courthouse in Buchanan. In Buchanan they had to find the judge, who with luck might be in his office, the nurse had told them. Violet hoped so. She hated to bother people at home with business things.

The courthouse was the only real building in town, a two-storey Gothic stone cube with a steeple and handless clock. A Confederate soldier at the foot of an obelisk guarded the bandstand and little square the courthouse fronted onto. The road around the square was dirt, with half a dozen gingerbreaded houses and two feed and mercantile stores facing it. Mud seethed around the courthouse like quicksand, and as Violet crawled out of the cab at the wide, cracked steps, she had a flash of fear that she would sink into it and never be found. The cab driver had to help Wick get out of the cab, and pretended to pick ticks off him to keep him calm as they climbed the steps behind Violet.

Violet led the way, her face still without expression, down the long, dim hallway that ran the length of the courthouse. The wide boards of the unvarnished floor, the olive wainscotting that rose halfway up the walls, and the cracked green plaster above swallowed the light from three naked bulbs dangling at intervals from the high and cobwebby ceiling. Gray light from the door at the other end of the hallway faded toward Violet into the dimness and made her feel as if she were in a tunnel or a mine shaft. Their footsteps thudded and echoed on the dust of the soft floorboards. Along the walls like souls in purgatory— though Violet didn't believe in purgatory, of course—sat a handful of old men in overalls and old women in bonnets, staring blankly from wooden benches at the walls opposite them, as if they were all waiting with incredible patience for something. Even as Violet stepped over a muddy dog asleep at the door labeled "Judge Cecil Bedsole," she couldn't get rid of the feeling that she was underground, that she was about to run out of air.

Judge Bedsole was in, sitting before a rolltop desk in a room far too large for an office, trying to catch enough light from the tall, leaded windows to read a sheaf of yellow legal papers. He didn't look up when Violet came in. Only when Wick groaned did he raise his eyes at them over his glasses. His heavy eyebrows, which hung like awnings over a tiny face with no chin, rose slightly when he saw Wick clutching the door frame, groaning and trying to show the cab driver where to find the ticks.

"He awright?" he asked Violet.

Violet was standing alone in the center of the huge room. "We want to get married," she said.

"Figured that. He gone live long enough?"

"He has a fever." Violet's knees kept trying to come unlocked.

"Blood tests?" Violet crossed the room and handed him the form the nurse had given her. Judge Bedsole put it down without looking at it. "Got a witness?" he asked.

Violet looked blank. The judge nodded toward the cab driver. "He gone be your witness?" Violet looked over her shoulder at the cab driver. He shrugged. With a sigh the judge heaved himself out of his swivel chair and walked past Violet to the door. He was shorter than she was, almost as short as Wick. At the door he stood patiently while the cab driver led Wick out of the way to a cane-bottomed chair and deposited him in it. Wick whimpered. Lord, Violet thought, if you've ever helped me carry it . . .

The judge buttoned his coat and shouted down the hallway, "Wedding, everybody!" The sound of slow bustling and of shuffling feet started up from the hall as the judge stalked back to his desk and began asking Violet questions for a form he filled out with an old black fountain pen. Violet felt a bowstring begin to tighten, sensed the dark hole yawn.

The judge finished the form and Violet turned to see a room full of the old men and women from the benches in the hall. One of the women, faceless beneath her bonnet and shapeless under her feedsack dress, handed Violet a small bunch of winter wild flowers and patted her arm. The men were solemnly shaking Wick's and the cab driver's hands. Three or four dogs milled around in the crowd, and one of them hiked his leg on Wick's chair. "Huzzah," one of the old men said, and kicked it. Violet hugged the old woman until the old woman had to push her away. The dark hole retreated a tiny bit. Violet stood as straight as she could and let a thin veil of tears slip between her and the room.

"Ready," Judge Bedsole said. "Let's get the bride and groom over by the door. Everybody else in place now. Who's gone give the bride away?"

"My turn!" one of the old men said.

"Reckon so, Riley," the judge said. "Best man?"

"Me!" another old man said.

"Ain't your time, Thurlow. It's Winston's, ain't it?"

"Thurlow can do hit," the old man who must have been Winston said, glowering at Wick. Wick was pulling up his pants leg to look for a tick. Thurlow stepped out of the crowd, lifted him up from his chair, and steered him to the door. The old lady with the flowers walked with Violet to the door, patting her all the way. Violet's lips were moving, saying the Twenty-third Psalm over and over. The rest of the old men and women stood in two ragged lines on either side of an imaginary aisle. Riley shuffled up, took Violet's arm, and smiled at her from a round, toothless mouth.

"Now," the judge said. One of the old men along the aisle began to sing something that sounded to Violet like *here-nor-hit-nernt-ner, here-nor-hit-nernt-ner*, over and over again, while the woman who had given her the flowers hummed, "Heaven Is Nearer Now That Mamma Is There." Riley marched Violet, lips still moving, toward the judge. As they walked, he watched Violet's lips. "Beg pardon, ma'am?" he said as they reached the judge. "You talking to me?"

"Yea though I walk through the valley of the shadow of death, thou art with me; thy rod and thy staff they comfort me," Violet said audibly.

"Yes ma'am. Praise Jesus!" Riley said and quit watching her lips. When they got to the judge, Thurlow started down the aisle with Wick. Oh, Lord, they've got it backwards, Violet thought. I'm not supposed to be here first! She looked to the judge to tell him how horrible it was, when one of the dogs darted across the aisle and Wick tripped and fell down on top of it. The dog yelped, the same old man as before stepped out of line, said, "Huzzah," kicked it, and Wick crawled off into the line of old women with his eyes closed. One of the old women screamed and two or three old men dove for Wick.

Violet could stand no more. She let herself sink down into the dark hole and began to fill its muddy bottom with tears. The next thing she knew Riley was holding her arm while the judge was asking Wick if he took this woman to be his lawfully wedded wife. Wick's eyes were focused somewhere outside the window beyond the judge, where it had started to rain again. He didn't answer. The judge reached out and shook him and repeated the question.

"Hot damn," Wick said softly.

"What? What's that?" the judge said, looking toward Violet.

Violet closed her eyes again. She treaded water in the black hole as hard as she could. "He says, 'I do,' your honor." Her voice didn't break. It didn't even quaver.

When she opened her eyes again, Riley's toothless face was poking a three-day beard at her.

"Git to kiss the bride," he said. He shifted his chewing tobacco further back in his cheek and took Violet's shoulders. Violet was a board. He kissed her full on the mouth and she gagged. It's done, Lord, she said to herself. Wick was taking a long drink of corn whiskey from a Mason jar Thurlow held up for him. It's done, Lord. Her mamma and daddy and her first husband peered down over the edge of the dark hole at her. I've got me a man again, Mamma, Violet said. A man! Just like you do.

"Fee's ten dollars, Miz Makewater," the judge said. "Two more if you want the engraved certificate. Most folks give a little something to these good people—" he waved toward the old men and women "—and congratulations. Need you two and the witness to sign my book now."

When they left the judge's office, Violet walked in front again, her face a mask, clutching the rolled-up engraved certificate. Wick came behind with Thurlow, the cab driver, and the Mason jar. On the steps, Violet felt that she'd come up above ground again from the dark courthouse. And in the dim wet dusk she gave quarters and dimes to the old men and women until she ran out. Thurlow helped stuff Wick into the cab and took back the empty Mason jar. Two teen-agers in a hot rod with Alabama plates pulled up to the steps behind them, the girl huddled wide-eyed under the skinny boy's arm. As the cab slid away through the mud, one of the old women threw a handful of rice. The last thing Violet could make out was Riley's toothless face as he waved her a good-bye kiss, then turned away to follow the teen-agers into the courthouse. It's done, Lord. They will be done. The bare tree limbs against the sky were what her mamma had told her they were when she was a little girl, witches' fingers.

The white whiskey seemed to have taken care of Wick's ticks for the time being. As they turned onto the main highway out of Buchanan, he tried to lean over to Violet and wound up sliding down in the seat beside her. "Hon?" he said without trying to get up.

"Yes, Wick. I'm here," Violet said.

"This supposed to mean we in love, don't it?"

"Yes."

"Good! I've always wondered what that felt like." He reached an arm for Violet's knees, but missed. By the time they reached Bremen he was asleep. All the rest of the way home, as night came on, the rain kept falling, kept turning the darkening fields to mud.

David Huddle

APACHE

She was a blue-eyed blonde, her name was Apache, and if you didn't like it, you could kiss her ass. Worked at the Pussy Cat, not the Naked Cabaret, which she and the other Pussy Cat girls considered tacky, though more than a few had worked there, too. Not Apache. When she came in from New York, she went straight to work for the Pussy Cat. Had the job before she even got there.

Up at the Naked they had one of those peach-skinned girls with silicone tits and light-brown hair, and her name was Miss Cheyenne, but anybody could tell that was bullshit. Apache was called Apache because she had a temper. "I'll jerk a knot in your ass," Apache said in a friendly voice to a clean-scrubbed M.I.T. sophomore if he ran a hand up her thigh. He stopped, too, because there was something back there, something that boy could tell from how she said it or how she looked.

Up on the bar Apache was damn sure no squaw. She started out with what looked like one of those old-fashioned two-piece bathing suits, the kind that just barely showed your navel. The bottom had zippers at each hip, the top had a zipper that came up in the middle. Apache did the zips up to the top first pass up and down the bar. By the end of "Nasty Girl," she was down to a pretty little white-crotched G-string. Blond hair was one of her best features, Apache knew that, and she didn't care if some of the other girls thought she showed it maybe a little too soon. Apache was twenty-nine and said she was twenty-five, but she still had some to spare. If you had style, you could work without resorting to implants.

But Apache knew that what got Lola and the Tucson Twister was the white peignoir and the bridal business. "I'll swear to God, girl, you look like a Barbie Doll up there," Tucson said, but Apache ignored her because her real name was Ida and God knew Apache didn't have to take anything from somebody named Ida.

"Barbie Doll that wants to fuck," murmured Lola, who was black and slinky as a hungry cat. Now that was true, but it didn't bother Apache because she had put some thought into looking kind of bride-like, even down to how she smiled when there was that long pause in the music and she opened the white peignoir and ran two fingers over her best feature.

Apache had been married and divorced three times, starting with when she was sixteen, and for all she knew, she was married a fourth time, too. At least the Chinaman said she was. And she said she was sometimes, when one of the shitheads who bought her a drink asked her. "Yeah, I'm married to a Chinese man," she said, ruefully or hatefully, depending on how she felt and how much more the shit-head was likely to spend on her. It didn't make a damn to her whether she was married or not, and the white peignoir struck her as funny.

"You feeding those little boys' dreams, honey. You jacking off twelve-year-olds," said Lola, and Apache turned on her.

"So what if I am?" said Apache, and she walked right up to Lola even though Lola was the one of all of them who scared her. Apache and Lola stared at each other, and then Apache laughed and said, "I'm a jack off all ages." And Lola laughed, too, and said she was, too, and the Tucson Twister sniffed and went on out to find herself what she in her ignorance called "a sweet thing."

Apache met this real bullshit guy who said that he was an Indian of the Osage tribe. This was on a rainy Tuesday night in June when it looked like nobody and all nobody's cousins was going to come into the Zone. There were five girls for every man who came through the

Pussy Cat door, there were empty spaces around the bar, and Apache felt spooked by the place when it was that way. She figured she'd do her ten o'clock number and ask Paulie if she could go home. He'd say yes. Paulie liked her. Apache never complained about anything, even about the night that West Virginia girl, the Coalminer's Daughter, puked all over Apache's locker. And Paulie had caught Apache's number a couple of nights when she's set that place on fire, had them stamping their feet and whistling. But on this particular night Apache was just sitting there having a vodka martini and telling Albert how she was going to leave early and go over and spend some time with the Chinaman, and Albert was telling her how maybe she ought to give the Chinaman a call first, when this guy in a pony-tail and a poncho sat down beside her and started wiping the rain off his glasses.

The guy told Albert he wanted coffee, and Albert of course enjoyed telling him he wasn't going to get no god damn cup of coffee at the Pussy Cat, maybe he ought to try up the street at the Naked. So the guy got his glasses on and ordered a coke, for which Albert charged him three bucks. Apache saw him eyeing her through those gold-rimmed spectacles of his, his poncho still dripping on the floor and on the bar. What the hell, she asked him if he wanted to buy her a drink. He said yes and told Albert to bring this lady a coke. Albert guffawed and walked on down the bar while Apache explained the system to him: he could buy her a "beer," which was a bottle of champagne that cost twenty-one bucks, or he could buy her a "drink," which cost seven bucks. The guy smiled at her, rustled around in his poncho, pulled out his wallet again, opened it, and showed it to her like some kind of rare treasure. It had an old raggedy-assed five in it, that's all, and the guy looked just pleased as could be. Albert came back up the bar and asked them if they'd got it worked out yet, which situation embarrassed Apache. So she said to Albert to bring her another vodka martini, she'd pay for it herself. She jerked her head toward the man in the poncho and said, "This guy's lost, he don't know where the fuck he is."

But the man didn't shrivel up and die just because she insulted him. He grinned at her and admitted that it was true, he was trying to walk back to Cambridge and took a wrong turn, he said. Apache was starting to get up and walk away because it ruins your reputation to sit with somebody who isn't spending money on you. But it was this rainy, dead-assed night, and it made sense to her right then just to keep her badelias parked on that bar-stool where at least she was safe and out of trouble. The guy asked her her name, and she told him Apache, but she didn't look at him any more. Who the fuck needed to look at some lost son of a bitch with a pony-tail who was dripping all over the bar and who couldn't buy her a drink, who was walking around with nothing but a five in his pocket? She damn sure didn't ask him his name, but he told her then anyway, it was John Chapman. Apache hardly ever asked anybody their name; even if they told her, she forgot it. Then John Chapman told her that bullshit about the Osage Indians in Kansas and Missouri.

Apache didn't listen. She was in a trance.

"Apache, you about to nod off there," said Lola, walking behind her, putting a bony hand on Apache's shoulder. "Somebody slip you some shit, honey?" she murmered close to Apache's ear, and when Apache blinked at her, Lola smiled and sauntered on down the bar a few places, Lola in her spike heels and fish-net stockings.

John Chapman pulled the poncho up over his head in a grand crinkling of heavy plastic, bashed that thing into a semi-folded state, and dropped it on the floor between himself and Apache. "I also have an Osage name," he told her, leaning in her direction to get her attention. The man obviously intended to carry on a conversation as long as she sat there.

"Hey, Apache!" Albert shouted at her from way down at the other end of the bar. "Paulie wants to know if you're going on welfare tomorrow or what?"

Apache sighed and stood up and walked back to do her number.

"Another time, and maybe we'll talk," Chapman murmered, watching her when she walked past him even though she kept her eyes on the floor.

"Hell of a night to get married," said Lola when Apache walked past her, and Apache wished she could give Lola a grin, but she didn't have one available.

Sometimes Apache was pretty fabulous. It didn't have anything to do with anything. Or else it did. She could be high and happy, step out there, and then start feeling sleazy and old for no reason. Those times she hated even to look at the shitheads at the bar, gaping at her like a bunch of retards at a retard convention. Or it could happen like tonight when she felt lower than whale shit and dreaded putting a foot through that curtain, and all of a sudden she was flying. She was energy and muscles, and her body was the music, the Pointer Sisters singing, "I'm so excited . . ." Even the few men who sat around the bar seemed acceptable to Apache, and she smiled at them in sweet romance, let her body make its moves. Just before the lights went down for her to twirl in the white peignoir under the silver strobe light, she saw Mr. John Chapman in his poncho, raising a hand to wave to her before he went out the door. The strobe divided her into a thousand spinning Apaches, and one or two of them said aloud into the blast of music, "Go get rained on, Indian. Go get your ass wet."

When she was out working through the tables and around the bar, Apache wore a red velveteen jacket, a black one-piece bathing suit split down to below her navel, smoke-colored tights, and heels. She never had trouble getting somebody to buy her a drink, and she usually had more "beer" tickets to turn in at the end of the evening than any of the other girls. Trouble was, Apache did have difficulty with her vision and her footwork before the evening was over. There weren't more than a few drops of rum in each drink, but she went through fifty or sixty drinks on a good night. She danced a lot of it out of her system, but even so, she usually felt pretty floaty by around midnight.

Which was about the time John Chapman came in, wearing a tie and a three-piece khaki suit. Just to wear that with a pony-tail took a lot of nerve, but to wear it into the Zone and then to wear it into the Pussy Cat on a Thursday at midnight meant the son of a bitch was from another planet. Apache was sitting close enough to the door when he came in to see that the suit was brand new. He'd washed that long black hair of his and tied up his pony-tail in a small silver and turquoise clip. But she was damned if she was going to talk with him. People seemed to be clearing a path for him to the one empty seat at the bar, and you could see every girl's eye on him when he took the stool, looked straight at Albert who was waiting in front of him, and ordered a coke.

"Money just walked in and sat down over there," said the Teenage Queen, moving through the crowd behind Apache.

"Ain't gonna spend none of it on you, bitch," whispered Lola moving briskly that way, too, just behind the Teenage Queen.

Apache had to laugh. This place was like something nobody could even dream of. Chapman was strafed in rapid succession by Tina, Erica Mahoney, Coco, Wonder Woman, Patsy Jones, the Teenage Queen, Sweet Anabel, Lola, Nurse Goodbody, and Gladys Garrett. The Teenage Queen tried to pick up one of his hands and lay it on her titty, which was one of several undignified things the Queen did all the time that Apache wouldn't stoop to. John Chapman shook off the Queen, told all of them no, he didn't want any company, and no, he wasn't lonely, and smiled at them to keep them happy and moving on down the bar away from him.

"Wants you," said Wonder Woman, circling back the other way around the bar, passing behind Apache. Apache shrugged, but Wonder Woman wasn't watching to catch her response.

"I'm up," said Apache to nobody. It wasn't even true. She had a while before she was up, but she walked back to the dressing room anyway. It was better to sit around back there than to have to watch the meat show.

Then she was up, and goddammit, she was too sober to get anything going. Everything all around her was so ridiculous it was all she could do not to stop dancing and just stand there giving them the finger, those god damn stupid open-mouthed faces around that bar, a stink rising from the floor of thirty years of spilled draft beer half mopped up every night. "I'm so excited! I'm so excited!" She was bored with the song. The strobe light split her up while she tried to make herself spin. She wished she could just dissolve that way, and when they turned up the lights there would be no more Apache.

"You auditioning for a nursing home?" asked Paulie when she came off. He was sitting on his stool just inside the door. She walked past him, the peignoir, the bathing suit, and the G-string all wadded up in one hand because she didn't give a damn.

"Fuck you, Paulie." She tried to sound friendly, but she really didn't want to talk to anybody right then.

"Man out there wants to talk to you," Paulie told her softly. Paulie was always doing isometrics, pushing one arm against another, flexing his legs, going up on the tips of his toes, and Apache didn't like to look at him, but she knew better than to ignore him.

"Nothing new about that," she murmured, standing there and waiting. "Well?" she said. She turned enough to see past Paulie through the two-way mirror, like a television screen, to where John Chapman sat with a little space around him in that crowded bar, as if everybody knew he didn't belong there.

"Lola's saving you a seat," Paulie said. Sure enough, she could see Lola sitting one seat down from Chapman, talking to somebody who hadn't bought her a drink, Apache could tell that even from that far away.

"I don't need it," Apache said.

"Talk to him or hit the street," Paulie told her and sighed and stood up and stretched.

Apache walked over and threw her clothes at her locker and sat down to take off her white heels. "I was gonna talk to him anyway," she muttered.

"Can I buy you a drink, Apache?" John Chapman asked her when she was walking toward him, before she'd even reached the empty seat beside him.

Apache shrugged and sat down. "Sure you can," she said. "Buy me a beer?" She didn't look at him. She hoped he'd say no. Albert was standing right there in front of them, waiting for the definite signal from one or the other of them. When John Chapman nodded at him, Albert was setting that little bottle of champagne up in front of Apache in ten seconds flat. Chapman put a fifty on the bar, and Albert hustled to make the change.

"So how come you're so dressed up?" Apache made herself sound like a lady who could kick some ass when she wanted to.

Chapman smiled at her but wouldn't say anything. Under the knot of his tie there was a gold pin that made it stand up from his collar; Apache looked at that while she talked to him. "I thought you said you were an Indian?" she said, still making a point of not giving him a smile. She tossed off the first glass of the champagne with Albert right there filling up her glass again when she set it down.

"An Indian can't dress up?" Chapman asked her.

"He teaches up at Harvard, Apache," said Albert, so polite she could have slapped his face.

"You talking to a professor, girl," said Lola on the other side of her.

Apache shook her head. What the hell do I care if he sells ice to the Eskimos? Apache started to say, but then she held her tongue because she could feel Paulie watching her from back behind the mirror.

"I've been trying to talk Albert here into enrolling in some night courses," John Chapman said. "He's thinking about changing jobs."

"Yeah," Albert said, hitching up his trousers and standing up straight, "I want to get into a field where I can screw a lot of women." Chapman grinned at him appreciatively, and Albert burst out laughing.

"You got some customers up that way," Apache told Albert and watched him hustle his silly ass up the bar. "So what do you teach?" She hated asking anybody any kind of a question, but she wanted to get this over with fast.

"Para-Sociology."

"Para what?" she said.

"Pair o' what? Pair o' what?" echoed Patsy Jones gliding along the dark wall behind them. Apache reached back there and tried to swat her ass, but she was gone.

"It's one of the social sciences," John Chapman told her. "It's very new."

"Never heard of it," said Apache. She looked all around the bar, getting ready to move away.

"She's just moody," Lola told Chapman, leaning around Apache to catch his eye. "You got to make an impression on her."

Apache grimly tossed off the last of her champagne. "Buy me another beer?" She knew he wasn't going to. When Apache didn't want to see somebody she had a trick of putting her eyes on him but focusing behind him.

"I have a suggestion," said Chapman, folding his hand on the bar and leaning toward Apache.

She cut him off. "I don't go out with anybody."

Albert had been standing in front of them, ready to serve Apache another drink but now he sidled back down the bar to the end where he and Paulie could talk with each other through the curtained doorway.

"This is special," Chapman told her. "I know a nice place. It's quiet. We can talk Indian to Indian, Apache to Osage. By the way, my Osage name is . . ."

Apache stood up and was starting to move away when Albert reached across the bar and caught her wrist.

"You're going out," Albert told her softly, grinning. "Paulie says for you to have a good time."

Apache let her arm go limp and wouldn't look at Albert. She stood there making her eyes blaze at Chapman. "I guess we have a date," she said.

"You don't have to go," Chapman told her. "I don't want you to make her go," he told Albert, and Albert raised his hands, palms open, smiling and shaking his head.

"Let's go," said Apache making for the door. She could get this over with in less than half an hour, even if they were going to make it tough on her.

"Wait," said Chapman behind her.

"What's wrong?"

"Don't you need to change clothes?" He was smiling.

"You want me to wear the G-string?"

"No." He was still smiling at her. "Your regular clothes. What you wore when you came to work."

"A denim skirt?"

"That's fine."

"Christ."

A room like that, shag-carpet-two-double-beds-sliding-glass-doors-to-the-balcony, Apache didn't need to see, and she told Chapman she thought the place sucked. Speaking of which, she said, "If you've got another one of those fifties, you can get out of your clothes, lie back there and relax, and I'll stop wasting your time and mine. How much did you pay Paulie?" she asked him, letting the denim skirt drop, pulling the little cotton sweater up over her head.

Chapman made a slight waving motion with his hand. She couldn't believe him. She hadn't seen a man yet who wouldn't turn his eyes toward a woman taking off a bra, but this one here had turned into a statue. "Traditionally," he said, "the Osage and the Apache nations were never able to agree on any terms of trade. It would have seemed, since the former were farmers and the latter hunters and warriors, that . . ."

"Jesus Christ!" Apache said. She refastened the bra, put the sweater back on, and wrapped the skirt around her waist. She dug a cigarette out of her purse, lit it, plumped up the pillows on one bed, and lay back to smoke and wait him out. Chapman stood, posed, at the far end of the room, his hands in his pockets.

"I don't actually teach at Harvard," he told her, folding his arms in front of him now and staring at her, "but I don't think that ought to matter."

Apache gave him a look, a snort, a sneer, some kind of noise she meant to let him know she could give less of a rat's ass what he did. There weren't many things she hated worse than being out of the bar during working hours, and this was useless, what was going on now.

Chapman took off his glasses, breathed on them, and rubbed them carefully on his vest. "I'm a research assistant," he said, holding the glasses up to the light.

Apache let the smoke from her cigarette curl around her face while she watched him. He kept looking at her as if he expected her to ask him a favor any minute.

"I work for a guy who's writing up pieces on working people in the city," he said. "I told him I wanted you to have an interview." He made it sound like he was giving her something.

Apache let some silence fall between them before she asked him how much he would pay her.

"I don't need a great deal of information," Chapman told her. "Just the standard background kind of thing, your hometown, your family, where you went to school . . ."

Apache asked him how much he would pay her.

"Preliminary expenses were higher than I estimated," he told her, smiling and walking toward her. "I got a deal on this room, but Paulie's fee was substantial. Albert's tip, that drink I bought for Lola, the cab, this suit . . ." He turned a little, modeling the suit for her.

"How much?"

Chapman stood next to her and pulled a ten and two ones out of his wallet, then showed her it was empty. He continued to smile at her, though she could see it was costing him some effort. Digging up two quarters and a nickel, he let change, bills, and wallet fall on the bed beside her. When she laughed at him, he turned away and walked over to pull the drapes and stare through the glass doors. The more Apache looked at his silly pony-tail and the back of his expensive suit, the more she had to laugh.

"You've got some nerve," she said. "I need some air." She walked over to the doors, too, unlatched one of them, and slipped out onto the balcony. It was high and cool and dark out there. She liked it immediately and didn't give a damn if Chapman did come out behind her.

"Mr. Bigshot Indian," she said. She wanted to laugh out loud again, into that open space off the balcony, but it seemed like all she could do was chuckle to herself.

"Ten minutes' worth of talk," Chapman said softly. The man was still coming on like he was doing something nice for her. "Easy Questions. What's your name? What are your hobbies?" He forced a laugh.

Apache glanced straight down from the balcony. She wasn't ready for all that space of darkness that fell away from the railing down to the lighted streets below. She felt her stomach go queasy. Then she shook her head and accepted Chapman's offer of his jacket—he was putting it around her shoulders before she even thought to herself that he was doing it to manipulate her. For a moment she understood what he must feel like being too broke to make her a decent offer and too full of pride to beg her. She shook her head again, to get rid of that understanding. "Make it all up," she told him. "Use any name. What difference does it make?"

A noise swelling around her kept Apache from hearing what he said and made her look up to her left where a huge jet was coasting in across the harbor to Logan Airport. Chapman shouted something, and then he came closer to her. "I have to have some facts," he said.

Apache hated how his face looked now, his mouth shaping the

words so carefully and then drawing down into a thin little grimace. She stepped toward the door, and he stepped in front of her. "I spent all that money," he said.

They stood staring at each other, Apache getting madder by the second. All of a sudden she pulled his jacket off her shoulders and flung it out into the air, off the balcony. She didn't know she was going to do that until she'd done it, and neither one of them watched it drop. She started toward him, meaning to scratch his face until he moved out of her way.

Chapman caught one of her hands and then the other. It wasn't that he seemed to know what he was doing, it was just protecting himself, she could tell that, but it was like a dance of when she moved, he moved, too. Then he had her. His left arm was hooked around her neck, not choking but holding her steady, his right hand holding her right hand back up behind her shoulder-blades, and there was such a pain in her right shoulder she thought she was going to black out. In spite of that, she felt herself breathing and sort of crying. She could hear him breathing hard, too, behind her.

Chapman pushed her to the railing where he bent her forward so that she had to look straight down the side of the building. "What's your name?" he rasped into her ear. Apache closed her eyes and wouldn't say a god damn word. "Do you want me to let you drop?" he asked her.

Apache felt herself pissing. She couldn't tell what she was seeing down the side of that building, but she couldn't keep her eyes closed, and her whole body hurt her. She was crying, and she didn't know if she could speak a word in any kind of language. But she tried. "Yes," she got out of herself. "Yes, let me drop."

Chapman let her go.

"Bitch!" he said. He turned away from her, put his hands against the glass door and leaned against it, panting, as if he'd been the one dangled over the edge.

"I pissed in my pants," Apache said. There was one reasonable thing to do, and she did that, took her wet underwear off. She didn't even think about what to do with them, she just flung those underpants right over the side where she'd sent Chapman's jacket. "Tell you what, Mr. Motherfucker Indian," she told his back. "You come with me. I'll give you a god damn interview."

In the taxi Apache told the driver, "Fourteen Ping On Street," and when Chapman raised his eyebrows at her, she told him that they were going to the Chinaman's. No need to go back to the Pussy Cat; it was past closing time. She had a plan now. She made up her mind to be a little more friendly to Chapman. "I go to fix the Chinaman his breakfast when I get off from work. He's my old man." She laughed at how startled Chapman looked.

"You're married?" he said.

She shrugged. "The Chinaman says we are. I can't remember it. He says we did it one morning a couple of years ago when we were both shitfaced."

"Did you?"

"I don't know. I remember drinking a lot, but I don't remember any wedding. He and I both get to laughing when we talk about it. You can ask him and see what he says." Apache felt o.k. now that she knew what she was going to do, but tiredness was coming down on her. She leaned back in the seat and closed her eyes, hugging herself to keep warm.

The sky was lightening when the cab let them out down at the end of a dead-end street, a little pocket of Chinatown. "Original, huh?" Apache stifled a yawn and cast her eyes up at the restaurant sign that blinked feebly, "The Golden Dragon." "The Chinaman says he's owned a dozen restaurants, and he's named every one of them 'The Golden Dragon.'" She had a key to a door at the side of the restaurant, which she opened and then locked behind them. She led Chapman down a steep, dimly-lit staircase. At the bottom of the steps she used another key to open the first door in the hallway. The Chinaman was sitting, just as she knew he would be, there at his kitchen table, facing the door.

"Apache," he shouted, "where the hell have you been?" He laughed. He was a short, stocky man, wearing a plain white shirt and an old Cleveland Indians baseball cap tipped back on his head. His kitchen was so brightly lit with flourescent tubes in the ceiling that even Apache, who was used to it, blinked at the light. Chapman took off his glasses and rubbed his eyes. "You gonna make me sit here and starve, woman?" said the Chinaman.

"The little shit-ass would sit here all day if I didn't come and fry up his breakfast for him," Apache said proudly. She knew the Chinaman was showing off for Chapman. He liked it when she brought him somebody to talk to. "Bill Po, this is John Chapman. Mr. Chapman is a . . . ?" She let it trail off just to see what Chapman would say.

"I do research," said Chapman. Apache could tell he was using his dignified tones. He and the Chinaman shook hands across the kitchen table, Bill Po rising slightly from his chair. "I work up at Harvard."

Apache watched Bill Po give a little bow of his head to express his reverence for Harvard, and it was all she could do to keep from laughing out loud. There were no windows in the Chinaman's kitchen, the walls were bare, and the door that led to the other rooms of the apartment was shut. But Apache still found the place comfortable. She hummed while she set out eggs and bacon and butter on the counter, keeping one eye on the men.

She savored the dignity with which Chapman accepted the chair the Chinaman scooted out for him with his foot. "So you're Apache's husband," he said. "I've heard a lot about you."

Apache couldn't help but snort, and Bill Po grinned at Chapman. "That god damn Apache," he said, shaking his head. "I don't think she knows anything about me. She don't ask me questions, and if I tell her something, she forgets it the next day. Wish somebody would tell me why I married that woman." He laughed up toward the kitchen ceiling.

"Blonde hair," Apache said and smacked the Chinaman's hat off with her spatula. "Come on, Bill," she said. "I told him about all your 'Golden Dragons.'" She turned back to her cooking, poking at the strips of bacon to make them lie evenly in the frying pan. "Why don't you tell Mr. Chapman about our wedding, Bill."

The Chinaman guffawed. Apache saw Chapman start to set his elbows on the blue and white checked tablecloth, then pull back when he noticed jelly drippings on it. "We had champagne," said the Chinaman. "And everybody sang." He and Apache broke up. Apache held on to Bill Po's shoulder. She could tell Chapman was trying to look casual while he sat there, but he wasn't succeeding at all.

She had to pay attention to the bacon because she liked to cook it at a high heat. The Chinaman had sworn she wanted to set the kitchen on fire, but Apache knew he didn't really care. She did things the way she wanted to, not like a god damn housewife, and she knew he liked that. "Oh, Bill! I gotta tell you this," she said. "Look at this," she said, turning to face him, pulling up her apron and skirt to her waist and holding them while Bill Po took a look. He raised his eyebrows at the sight and turned to Chapman. Apache saw Chapman glance back at the door, as if measuring the distance to it from where he sat.

"She, ah . . . ," said Chapman.

"See, he doesn't have a jacket on," explained Apache. She broke eggs into the sputtering grease.

"Yes?" said Bill Po.

"Apache is the subject of an interview I've been commissioned to conduct," Chapman said. He was straining for poise. She was going to fix his ass.

"Yes?" said Bill Po, looking from one to the other of them.

"We were up in his hotel room," Apache said, setting two slices of bread into the Chinaman's toaster and slapping the handle down. "And Mr. Chapman here offered me twelve dollars to tell him about my life. I walked out onto the balcony, and Mr. Chapman followed me out there and gave me his jacket, the gentleman, you know, trying to keep me warm and get me to answer his questions. I wouldn't talk, and he wouldn't let me leave. So I threw his jacket over the side. He grabbed me and held me over the edge, asked me if I wanted him to drop me off the side of that building. He scared me so bad I pissed in my pants, and then he let me go and called me a bitch. I threw my underwear over the side, too." She and Bill Po both stared at Chapman.

"These interviews will be published . . ." Chapman began, but he trailed off, and Apache was satisfied to see him squirming in his chair, facing the Chinaman with nothing to say for himself. She turned and scooped the eggs out of the skillet, laid the bacon on the plate beside the eggs and nudged the toaster handle until it popped. This was the one moment she liked best at the Chinaman's every morning, when she produced that breakfast like a magic trick and set the plate down in front of Bill Po.

"Thanks, Apache." Bill took off his hat and set it beside his plate. Then he reached behind him to a drawer in a kitchen cabinet. She watched him shuffle a batch of tools out of the way before he got hold of what he was looking for, his army-issue forty-five. It looked huge in his thin hands. He kept groping around in the drawer, tossing aside a screwdriver and some pliers and some wire and wrenches. "Apache, have you seen my . . . .," he said. But then he dug out the clip and whispered to himself as if he were alone in the room, "Here you are." He checked the cartridges, popped the clip into the handle, chambered a round and pointed that thing across the table at Chapman's face.

"Bill," said Apache softly. She knew she had to be careful not to provoke him too much.

"All right," Bill told her. He held the pistol steady while Chapman eased himself back down into his chair. Apache watched him open and then close his mouth. The forty-five was three feet from Chapman's forehead. "Mr. Chapman," Bill said, "Apache has left all that shit behind." Bill Po's diction was very precise. "She don't have a background any more. If she did, it would cost you more than twelve dollars. Do you understand?"

"Yes sir," said Chapman, except that he said it with just his mouth, so that you could see what he was saying, but you couldn't hear it.

The Chinaman raised the barrel and squeezed off a round into the transom behind Chapman, shattering glass down onto the floor outside in the hallway.

"Jesus fucking God, Billy!" said Apache, holding both hands over her ringing ears. "Did you have to pull the god damn trigger? Now you're gonna have the cops over here."

Bill Po gave her a quick grin and brought the pistol down. Chapman sat shivering. Apache went over beside him and shouted at him. "You haven't been shot, John! You're all right!" She patted him on the shoulder, but she couldn't get him to look at her.

The Chinaman dropped the clip out of the forty-five and cleared the chamber. He reached behind him and tossed both the clip and the pistol into the tool drawer. He shoved the drawer closed, turned, and picked up his fork. "Nobody in the whole building but us," he said. He took a couple of quick bites of his breakfast while Chapman and Apache watched him. "Check him out, Apache," he said. "See if he pissed in his pants."

Apache peered into Chapman's lap. "Don't think so," she said. She put a hand lightly on his crotch. "Nope."

"Too bad," said the Chinaman. He ate with astonishing speed. Then he put his cap back on and pushed his chair away from the table. He reached behind him into another drawer, at this time, without looking, he pulled out a toothpick. "Do you have any questions?" he asked Chapman.

"No sir," said Chapman with just his lips.

"Apache, you going over to your place now?" Bill Po asked her. Apache nodded and gave him enough of a smile to let him know she appreciated what he'd done for her. Bill Po examined the results of the preliminary pickings of his teeth. "Why don't you walk the man back upstairs?"

Apache took off her apron, retrieved her purse, and with her hands on his arms and back, she directed Chapman back out into the hallway. She couldn't hate him any more now, but she did want to get him on his way. She waved to Bill Po, who had a leg up on the table, digging with the toothpick at a molar far back in his jaw. He winked at Apache just as she closed the door.

Apache steered Chapman up the steps. He seemed willing enough to move as she directed him. "Wasn't that the loudest god damn thing you ever heard in your life?" she asked, giving his elbow a little shake.

Chapman tried to say something, but she couldn't get it.

Apache rattled the key in the door at the top of the steps. The damn lock was half-busted, but the Chinaman had refused to do anything about it when she complained to him. And when she finally did get the door open, Chapman just stood still, looking at the street and the people walking along in the sunshine, but he didn't look like he was planning to go out there any time soon.

"What's wrong?" she asked him.

"I don't know . . ." His voice was feeble, but she could hear him now.

Apache stared at him. "Move out, John," she said softly.

But Chapman just stared at the floor, his hands shoved down into his pockets. His clothes drooped. His pony-tail was snarled and skewed to one side. He really did look like somebody who didn't have but twelve dollars and change to his name. Apache thought for a moment, then pulled the door closed again. A little roughly she tugged him toward her and leaned back against the wall there in the hallway. "Where are you from anyway, John?" she asked him. She was untucking the little pullover from her skirt, reaching up under it behind herself and arching her back. "What's your hometown?"

"Parmalee, South Dakota," Chapman told her. She pulled at his hands and put them where she wanted them, up under her sweater.

His glasses were smudged, but it interested her to watch his eyes while she made him touch her. She undid his pony-tail and impatiently combed through its snarls with her fingers. "Did you say you had an Osage name?" she asked him.

"Little Cougar," he whispered, his voice like a hypnotized man's. "I don't know if I want this," he said.

Bending, she unzipped and unbuckled him. "Go down one step, John," she instructed. She moved him down where she wanted him. "There we go," she said. It took a good bit more adjusting of how they were standing and how she leaned against the wall. Chapman wasn't making it easy for her either, but she was determined to make it work.

"Tell you what," she said, softly now that they were so close. "You just relax and tell me what your hobbies are. One at a time." She felt a little jolt of surprise run through his shoulders, but then he really did brace up, and she knew she could make it work now.

"Give me a hobby, John," she rasped into his ear.

"Hiking," he responded.

They each inhaled sharply.

"Yes," she said. "Yes, keep going."

"Horseback riding," he plunged on.

"Good, John," she urged him. "That's good."

"Archery!" he blurted, as if he were running out of time.

"Oh God! Little Cougar!" Apache sang. "That's exactly right!"

John Irving

TRYING TO SAVE PIGGY SNEED

This is a memoir, but please understand that (to any writer with a good imagination) all memoirs are false. A fiction writer's memory is an especially imperfect provider of detail; we can always imagine a better detail than the one we can remember. The correct detail is rarely, exactly, what happened; the most truthful detail is what *could* have happened, or what *should* have. Half my life is an act of revision; more than half the act is performed with small changes. Being a writer is a strenuous marriage between careful observation and just-as-carefully imagining the truths you haven't had the opportunity to see. The rest is the necessary, strict toiling with the language; for me this means writing and rewriting the sentences until they sound as spontaneous as good conversation.

With that in mind, I think that I have become a writer because of my grandmother's good manners, and—more specifically—because of a retarded garbage collector to whom my grandmother was always polite and kind.

My grandmother is the oldest living English Literature Major to have graduated from Wellesley. She lives in an old people's home, now, and her memory is fading; she doesn't remember the garbage collector who helped me become a writer, but she has retained her good manners and her kindness. When other old people wander into her room, by mistake—looking for their own rooms, or perhaps for their previous residences—my grandmother always says, "Are you lost, dear? Can I help you find where you're *supposed* to be?"

I lived with my grandmother, in her house, until I was almost seven; for this reason, my grandmother has always called me "her boy." In fact, she never had a boy of her own; she has three daughters. Whenever I have to say good-bye to her, now, we both know she might not live for another visit, and she always says, "Come back soon, dear. You're *my boy*, you know"—insisting, quite properly, that she is more than a grandmother to me.

Despite her being a English Literature Major, she has not read my work with much pleasure; in fact, she read my first novel and stopped (for life) with that. She disapproved of the langauge and the subject matter, she told me; from what she's read about the others, she's learned that my language and my subject matter utterly degenerate as my work matures. She's made no effort to read the four novels that followed the first (she and I agree this is for the best). She's very proud of me, she says; I've never probed too deeply concerning *what* she's proud of me *for*—for growing up, at all, perhaps, or just for being "her boy"—but she's certainly never made me feel uninteresting or unloved.

I grew up on Front Street in Exeter, New Hampshire. When I was a boy, Front Street was lined with elms; it wasn't Dutch elm disease that killed most of them. The two hurricanes that struck back-to-back, in the fifties, wiped out the elms and strangely modernized the street. First Carol came and weakened their roots; then Edna came and knocked them down. My grandmother used to tease me by saying that she hoped this would contribute to my respect for women.

When I was a boy, Front Street was a dark, cool street—even in the summer—and none of the back yards were fenced; everyone's dog ran free, and got into trouble. A man named Poggio delivered groceries to my grandmother's house. A man named Strout delivered the ice for the ice box (my grandmother resisted refrigerators until the very end). Mr. Strout was unpopular with the neighborhood dogs—perhaps because he would go after them with the ice tongs. We children of Front Street never bothered Mr. Poggio, because he used to let us hang around his store—and he was liberal with treats. We never bothered Mr. Strout, either (because of his ice tongs and his fabulous aggression toward dogs, which we could easily imagine being turned toward us). But the garbage collector had nothing for us—no treats, no aggression—and so we children reserved our capacity for teasing and taunting (and otherwise making trouble) for him.

His name was Piggy Sneed. He smelled worse than any man I *ever* smelled—with the possible exception of a dead man I caught the scent of, once, in Istanbul. And you would have to be dead to look worse than Piggy Sneed looked to us children on Front Street. There were so many reasons for calling him "Piggy," I wonder why one of us didn't think of a more original name. To begin with, he lived on a pig farm. He raised pigs, he slaughtered pigs; more importantly, he lived *with* his pigs—it was *just* a pig farm, there was no farmhouse, there was *only* the barn. There was a single stovepipe running into one of the stalls. That stall was heated by a wood stove for Piggy Sneed's comfort— and, we children imagined, his pigs (in the winter) would crowd around him for warmth. He certainly smelled that way.

Also he had absorbed, by the uniqueness of his retardation and by his proximity to his animal-friends, certain pig-like expressions and gestures. His face would jut in front of his body when he approached the garbage cans, as if he were rooting (hungrily) underground; he squinted his small, red eyes; his nose twitched with all the vigor of a snout; there were deep, pink wrinkles on the back of his neck—and the pale bristles, which sprouted at random along his jawline, in no way resembled a beard. He was short, heavy, and strong—he *heaved* the garbage cans to his back, he *hurled* their contents into the wooden, slat-sided truck bed. In the truck, ever eager to receive the garbage, there were always a few pigs. Perhaps he took different pigs with him on different days; perhaps it was a treat for them—they didn't have to wait to eat the garbage until Piggy Sneed drove it home. He took *only* garbage—no paper, plastic, or metal trash—and it was *all* for his pigs. This was all he did; he had a very exclusive line of work. He was paid to pick up garbage, which he fed to his pigs. When *he* got hungry (we imagined), he ate a pig. "A whole pig, at once," we used to say on Front Street. But the *piggiest* thing about him was that he couldn't talk. His retardation either had deprived him of his human speech or had deprived him, earlier, of the ability to learn human speech. Piggy Sneed didn't talk. He grunted. He squealed. He *oinked*—that was his language; he learned it from his friends, as we learn ours.

We children, on Front Street, would sneak up on him when he was raining the garbage down on his pigs—we'd surprise him: from behind hedges, from under porches, from behind parked cars, from out of garages and cellar bulkheads. We'd leap out at him (we never got too close) and we'd squeal at him: "Piggy! Piggy! Piggy! Piggy! OINK! WEEEE!" And, like a pig—panicked, lurching at random, mindlessly startled (*every time* he was startled, as if he had no memory)—Piggy Sneed would squeal back at us as if we'd stuck him with the slaughtering knife, he'd bellow OINKS! out at us as if he'd caught us trying to bleed him in his sleep.

I can't imitate his sound; it was awful, it made all us Front Street children scream and run and hide. When the terror passed, we couldn't wait for him to come again. He came twice a week. What a luxury! And every week or so my grandmother would pay him. She'd come out to the back where his truck was—where we'd often just startled him and left him snorting—and she'd say, "Good day, Mr. Sneed!"

Piggy Sneed would become instantly childlike—falsely busy, painfully shy, excruciatingly awkward. Once he hid his face in his hands, but his hands were covered with coffee grounds; once he crossed his legs so suddenly, while he tried to turn his face away from Grandmother, that he fell down at her feet.

"It's nice to see you, Mr. Sneed," Grandmother would say—not flinching, not in the slightest, from his stench. "I hope the children aren't being rude to you," she'd say. "You don't have to tolerate any rudeness from them, you know," she would add. And then she'd pay him his money and peer through the wooden slats of the truck bed, where his pigs were savagely attacking the new garbage—and, occasionally, each other—and she'd say, "What beautiful pigs these are! Are these your *own* pigs, Mr. Sneed? Are they *new* pigs? Are these the same pigs as the other week?" But despite her enthusiasm for his pigs, she could never entice Piggy Sneed to answer her. He would stumble, and trip, and twist his way around her, barely able to contain his pleasure: that my grandmother clearly approved of his pigs, that she even appeared to approve (wholeheartedly!) of *him*. He would grunt softly to her.

When she'd go back in the house, of course—when Piggy Sneed would begin to back his ripe truck out the driveway—we Front Street children would surprise him again, popping up on both sides of the truck, making both Piggy and his pigs squeal in alarm, and snort with protective rage.

"Piggy! Piggy! Piggy! Piggy! OINK! WEEEE!"

He lived in Stratham—on a road out of our town that ran to the ocean, about eight miles away. I moved (with my father and mother) out of Grandmother's house (before I was seven, as I told you). Because my father was a teacher, we moved into academy housing— Exeter was an all-boys' school, then—and so our garbage (together with our nonorganic trash) was picked up by the school.

Now I would like to say that I grew older and realized (with regret) the cruelty of children, and that I joined some civic organization dedicated to caring for people like Piggy Sneed. I can't claim that. The code of small towns is simple but encompassing: if many forms of craziness are allowed, many forms of cruelty are ignored. Piggy Sneed was tolerated; he went on being himself, living like a pig. He was tolerated as a harmless animal is tolerated—by children, he was indulged; he was even encouraged to be a pig.

Of course, growing older, we Front Street children knew that he was retarded—and gradually we learned that he drank a bit. The slat-sided truck, reeking of pig, of waste, or *worse* than waste, careened through town all the years I was growing up. It was permitted, it was given room to spill over—en route to Stratham. Now there was a town, Stratham! In small-town life is there anything more provincial than the tendency to sneer at *smaller* towns? Stratham was not Exeter (not that Exeter was much).

In Robertson Davies' novel, *Fifth Business*, he writes about the townspeople of Deptford: "We were serious people, missing nothing in our community and feeling ourselves in no way inferior to larger places. We did, however, look with pitying amusement on Bowles Corners, four miles distant and with a population of one hundred and fifty. To live in Bowles Corners, we felt, was to be rustic beyond redemption."

Stratham was Bowles Corners to us Front Street children—it was "rustic beyond redemption." When I was 15, and began my association with the academy—where there were students from abroad, from New York, even from California—I felt so superior to Stratham that it surprises me, now, that I joined the Stratham Volunteer Fire Department; I don't remember *how* I joined. I think I remember that there was no Exeter Volunteer Fire Department; Exeter had the other kind of fire department, I guess. There were several Exeter residents— apparently in need of something to volunteer *for?*—who joined the Stratham Volunteers. Perhaps our contempt for the people of Stratham was so vast that we believed they could not even be relied upon to properly put out their own fires.

There was also an undeniable thrill, midst the routine rigors of prep school life, to be a part of something that could call upon one's services without the slightest warning: that burglar alarm in the heart, which is the late-night ringing telephone—that call to danger, like a doctor's beeper shocking the orderly solitude and safety of the squash court. It made us Front Street children important; and, as we grew only slightly older, it gave us a status that only disasters can create for the young.

In my years as a firefighter, I never rescued anyone—I never even rescued anyone's pet. I never inhaled smoke, I never suffered a burn, I never saw a soul fall beyond the reach of the safety bag. Forest fires are the worst and I was only in one, and only on the periphery. My only injury—"in action"—was caused by a fellow-firefighter throwing his Indian pump into a storage room where I was trying to locate my baseball cap. The pump hit me in the face and I had a bloody nose for about three minutes.

There were occasional fires of some magnitude at Hampton Beach (one night an unemployed saxophone player, reportedly wearing a pink tuxedo, tried to burn down the casino), but we were always called to the big fires as a last measure. When there was an eight- or a ten-alarm fire, Stratham seemed to be called last; it was more an invitation to the spectacle than a call to arms. And the local fires in Stratham were either mistakes or lost causes. One night Mr. Skully, the meter reader, set his station wagon on fire by pouring vodka in the carburetor—because, he said, the car wouldn't start. One night Grant's dairy barn was ablaze, but all the cows—and even most of the hay—had been rescued before we arrived. There was nothing to do but let the barn burn, and hose it down so that cinders from it wouldn't catch the adjacent farmhouse on fire.

But the boots, the heavy hard hat (with your own number), the glossy black slicker—*your own ax!*—these were pleasures because they represented a kind of adult responsibility in a world where we were considered (still) too young to drink. And one night, when I was 16, I rode a hook-and-ladder truck out the coast road, chasing down a fire in a summer house near the beach (which turned out to be the result of children detonating a lawn mower with barbecue fluid), and there— weaving on the road in his stinking pickup, blocking our importance, as independent of civic responsibility (or any other kind) as any pig—was a drunk-driving Piggy Sneed, heading home with his garbage for his big-eating friends.

We gave him the lights, we gave him the siren—I wonder, now, what he thought was behind him. God, the red-eyed screaming monster over Piggy Sneed's shoulder—the great robot pig of the universe and of outer space! Poor Piggy Sneed, near home, so drunk and foul as to be barely human, veered off the road to let us pass, and as we overtook him—we Front Street children—I distinctly heard us calling, "Piggy! Piggy! Piggy! Piggy! OINK! WEEEE!" I suppose I heard my voice, too.

Clinging to the hook-and-ladder, our heads thrown back so that the trees above the narrow road appeared to veil the stars with a black, moving lace—the pig smell faded to the raw, fuel-burning stink of the sabotaged lawn mower, which faded finally to the clean salt wind off the sea.

In the dark, driving back, past the pig barn, we noted the surprisingly warm glow from the kerosene lamp in Piggy Sneed's stall. He had gotten safely home. And was he up, reading? we wondered. And once again I heard our grunts, our squeals, our oinks—our strictly animal communication with him.

The night his pig barn burned, we were so surprised.

The Stratham Volunteers were used to thinking of Piggy Sneed's place as a necessary, reeking ruin on the road between Exeter and the beach—a foul-smelling landmark on warm summer evenings, passing it always engendered the obligatory groans. In winter, the smoke from the wood stove pumped regularly from the pipe above Piggy's stall, and from the outdoor pens, stamping routinely in a wallow of beshitted snow, his pigs breathed in little puffs as if they were furnaces of flesh. A blast from the siren could scatter them. At night, coming home, when whatever fire there was was out, we couldn't resist hitting the siren when we passed by Piggy Sneed's place. It was too exciting to imagine the damage done by that sound: the panic among the pigs, Piggy himself in a panic, all of them hipping up to each other with their wheezy squeals, seeking the protection of the herd.

The night Piggy Sneed's place burned, we Front Street children were imagining a larkish, if somewhat retarded spectacle. Out the coast road, lights up full and flashing, siren up high—driving all those pigs crazy—we were in high spirits, telling lots of pig jokes: about how we imagined the fire was started, how they'd been having a drinking party, Piggy *and* his pigs, and Piggy was cooking one (on a spit) and dancing with another one, and some pig backed into the wood stove and burned his tail, knocked over the bar, and the pig that Piggy danced with *most* nights was ill-humored because Piggy *wasn't* dancing with *her* . . . but then we arrived, and we saw that this fire wasn't a party; it wasn't even the tail-end of a bad party. It was the biggest fire that we Front Street children, and even the veterans among the Stratham Volunteers, had ever seen.

The low, adjoining sheds of the pig barn appeared to have burst, or melted, their tin roofs. There was nothing in the barn that wouldn't burn—there was wood for the wood stove, there was hay, there were eighteen pigs and Piggy Sneed. There was all that kerosene. Most of the stalls in the pig barn were a couple of feet deep in manure, too. As one of the veterans of the Stratham Volunteers told me, "You get it hot enough, even shit will burn."

It was hot enough. We had to move the fire trucks down the road; we were afraid the new paint, or the new tires, would blister in the heat. "No point wasting the water," our captain told us. We sprayed the trees across the road; we sprayed the woods beyond the pig barn. It was a windless, bitter-cold night, the snow as dry and fine as talcum powder. The trees drooped with icicles and cracked as soon as we sprayed them. The captain decided to let the fire burn itself out; there would be less of a mess that way. It might be dramatic to say that we heard squeals, to say that we heard the pigs' intestines swelling and exploding—or before that, their hooves hammering on the stall doors. But by the time we arrived, those sounds were over; they were history; we could only imagine them.

This is a writer's lesson: to learn that the sounds we imagine can be the clearest, loudest sounds of all. By the time we arrived, even the tires on Piggy's truck had burst, the gas tank had exploded, the windshield had caved in. Since we hadn't been present for those events, we could only guess at the order in which they had taken place.

If you stood too close to the pig barn, the heat curled your eyelashes—the fluid under your eyelids felt searing hot. If you stood too far back, the chill of the winter night air, drawn toward the flames, would cut through you. The coast road iced over, because of spillage from our hoses, and (about midnight) a man with a Texaco emblem on his cap and parka skidded off the road and needed assistance. He was drunk and was with a woman who looked much too young for him—or perhaps it was his daughter. "Piggy!" the Texaco man hollered. "Piggy!" he called, into the blaze. "If you're in there, Piggy— you *moron*—you better get the hell out!"

The only other sound, until about two in the morning, was the occasional *twang* from the tin roof contorting—as it writhed free of the barn. About two the roof fell in; it made a whispering noise. By three there were no walls standing. The surrounding, melted snow had formed a lake that seemed to be rising on all sides of the fire, almost reaching the level of heaped coals. As more snow melted, the fire was being extinguished from underneath itself.

And what did we smell? That cooked-barnyard smell of mid summer, the conflicting rankness of ashes in snow, the determined baking of manure—the imagination of bacon, or roast pork. Since there was no wind, and we weren't trying to put the fire out, we suffered no smoke abuse. The men (that is to say, the veterans) left us boys to watch after things for an hour before dawn. That is what men do when they share work with boys: they do what they want to do, they have the boys tend to what they don't want to tend to. The men went out for coffee, they said, but they came back smelling of beer. By then the fire was low enough to be doused down. The men initiated this procedure; when they tired of it, they turned it over to us boys. The men went off again, at first light—for breakfast, they said. In the light I could recognize a few of my comrades, the Front Street children.

With the men away, one of the Front Street children started it—at first, very softly. It may have been me. "Piggy, Piggy," one of us called. One reason I'm a writer is that I sympathized with our need to do this; I have never been interested in what nonwriters call good and bad "taste."

"Piggy! Piggy! Piggy! Piggy! OINK! WEEEE!" we called. That was when I understood that comedy was just another form of condolence. And then I started it; I began my first story.

"Shit," I said—because everyone in the Stratham volunteers began every sentence with the word "shit."

"Shit," I said. "Piggy Sneed isn't in there. He's crazy," I added, "but nobody's that stupid."

"His truck's there," said one of the least imaginative of the Front Street children.

"He just got sick of pigs," I said. "He left town, I know it. He was sick of the whole thing. He probably planned this—for weeks."

Miraculously, I had their attention. Admittedly, it had been a long night. *Anyone* with almost *anything* to say might have easily captured the attention of the Stratham Volunteers. But I felt the thrill of a rescue coming—my first.

"I bet there's not a pig in there, either," I said. "I bet he ate half of them—in just a few days. You know, he stuffed himself! And then he sold the rest. He's been putting some money away, for precisely this occasion."

"For *what* occasion?" some skeptic asked me. "If Piggy isn't in there, where is he?"

"If he's been out all night," another said, "then he's *frozen* to death."

"He's in Florida," I said. "He's retired." I said it just that simply—I said it as if it were a *fact*. "Look around you!" I shouted to them. "What's he been spending his money on? He's saved a bundle. He set fire to his own place," I said, "just to give us a hard time. Think of the hard time we gave *him*," I said, and I could see everyone thinking about that; that was, at least, the truth. A little truth never hurt a story.

"Well," I concluded. "He's paid us back—that's clear. He's kept us standing around all night."

This made us Front Street children thoughtful, and in that thoughtful moment I started my first act of revision; I tried to make the story better, and more believable. It was essential to rescue Piggy Sneed, of course, but what would a man who couldn't talk do in *Florida?* I imagined they had tougher zoning laws than we had in New Hampshire—especially regarding pigs.

"You know," I said, "I bet he *could* talk—all the time. He's probably *European,*" I decided. "I mean, what kind of name is *Sneed?* And he first appeared here around the war, didn't he? Whatever his native language is, anyway, I bet he speaks it pretty well. He just never learned *ours.* Somehow, pigs were easier. Maybe *friendlier,*" I added, thinking of us all. "And now he's saved up enough to go home. That's where he is!" I said. "Not Florida—he's gone back to *Europe!*"

"'Atta boy, Piggy," someone cheered.

"Look out, Europe," someone said, facetiously.

Enviously, we imagined how Piggy Sneed had gotten "out"—how he'd escaped the harrowing small-town loneliness (and fantasies) that threatened us all. But when the men came back, I was confronted with the general public's dubious regard for fiction.

"Irving thinks Piggy Sneed is in Europe," one of the Front Street boys told the captain.

"He first appeared here around the war, didn't he, Sir?" I asked the captain, who was staring at me as if I were the first *body* to be recovered from this fire.

"Piggy Sneed was *born* here, Irving," the captain told me. "His mother was a half-wit, she got hit by a car going the wrong way around the bandstand. Piggy was born on Water Street," the captain told us. Water Street, I knew perfectly well, ran into Front Street— quite close to home.

So, I thought, Piggy was in Florida, after all. In stories, you must make the best thing that *can* happen happen (or the worst, if that is your aim), but it still has to be true.

When the coals were cool enough to walk on, the men started looking for him; discovery was a job for the men—it being more interesting than waiting, which was boys' work.

After a while, the captain called me over to him. "Irving," he said. "Since you think Piggy Sneed is in Europe, then you won't mind taking whatever *this* is out of here."

It required little effort, the removal of this shrunken cinder of a man; I doused down a tarp and dragged the body, which was extraordinarily light, onto the tarp with first the long and then the short gaff. We found all 18 of his pigs, too. But even today I can imagine him more vividly in Florida than I can imagine him existing in that impossibly small shape of charcoal I extricated from the ashes.

Of course I told my grandmother the *plain* truth, just the boring facts. "Piggy Sneed died in that fire last night, Nana," I told her.

"Poor Mr. Sneed," she said. With great wonder, and sympathy, she added: "What awful circumstances forced him to live such a savage life!"

What I would realize, later, is that the writer's business is *both* to imagine the possible rescue of Piggy Sneed *and* to set the fire that will trap him. It was *much* later—but before my grandmother was moved to the old people's home, when she still remembered who Piggy Sneed was—when Grandmother asked me, "Why, in Heaven's Name, have you become a *writer*?"

I was "her boy," as I've told you, and she was sincerely worried about me. Perhaps being an English Literature Major had convinced her that being a writer was a lawless and destructive thing to be. And so I told her everything about the night of the fire, about how I imagined that if I could have invented well enough—if I could have made up something truthful enough—that I could have (in some sense) saved Piggy Sneed. At least saved him for another fire—of my own making.

Well, my grandmother is a Yankee—*and* Wellesley's oldest living English Literature Major. Fancy answers, especially of an aesthetic nature, are not for her. Her late husband—my grandfather—was in the shoe business; he made things people really needed: practical protection for their feet. Even so, I insisted to Grandmother that her kindness to Piggy Sneed had not been overlooked by me—and that this, in combination with the helplessness of Piggy Sneed's special human condition, and the night of the fire, which had introduced me to the possible power of my own imagination . . . and so forth. My grandmother cut me off.

With more pity than vexation, she patted my hand, she shook her head. "Johnny, *dear*," she said. "You surely could have saved yourself a lot of *bother*, if you'd only treated Mr. Sneed with a little human decency when he was alive."

Failing that, I realize that a writer's business is setting fire to Piggy Sneed—*and* trying to save him—again and again; forever.

THE FALL OF TEXAS

The world was supposed to end on a Saturday night in March of 1962. Some Medieval astrologer had absolutely predicted it, and for a while the approaching cataclysm got a lot of play in the pages of the *Daily News*. You never believe such things, of course, but you don't entirely disbelieve them either. People made jokes or decided to have parties. The idea was to go out with a bang.

I was twenty-six. I don't think I've ever felt older. In three years I'd had thirteen lovers. The count may even have been higher. There were the serious ones who took months of your life and all the transitional ones in between when you were trying to recover. Those were the ones you tended to forget, and if you passed one on Second Avenue, you'd give a distant nod and walk on too fast for any conversation. I once asked one of them, "Why are we here?" as we were taking off our clothes, and I remember his answer, though not his name. "If you don't know," he said, "I can't help you."

I was living then in a two-room walkup on East Seventh Street above a linoleum store. My landlord was the linoleum king of the Lower East Side. Linoleum was his passion; he took no interest in his real estate. I'd moved into his place with a saxophone player named Arnie Raff, who met a rich girl in East Hampton one weekend and moved in with her and never returned—even to pick up his records, which I kept in boxes for a while, then put back on their shelves and played until the music wore out all Arnie Raff associations and became mine. Finally he remembered where his records were, the great sides he'd had ever since he was a kid and had to steal his brother's draft card to get into Birdland to hear Charlie Parker. "Hey, why don't I just come on by and get them?" he said, and I said, "No, you can't ever walk in here again, Arnie. There's nothing you can take out of here." I'd always thought of myself as a gentle person and now here was a piece of someone's life and identity I wasn't giving back, as if I'd hardened without realizing it. It's better to be tough than sad, I thought.

I would have married Arnie Raff, although it seems incredible now. The illusion of kindness was in the chestnut color of his hair and eyes and the warm, Russian-looking mustache over his lips, which hid, as it turned out, a small mouth of real meanness. I could never have loved him cleanshaven. He was much more bourgeois than I was, which made me feel safe. He yelled at me about my cooking and sanded the floorboards of our apartment and stripped most of the plaster off a wall of brick, as if he meant to live there forever.

After he left, I became aware that the apartment had begun to disintegrate. Little pieces of it kept breaking off or falling down. There was a crack in the ceiling above the bed. I used to lie there and stare up at it. First it looked like the outline of a cloud drawn by a fine black pen, then the cloud began to resemble Texas. Gradually Texas began to look three-dimensional. It made my various lovers nervous. "That ceiling's going to fall," they'd point out accusingly, as if by inviting them there I'd endangered them deliberately. I believed Texas would fall someday, but I didn't believe it would fall on me. So far something had held it up, and no one I personally knew had ever been crushed by a falling ceiling. I thought when it did fall, I'd be in Rome. A friend of mine had just found an apartment there with room enough for me, and at black times I'd remember to say "Rome" to myself as if I were really going to get an airplane ticket and go there. It was the most exotic of the ideas I had about turning myself into a luckier person.

I was home the night Texas came down. The man I was with was married and was always holding up his wrist so I could look at the luminous numbers on his watch in the dark and tell him what time it was. He was a very nearsighted poet who could see nothing without his glasses, and he'd put them on top of a bookcase that jutted out from the wall behind the bed. As I lay in his embrace, I heard a loud ticking, as if he were wearing a grandfather clock. The ticking grew louder and faster and he said, "My God, what's that?" and we both sat up. Plaster rained down around us, falling on the pillow where our heads had been, crashing onto the bookcase, severing his glasses neatly at the bridge but amazingly leaving the lenses intact. He put on both halves of the glasses and said in an awed voice, "I guess I'd better go. I've never had an experience like this. That was a close one, wasn't it?" I helped him find his clothes and we brushed off the white dust as best we could, and pinching his glasses together so they wouldn't fall off, he made his way home to his wife.

I turned on all the lights and sat up the rest of the night staring at the enormous hole where Texas had been, wondering what it meant to find yourself alive when you'd done nothing in particular to ensure your self-preservation.

That week a card arrived in the mail, silver print on black paper:

DANCE THE END OF THE WORLD AWAY.
MAKE THE APOCALYPSE A NIGHT TO REMEMBER.
R.S.V.P. REGRETS ONLY

You had to pay attention to an invitation like that. It made me feel hopeful, though by then I'd been to enough parties to know whom you could expect to see—Arnie Raff, for example, or the poet in his new glasses turning up with his wife, or the old painters who liked to dance with you ostentatiously, wheezing for breath while their women exchanged ironies near the wine table.

I took some of the rent money, since the landlord wasn't rushing to make repairs, and went to Klein's on Fourteenth Street and bought a dress. A slithery shift of something that looked like silk and was so much brighter than anything I had—all zigzags of purple, blue and green—that I didn't quite know who I was in it. I could imagine wearing it in Rome if the world didn't blow up.

I wasn't one of those who flourished at those famous downtown parties of the sixties. I knew what they were about, aside from abandon and ambition. You put yourself out there to be seen, to be taken up, to be judged in the flickering of an eye. I'd slip into watching and become, I thought, invisible. Then someone would accuse me of checking out and I'd make an effort for a while to simulate presence. Watchers stand alone, which is against the rules of parties. They're like pieces that have fallen out of a kaleidoscope when all the other pieces are being shaken up so new patterns can be formed. It's the kaleidoscopic nature of parties that makes them necessary or things might stay too much the same.

The art scene never stood still for long. There were always people coming and going, surfacing overnight, disappearing into thin air without ever sending a postcard to a friend. People gave up on New York and went to Paris, California, Majorca, Mexico City. Some started dropping out of life altogether, people as young as I was mostly, leaping off rooftops into space, diving from windows and landing so gracefully there was only a little blood around the corners of the mouth.

I remember the tall, beautiful, coffee-colored girl with strange green eyes who'd appeared out of nowhere that winter and was seen at all the artists' parties for a while, wildest of all the dancers. Her name was Annabel, it was the season of Annabel. She had a little baby named Anton, whom she'd carry everywhere in her arms and put to sleep in back bedrooms among piles of coats and ride home with at dawn in taxis with various infatuated strangers. She moved into a railroad flat on St. Mark's Place where immediately there were surprising numbers of hangers-on, smoking joints and drinking wine while Annabel made big pots of rice and beans, West Texas style, on her three-burner stove as if she were everyone's mother. You could go there on Sundays for brunch and eat bacon and grits and dance to Ray Charles on the phonograph at eleven-thirty in the morning. "Ooh, don't go," Annabel would say if she caught you heading for the door. "I hate an empty house worse than anything."

The story went around that Annabel was in hiding from her ex-husband, a remittance man from an old Boston family whom she'd met in Paris while she was modeling. But she never acted like someone who was hiding.

One week, though, at the beginning of the summer, people were asking, "Has anyone seen Annabel?" Nobody had. Annabel left her baby with a friend one afternoon and never came back for him. She told the friend she had an important date. She wore an armful of ivory bracelets and a little green silk shift and new gold sandals. She went rushing off to meet some deadbeat, who gave her an overdose of heroin. After several days an electrician found her body in a cellar on Avenue C.

I realized later that in an indirect way Annabel helped to change the direction of my life, though I might never have thought it if she hadn't died the way she did. We always smiled at each other, but I can't recall that we ever had a conversation. I was never even sure she knew my name. It surprised me, in fact, to get one of those black and silver cards.

She sent out so many—to more people than could ever have fitted into her apartment. Even early in the evening there was a fancy uptown crowd no one knew, piling out of taxis in the rain, pushing their way in past Annabel's friends, drinking wine out of paper cups on the stairs. In her brief season, this was the big event.

Upstairs it looked like Halloween. Annabel had draped all the furniture in black sheets and lit candles. She wafted from room to room, very high and giggly, a lost child in a silver gown. People milled around in the dark in their wet coats, spilling beer on each other and saying, "Hi, I didn't know it was you," in hushed voices. Somewhere in the back the baby woke up and started crying. "What is this shit anyway?" someone said drunkenly and turned on the lights.

Too much had been expected, of course, so all the guests felt cheated. They also hated being caught with their imaginations down. Where was the gaiety, the wit, the inspired madness, with which artists would greet the apocalypse? "Tonight Marcel Duchamp would not be impressed," one of the old painters commented loudly.

From then on it was like a party for someone going away whom no one gave a damn about anymore, not even Annabel, who drifted into a room with someone and locked the door. Later people said she'd been trying to tell the rest of us she saw doom up ahead, but that night no one cared.

I didn't feel much like dancing, so I walked back to where the baby was. I wanted him to stop crying. His head banged against my shoulder when I picked him up. I kept repeating, "Shh, Mommy's coming soon," though I knew that wasn't the case, and patted his bottom which was very wet. I felt utterly inept. Suddenly he was quiet, so I put him down in his crib. "Go to sleep, Anton," I said, pretending authority, but I heard him wail as soon as I walked back into the party.

People were doing the latest thing, something called the Twist, in which a man and woman rotated their hips in front of each other but never touched. I poured a glass of wine, looked around the room, and thought very calmly, "There is no one."

A man came up from the street. I noticed him because he wasn't wearing a coat, just a heavy grey sweater and a green scarf around his neck, and I remember thinking he must be cold. He had thick brown hair wet from the rain and a face that had been used a lot, fierce eyes set deep in smashed bone, the right one angled down sharply. He was a very good-looking man, so I decided he would be dangerous, spoiled rotten by women no doubt. For a while he stood near the door at the edge of things, like a player waiting his turn in a game, sizing up his next move. Now and then he'd tighten his lips, pressing them together as if against some oblique thought he couldn't voice to anyone. He caught me staring, so I stepped back a little behind a dancing couple. When I looked again, the party had swallowed him up.

A little later he was standing right in front of me. He took me in, I don't know how else to say it. My tremendous uncertainty, my habit of watching, my ridiculously bright dress. It was as if he could read my bones, it wasn't that he wanted anything. "Why do you hang back?" he said and walked away.

I stood amazed where he left me, wanting to run after him and find out who he was. But his fierceness really scared me. I didn't want him telling me I'd made a mistake, that he'd said all he was ever going to say to me in one question I couldn't even answer, that suddenly seemed the entire painful puzzle of my life.

He was one of those people who'd probably never surface again, who kept wandering in and out. He'd disappeared by the time I got brave enough to look for him.

To tell the truth, I wasn't sorry. I thought of his blue eyes and his handsomeness and how the night might have gone.

Down on St. Mark's Place in the cold darkness the world was still intact, and I carried his question all the way home.

David Madden

WILLIS CARR AT BLEAK HOUSE

The minutes of the October 21, 1927, semi-annual, Special Meeting of the Knoxville Chapter of the Daughters of the Confederacy were read and approved. On March 21, 1928, the Chapter met at Bleak House in the Music Room. There being no new business, Professor Jeffrey Arnow of the University of Tennessee History Department introduced his friend Willis Carr of Carter County, who shared his reminiscences of his role in the War Between the States as follows:

Lota people wanted me to talk about it, but I haven't talked about it all these years. I *heard* a lot of people talk about it, I listened to people talk, but this is the first time that I've opened *my* trap.

And Professor Arnow doesn't even know *why* that I *finally* said I *would* and that's because—right upstairs—I mean we're sitting in the music room and you all know about that ball that the Yankees fired into the wall. General Longstreet's walking up and down in them big boots down here, I could hear him, and there was a man in the back, painting a fresco while that whole thing was going on between General Longstreet and General Sanders, and the reason I came is because I was up there in the tower.

And I wanted to come *back*, and just sorta be where General Longstreet was, where ol' Pete was. I'm not even sure I'll be able to go *up* in that tower.

I tell you, I had a fever from we had marched through the mud and the rain and November cold. And I had a fever, and I didn't quite know what was going on, I was barefoot, most of us barefoot. And sharpshooter, see, he can go wherever he wants to, he's a free agent, that's part of it. So you just naturally gravitate to high places. We saw a house on a hill, highest hill, the highest house, I saw the tower up there, I didn't even *think* about it, I just went on through, past that man that was painting that fresco on the wall, smelled the paint, and I climbed that staircase, and bunch of 'em came behind me, four, five, or six of 'em, we went up there—windows faced East, West—no, East—North, South, but blind toward the West.

From up there, we could look all around, down on the Tennessee River, down there on what I later learned was Kingston Pike, but I didn't know it was *called* Kingston Pike, I didn't know nothing. I was thirteen, I was fourteen, I was thirteen when I went in, but I was fourteen time we got here. Looked old for my age. And so we got up there, and I had a fever, and this old boy from Virginia, he was— during a skirmish, wasn't a battle, was a skirmish—he was sighting through the window, and he said, he didn't turn around to me, but he said, "I *got* him!"

And so then he aimed again. I was in a fever, leaning up against the West wall, you know, and I was thinking, I was watching him real tight, like *I* was sighting through that telescope lens, and I was waiting for him to say, "I *got* him!" because he's focusing like he really had this fellow, whoever might be out there. But he didn't. And I noticed between his legs where he was kneeling down, I noticed a little trickle of blood. It come down the wainscoting—kinda fancy up there—flowing out on the floor between his legs. So I thought, well, I'll see what's going on out there, and I got up there in the other window—two of 'em's already wounded, laying over there to the side—and I got up there, and I sighted through the sights of my telescopic lens. And I saw a man, an officer, riding a white horse, *charging* back and forth in front of the Yankees that was firing at us. He's going back and forth like he's daring 'em to kill him. Shoot!

Shoot! I'm here! Shoot! See if you can *do* it! Yeah. Riding back and forth. And I thought, Nobody, on their side or our side, is crazy enough to be doing what I'm watching, it's fever, it's fever got me, you know. Why, hell—pardon my talk here—I can just shoot at that feller and it won't even hurt him. That's kinda nice, shoot somebody that you can see plain as day, know it's a fever, you shoot at him, won't even hurt him, I just shoot 'im, won't bother 'im, you know. I pulled the trigger, and I just turned away, I didn't even see if I *got* 'im.

But two years after the war was over, I was coming back from out West, where I'd been out there on a two-year drunk, just drunk—bar, barroom *brawls*—you say that word *brawls*, you almost got the whole thing right there in your mouth, need to spit it out. And I made my living by drawing people. I had the knack for drawing, people say, "Draw my picture," I draw their picture in the barroom, I get a drink, made it to my eighteenth birthday that way, just drawing 'n drinking 'n brawling, and I got enough of it, said, "Hell—'scuse me—I'm going back to Carter County." So coming back through, I stopped in this little ol' town, Pulaski, think it was, and these ol' boys were telling about the war, sitting around telling stories. One ol' boy said—well, I was drawing, that's what it was, I was drawing a man, and this other says, "There's the one's picture you *ought* to draw."

And I said, "Why?"

He said, "Well, he's the one—"

"Don't you start that! That's *private*."

He said, "Private, hell, you told everybody that comes through this town, you told *us* thirty times, can't you tell him onc't?"

And he's sitting there mumbling.

So I started to draw his picture, he said, "I ain't gonna pay for it."

I said, "You don't *have* to pay for it, 'less you like it."

I kept drawing his picture, he got to talking, he said, "Well, what these boys talking about, what made *me* famous in the war was that I'm the one that shot General Sanders."

I didn't know who General Sanders *was*. I didn't know what he's talking about. Said, "Where?"

He said, "At Knoxville."

So, I says, "I think I was *in* Knoxville." You know, my brain rotted from drinking, I was too young to remember everything anyway, so I said, "I think I was *in* Knoxville."

He said. "Big ol' house that they got down there called Bleak House, I got up in the tower, I shot down, and I killed him, I'm the one, very one that you're drawing a picture of."

I believed him, cause I didn't remember a dern thing, who'd remember a fe-ver dream, so. . . .

I just went on, I met a lot of other people, I heard a lot of other people, talking about this and that, the Civil War, and I was wondering, "Well, you know, I was there, but I don't remember all *this*, and why are these people so. . . . Why they talk about this all the time, why they want to sit around talk about this, what is it *about* it? That was just something I did, then I went out West."

And so I went back up on Holston Mountain to the cabin where we always lived. I was born up there in 1846, the year that the Mexican war ended. I learned that about thirty years later, I didn't know that then. And my great-grandfather, he *stayed* up there when all the rest of 'em went down to fight. He's old, you know, fact he'd been sitting there beside the fire the whole time since before I was born. One day he came in, said, "I'm a-cold," went over there and stirred up the fire, sat down by the fire, and they say he never got up, just stayed there. "Why don't you go sit in the doorway where you can get some sun? Gran' paw, you worrying us to death sitting over there, staring at the fire all the time."

He said, "I got my own sun right here, it goes down at night, and I poke it up in the morning, all I need."

So my grandfather and my daddy and my big brothers and me went off to war, and time I come back, my great-gran'paw was the only one left. When I come in the door two years after the war was over, he was of course dead, sitting there by the fire, dead. And I said, "Well, that's the way he'd want to go." I went over and I—I'd been civilized, you know, and I was going to bury him, so I pick him up like he's gonna be heavy, like I was still that little kid, you know, still big man in my memory, you know, I picked him up and jerked up on that chair too quick and he spilled out all over the floor. And somehow that aggravated the fool out of me, and I got the broom and I swept him right in the fireplace. His bones been there, ever since, burned down now, of course.

Anyway, I come back home and I went back to hunting—hunting skins and hunting my meat and everything, and I wished I had my old sharpshooter sights to get bear with. And one time I got a bear in my sights and I—he was coming toward me like—I was looking for my dinner—and he was coming towards me like he was looking at *his* dinner, and I sighted on him and I was about to pull the trigger—and I remember sighting on that man, that officer on the white horse, and I said, "My God, that was General Sanders," that they all a-talking about, cause I'd heard a lot of talk about him. General Sanders. I *think*. I'm not sure.

So that has bothered me, what I been thinking about, studying about for years is—sitting up there on Holston Mountain—trying to understand, you know. Why is it, if, if I was the man that shot General Sanders, and I'm *reasonably* certain that I was, I'm not sure, why is it that I feel that I missed the war? That I missed the war?

So one thing that drew me back *here*—I *walked* all the way here from Carter County, Holston Mountain. Cause I wanted to think more about *why* did I want to go back there, why do I want to come back to that place? I *been* in Knoxville a number of times over the years, and I never had the desire to go up in the tower before, and I wonder *why*.

So I came back, trying to see if I can find a way, over here, that I could get some kind of answer I hadn't got—

So maybe I need to go back and just kind of go *over* what I *did* in the war. The events: Lota people writing their memoirs and—you know, people publishing them, and after I learned how to read, I read a lot of it.

Well, we were up on the Mountain, and I was thirteen years old. We

were all Union, you see, 'cept my mother, she was from Elizabethton, she was from a family of rebel sympathizers. And one day Colonel Stover, Andrew Johnson's son-in-law, came up South Holston
Mountain and said to my daddy, my gran'paw, he said, "I want you to
go *with* us . . . tonight, because we're gonna burn the railroad bridge
over Watauga River. Want you all to come and go with us."

And they got ready, they got ready to go, you know, I did everything they did, I hunted with 'em, you know, I did everything that
they did, even though I was thirteen years old, and so they got ready
to go, and they got on their horses, and started down the mountain,
and I went right on with 'em, you know, we gonna go burn the
bridge, whatever that is, we gonna do something for the Civil War,
whatever that is, we gonna do something for the Union, whatever
that is, I didn't know, but I thought it'd be a good idea, it'd be
something *different*. "What you doing coming with us!" they said,
turn around look at me, "What you think you're doing, you get on
back up with the women, your great gran'paw, and take care of 'em till
we get back!"

And *me* the best shot in the family. Not supposed to say that, see,
because—My gran'paw once said, "Don't brag on what you can do,
Davy Crockett done took care all *that*. *You* don't have to brag nothing, you just *do* it, and go bout your business." So nobody ever said,
"You the best," and I never said I was the best either, but I knew it.
What the hell—'scuse me—they gonna do without me? So, I—they
forgot that I was the best runner, too, cause when they took off on
their horses, I kept right up with 'em round those mountain paths, I
kept right up, running. And my brothers pulled up and they reached
down in the path and picked up rocks and started throwing rocks at
me like I's a mad dog.

Well, I *was* a mad dog by the time they got out of sight. I was so
mad, I said, "Hell, I'm gonna go look"—'scuse me—"look for the war
by myself, on my lonesome." So I took out and I—Knoxville, let's see,
that's probably where they got that war. How'd I know? Because my

great-gran'paw used to sit by the fire, as I say, and when my grand-daddy and my daddy would come back from down in Elizabethton or someplace, they'd bring the Knoxville *Whig*. You all read the *Journal* now, but it was the Knoxville *Whig* then. Edited by Parson Brown-low. "The meanest man to walk the streets of Knoxville," *some* of 'em said. "That vile serpent Brownlow," Doctor Ramsey said. "The ugliest man to come out of East Tennessee," Brownlow himself said. And he couldn't wait to get that paper, and when he'd get the paper, I'd be up there asleep in the sleeping loft, you know, and when the rafters went to shaking, I knew he'd got his paper, because he'd read that thing aloud. Only books we had up there was Milton's *Paradise Lost*, the works of Shakespeare, Paul Bunyan's *Pilgrim's Progress*, and the *Whig*. He's the only one could read. He was too mean to teach *me*. I just didn't know *how* to read. Didn't teach anybody else. And he'd yell out, and they'd say, "Can't you read that paper without all that screaming and yelling?" He didn't want words on the paper when it come to Parson Brownlow, he wanted fire, he wanted explosion, he wanted *force*! When he'd get done with the *Whig,* he'd take a hammer and he'd nail it to the wall, just to say, "Look yander. That's it. Right there! What the man said." And one time, he read it out of the paper, "They're taking the Union men down to Montgomery on the railroad and they're putting 'em in prison, and we ought to let the railroad, from Alabama to Bristol, be burned and every bridge on that railroad be burned—cut off the supplies to General Lee." And they listened to him, and that's why they were burning. That night, I learned later on, years later, that when they were burning that one bridge, Reverend William Blount Carter was co-ordinating the burning of nine strategic bridges—Strawberry Plains, up here at Bull's Gap—burning all those bridges at the same moment. 1862.

So . . . I went down there to Knoxville, I thought, Well, I'd find the war. Walked up to this feller on Gay Street, and I said, "Which way is the army?"

And he said—kidding like, I guess, I wasn't paying any attention—"Which one you talking about?"

I said, "Why, the *Union* army."

Said, "Young'un, come with *me*. I'll show you where we got some Union boys."

Took me down on Gay Street, back towards the river, took me in some old place they called Castle Fox, and some of 'em call Castle Thunder after the one they got in Richmond, and took me down in the basement of this place, they's hundred men laying around, all over, talking to each other, and getting sick, and dying, and scared to death.

Put me in there with them, said, "Get in there with *them* people. S'where *you* belong."

And everybody's so sad, didn't have any, you know, they didn't have any vim and vigor, you know, they just all loping around, moping around, you know, and suddenly the doors open, and these Negro soldiers that was guarding us stood aside, in walked this old man. He walked in with his head up and he had fire in his eyes, and they greeted him like he was a prince. I thought, "Who in the world is *that* man? He's gonna turn us all loose or something. Somebody look like that." Turned out it was Parson Brownlow. They arrested him for inciting those men to burn bridges—in that newspaper.

He said, "This is the proudest day of my life. And none a you people should be sad here tonight, you die in a great cause." And he'd raise his arms, and he'd raise his voice, and he'd lower his voice—because he used to be a Methodist circuit rider, you know—and he would dip up and down, and he would go among 'em and touch 'em, and he had 'em all pacified, and then he had 'em all fired up, and then he had 'em all proud, and he had 'em all the way he wanted 'em, and then he laid down and went to sleep.

And they come in and they says, "All right, you and you and you."

And I said, "What's that for?"

And they said, "They taking them out and gonna hang them, too, for burning them bridges."

And I heard one telling that they had already hung three of 'em by the railroad track, where people passing in the train could reach out with a stick and beat 'em, hanging from the trees. Colonel Leadbetter did it.

And so, they said, "Well, young'un, you want to go with these people we putting on the train?"

I said, "Hell, no."

And he said, "Well, then, you got your choice. You want to fight in the Rebel army with *us,* or do you want to go with *these* people?"

And I thought, "These people are dummer'n hell"—can't get over saying that—"These people are dumb. They are too dumb to know that as soon as I get out of here in their army, I'm gonna light out for the Union side, because my daddy said that's where I ought to be. And I'll probably find some of *them* over there, too," you know, "I'll just get out of here."

So I said, "Yeah, I'll be a Rebel soldier."

They put a uniform on me, they put me on a train, they put me under General Longstreet, they put me in a camp, and that was nice, because it was like camping up on Holston with my gran'daddy and my daddy and my brothers, and I enjoyed that, just sitting around, those fellers nice fellers, you know, and they was some of 'em our people, and I got to liking *that*. They had tin cans there, you know, lying around, and I'd take some feller's rifle and I'd do a little target practice, and a officer come up to me one day and said, "Son, you got the *eye* for it."

And I said, "For what?"

And he said, "To be a sharpshooter."

That sounded good to me. A *sharp*shooter. Yeah, that's me. A *Sharp*shooter. All right, I'll desert tomorrow or the next day. I'll see what this sharpshooter stuff's like. And what I saw it was like, it was good, it made me feel good, and everybody was proud of me, everybody looked up to me, and I's only thirteen years old. And so I went with *them*. And I *stayed* with them. Stayed with General Longstreet. I was at Gettysburg with him. I was in the Wilderness with him.

Bragg was facing Grant down there in Chattanooga, and he said, "Bring up Longstreet." Lee detached him, and they put us on a train, and we went over there, and we *arrived* just in time at Chickamauga to make a difference. We felt pretty good about that.

Then Bragg didn't much like having a man like General Longstreet around him, so he says, "Why don't you go up to Knoxville and run Burnside out of Knoxville? Cause he's taken over up there." So they put us on the trains, we got on the train, and we got up to Sweetwater, and the railroad was all *knocked out,* and so we started marching—in the rain and sleet, November, cold, no shoes. Came to Bleak House, went up in the tower.

And Burnside, who thought a awful lot of General Sanders, said— you know, as I figure it out—he said, "You go out there and you hold 'em off till we get the fortifications up here on this big hill that overlooks Kingston Pike. We gonna get that all fortified. The Rebels started it and we haven't quite finished it. You give us time to finish the fortification and hold 'em off, just long enough. You think you can do that?"

And General Sanders says, "I can do it."

So we went up against him.

And one of us—or somebody—shot him. Way what I've heard it, they took him to the Lamar House over there on Gay Street, up in the bridal suite of the hotel, and he laid there for a long time, and finally died, and they didn't want the soldiers that loved him to know that he died, so they buried him at night. They didn't give him any music or anything like that, because they didn't want to let us know that some officer had died.

But this good friend from West Point, Captain Orlando Poe, who was the engineer fixing the fortifications, he couldn't stand it, so when they let General Sanders down into the grave at Second Presbyterian churchyard, Captain Poe fired a pistol off as a salute. Some others started singing hymns.

I was still up in the tower, afire with fever.

Seems like I remember drawing the faces of the wounded and the dead Virginia boy on the wall of the tower, but if I wanted to make certain, I'd have to climb up there and look.

Then they called us to go down and take up sharpshooter positions around Fort Sanders. Sleeting and raining, and the next morning, we were to rest up, and attack that fort, which they had renamed Fort Sanders.

And what they did, in the night, they went out and strung telegraph wires among the stobs in the ground, so that we'd trip on 'em, in the early morning hours when they expected the attack. They took boiling water and poured it over the parapet so that it would freeze fast and create ice on the slopes. And General Longstreet said, "The ditch—" We would come up to a ditch and "It's very shallow. You can get right across it very easily and you can just climb on up that bank. You won't need the pioneers to go in and cut a place in the bank because that normally has something to grab holt of. You can just stand up in that shallow ditch," because he'd observed a man walk across that ditch through field glasses.

So the men rushed past us—sharpshooter's positions—the men rushed past us and they were ready to take Fort Sanders, they rushed through, they fell in the telegraph wires, got entangled, they fell on each other, they fell on the sharp stobs that were sticking up out of the ground, they all just piled up, and I had to stay where I was and *watch* all that, and there was some officer up there throwing hand grenades—what you call hand grenades now—that he had made, that he had created, fashioned, and he was throwing 'em down at the men. And what happened was that not only was the ditch not shallow, it was *deep*, and what General Longstreet had seen was a man walking across a plank to get across that deep ditch.

And not only was the ditch deep, but Orlando Poe was a very smart man, he said, "It's the tendency of men"—I heard this later—"the tendency of men charging a place to follow the line of least resistance. So we will plow the field in front of it and they will follow between the furrows." And what he did was to lead them into a position where the crossfire could get them.

And we were just slaughtered. All there was to it. Only one man got in there. And I was a sharpshooter just watching all that, wishing I was back up in that tower.

So then we got the word to go on, march away, and we went on up the Valley of Virginia, and we rejoined General Lee, and we were there in the battle of the Wilderness.

And I was up in a tree, as a sharpshooter, good position. The woods were on fire and wounded men were screaming, on fire. Burning limbs falling down on 'em. The woods were burning, and I was up above it, getting the smoke, able to see everything, but not able to see well enough to shoot anybody, and afraid I might shoot one of our own men, and somebody yelled up the tree and said, "We have *shot* General Longstreet! Old Pete!"

I said, "*We* have shot Old Pete, what you mean *we* have shot him?"

He said, "One of our own men mistook and shot 'im in the throat."

And I looked out over—looked out over—looked out over all that, you know. Smoke. Listening to all that screaming. And I said, "Willis Carr, it's time you went home."

I was pretty sure that I could go back the way that we had marched *in*to the Wilderness and find my way to Holston Mountain in Carter County.

But I got lost somehow. It looked like I was pretty deep into Yankee held territory, so I figured I'd better become a Yankee. I shot a stray Yankee soldier and took his uniform. Then I got captured by the Rebels, and they took me to some town called Anderson and took me before a captain who talked with some kind of accent.

Said, "What do you have to say for yourself?"

Said, "Well, I'm just a poor little boy, only fifteen, looking for my daddy and my brothers, trying to find 'em, and so that's why I put on this Yankee uniform so that I could get through Yankee territory, and look for 'em, sir."

He looked in my eyes and I reckon he knew they had seen the war. I didn't look fifteen at all to him. He said. "I believe you that you're not a Yankee, but I'm convinced you're a rebel deserter in a Yankee uniform, take him out and shoot him."

So they marched me to this outdoor prison with walls made of logs, great big open area on a hillside covered with ragged, starved men and a creek running athrawt it that I could see from a distance, and they took me over to what they called the dead house, and they stood me up against a wall, but before they could get lined up to shoot me, there was a work detail coming in of Yankee prisoners, and one of 'em yelled, "Hello, Sharpshooter, what they about to do to you?"

And I said, "Well, where did I know *you*?"

And he said, "Don't you remember that time we met in the middle of the Tennessee River, swimming, and exchanged coffee and tobacco and stuff out there?" And said, "We knew you for one of the best sharpshooters in Longstreet's whole army."

And so they marched him on inside the prison there, and the Rebel captain who was getting the men lined up straight to shoot me, turned to me, says, "Is he telling the truth, are you a sharpshooter?"

And I said, "Well, I can prove it."

And so he took a rifle off the firing squad and handed it to me, and I shot down everything he threw in the air. And he said, "We need guards here that shoot that way, we got just little kids and old men and they want to shoot everybody that even sneezes. So we need you up in one of them towers."

So he took me back to the captain and praised me to him, and Captain Wirtz said in that accent, "The first one you let escape, it's right back in front of that firing squad."

So I went up into a guard tower and one day I looked down and this Negro was leaning up against the dead line post, playing, looked to me, like he was reading a newspaper! A newspaper! Brazen as hell, 'scuse me. Well, now that made me mad. Teasing a poor ol' ignorant mountain boy, by pretending to read that newspaper in front of me, knowing I couldn't read myself. I yelled down, "Nigger, you asking for it."

Said, "What?"

I says, "Acting like you reading that thing."

Said, "Well, I *can* read it, and I'll teach *you* how, if you want me to."

And so he did, taught me how to read, but what he was reading was Cherokee writing that he told me was made up out of nothing by an Indian of the Cherokee nation. Named Sequoyah. Only man in recorded history ever made up a whole new set of letters, and he did it to free his people from the power of the white man's language. This Negro Yankee soldier had been a slave to a Cherokee Indian plantation owner, and his master taught him how to read and used him as a translator between his family and the white man. And when the war started, his master went into the Rebel army and took him with him to translate, and they got captured, and this Negro was forced into the Yankee army, and that's how he ended up in Andersonville prison, with me guarding over him.

He told me that story about Sequoyah making up that new set of letters and I loved to hear it more than once. Got so it made me want to read and write Cherokee, and that's how I learned to read and write. After a few months though, he stepped over that dead line and I shot him, without thinking. I wondered, Why did he do that? knowing I'd have to shoot him, and I guessed he thought I wouldn't shoot the man who taught me to read and write. Sure as the world, even though he was a nigger and I was a white boy, I wouldn't shoot him. I've had sixty-five years to wonder about that, and maybe fifteen more to go.

When it looked like we was going to lose the war, we broke up that prison, and most went to surrender, but I sort of drifted West with some that wanted to start a new nation in the West. Ended up on the border of Mexico in what was the last battle of the war—well, after the surrender was already over—in Palmetto, Texas.

And I just stayed out in the West, wandering, scratching a living and the price of a drink in saloons by drawing folks' faces to send back East, as I was saying when I first walked in here.

And then after about two years of all that drinking and drawing and brawling and living like a desert rat, I decided, again, "Willis Carr, it's time you went home," to Carter County, up Holston Mountain. So I struck out, and that's where I've been for the last sixty-five years, some odd. And in all that time, what's preyed on my mind is why I shot that Cherokee Negro, and whether I did shoot General Sanders or I didn't.

Nobody can really tell me who shot General Sanders. Folks tell it that General Sanders was riding a white horse down Kingston Pike, scouting out front of his men, when a sharpshooter shot him. But facts have come out that there was this young captain, Winthrop, come over from England to fight for the Confederacy, who, when Colonel Nance's charge up the hill went wrong, leapt on his white horse and went charging on his lonesome up that hill, and back and forth, back and forth in front of these fence rails where the Yankees had taken up position. The Yankees was shooting at him as he rode back and forth, and they wounded him and he rode back down to Bleak House—but he lived. And all this while, General Sanders stood on the brow of the hill, watching Captain Winthrop dash back and forth, and he turned to his aide—who told about it in the Knoxville *Journal* twenty-five years later—and said, "What a gallant fellow he was!" And as they started down the far side of the hill, to get out of the firing, somebody shot General Sanders. "I'm hit!" They say his last words were, "I am glad I was not shot in the back." I cannot figure out why he said that.

And I always had this feeling, all my life since, that I missed the war. So my mouth is down here in the music room telling you my experiences in the war, but seems like my mind is always in that tower above our heads, me fifteen, watching the blood of that Virginia sharpshooter drip down the wall under the window and between his legs, smelling the paint from the fresco that man kept painting at the foot of the steps all during the skirmish, and I'm drawing the faces of the wounded sharpshooters on the wall and looking out that window through my sniper's sights at that General on a white horse that I was certain come out of fever. I've dug my body one hundred miles awalking it, to try to match up my body and my mind, and tell the first and last time about it, but I don't reckon I can climb those steps.

Respectfully submitted, with thanks to Lois McClung, stenographer for this occasion, Musetta White, Secretary.

Mary Morris

THE LURE

The first time Ben asked Laurel to fly to Wisconsin with him to spend a week with his father, Laurel said no. She wasn't partial to fathers. During the sixties Laurel's father left her mother for a famous activist. Laurel had tried to stay away from fathers ever since. While Ben went home to visit his father, Laurel traveled through Europe with a friend on a Eurail pass for two weeks. She came back from Europe with snapshots of dozens of Gothic cathedrals, dull gray and stately, which had withstood many centuries. Ben returned with glowing reports of an old timber lodge with a huge fireplace set on the shore of Lake Michigan. Reports of a million berries on the shrubs in the woods, of long walks to pick them.

"So, how was Martha?" Laurel asked after he finished telling her about the house. Ben could go on for hours talking about the house, barely mentioning his father and never mentioning Martha. Two years after his mother died, Ben's father married a beautiful woman named Martha.

"She's alright," Ben replied. "They fight a lot."

"That doesn't mean they're unhappy." Laurel actually was defending herself. She and Ben fought a lot as well.

"My parents never fought." He gave his pat reply. Laurel was a reporter for a mediocre New York newspaper and she'd learned a few things. She learned that what gets left out is often more interesting than what gets put in. She looked at Ben. His fingers tugged at his thin, sandy hair, a gesture Laurel knew meant he didn't want to talk about something.

He didn't want to talk about how he used to sit on his hands to prevent himself from putting them tightly around Martha's throat. Ben passed time when he was younger imagining all the terrible accidents that could happen to Martha in the course of the day. Sometimes he waited for the phone to ring with the bad news that never came.

Ben began waiting for the bad news right after Harry married Martha. Harry met her in the pathology lab where they both worked. "You know," Ben said to Laurel once, "I think she was just waiting for Mom to die." It didn't do any good when Laurel pointed out that they married two years later. "That was for appearances' sake," Ben always said.

After Ben's mother died, Harry took him fishing and camping alone for a month on Green Bay. Harry taught Ben all he knew about the different kinds of tackle, bait, and lures. He showed Ben how to bring a fish up from down deep and how to coax it out of a rocky place. He taught him how to pick a fly and cast in a stream. He taught him which plastic lures will snare a pike in the middle of the lake. At night Harry cooked the fish they'd caught in the day over an open fire. One night as Harry cooked, Ben saw two tears slide down his face and evaporate in the heat of the fire. Shortly after that trip, Harry met Martha. Ben hadn't been alone with his father again since he married her.

Ben didn't tell Laurel then, though he'd tell her later, that he felt as if he could choke Martha. But he did confide in her one night shortly after he returned that he saw his mother from time to time. Ben and Laurel were lying in bed together and he stroked her hair as he told her this. "Sometimes I'll be in the laundromat and I'll see her sorting my socks. Or in a restaurant, she'll be laughing at the next table."

A few days before she died from a hideous and extended illness, Ben woke in the night and found his mother standing in her nightgown at the foot of his bed. She said she was cold, so Ben pulled back the covers and made a comfortable place for her to lie down. She curled beside him like a lover, hugging him and shivering. In the morning when Ben woke, she was gone. When he asked her what time she'd gotten up, his mother said she had no idea what he was talking about. She'd spent the entire night on the sofa in the den.

On Thanksgiving Laurel found herself in a plane flying with Ben to Green Bay. When Ben had told her they were going to Wisconsin for Thanksgiving, she'd said no, but Ben wasn't asking. He was telling. They sat in silence during most of the flight. They'd had a fight in the cab to the airport. They'd fought over the fact that Laurel didn't want to make this trip. She'd said to him in the cab, "I wish you hadn't said yes for me."

But his father had already made the reservations and had gotten tickets for the Packers game. "He didn't give me much choice," Ben replied.

Laurel sighed and wondered how she'd gotten herself into this mess. She didn't want to be involved in somebody's family. She didn't want to be involved with anyone in this way. Laurel met Ben through a friend of hers named Stefanie. Stefanie worked on the police blotter and one day Laurel told her she wanted to meet a man because she was dying from boredom on the weekends. So a week later Stefanie said, "I've got a great guy for you. Handsome, sexy, smart, talented, runs his own graphic design studio, loves to travel . . ."

"What's wrong with him?" Laurel asked.

Stefanie had hesitated. "He doesn't get involved." It seemed he'd been Stefanie's boyfriend for a long time and finally she gave up trying. When Stefanie gave Ben Laurel's number, he wasn't interested at first. But then he noticed that they both had a 260 telephone exchange which meant that if they started seeing one another, he could walk home in the morning.

It began as a matter of convenience. Then one morning as Ben was buttoning his shirt, he told Laurel. "Listen, I think I better warn you. I don't get serious."

"Don't worry," Laurel had said. "I don't either."

From New York to Green Bay, Laurel played the scene over and over in her mind. She couldn't understand how they'd gone from that to this. She couldn't understand how he'd gotten her on to this plane.

Harry was a tall, elegant man, like Ben, only with silver hair that seemed to shimmer as he walked. Harry and Ben had the same soft brown eyes, the same wide smile. Harry was a research scientist until he retired a few years before. He had a vaccine named after him, Bancroft's serum, something he discovered that saves the lives of infants who had a mysterious, and now, thanks to the serum, nonexistent disease.

Martha kissed Ben, who took it the way a corporal might take a command from his immediate superior. Martha and Laurel shook hands, but then Martha, as if in an afterthought, leaned over and kissed Laurel as well. Martha was fifty-five but she didn't look forty. Laurel expected that. What she didn't expect was that Martha would look like the picture of Ben's mother he kept on his dresser and she wondered why he'd never mentioned it before.

When they got into the car, Martha said, "Shall we take them for a ride around town first? I want to show Laurel our little shops."

Harry shook his head. "They're only here for a few days. They don't need to shop. They can shop in New York."

"Oh, well, I just thought . . ."

Ben nudged Laurel slightly, making certain she didn't miss this minor point. But Harry took the route through town anyway. He drove down Main Street and helped as Martha pointed out the boutiques, the small grocers, the fish and tackle shop. Then they drove home. The house was a few miles outside of town and it sat right on the bluff overlooking Lake Michigan. The Bancrofts had their own beach. The house was an old hunting lodge that Harry and Martha bought a few years before when he decided to give up his teaching post in Madison. As they drove up, Martha said, "Well, this is our little cottage."

They walked into the main room, a large, two-story living room with a moose head staring down at them from above the mantel. The moose had glassy, maudlin eyes. Laurel thought the moose had as much business being here as she did. On the wall were paintings, the kind a child had obviously done. Paintings of fish and birds and the lake. There were bright-colored paintings of dunes, sloping gently to the sea, of starfish and whales, swimming with lake trout, mixed with coral.

Then there were other paintings that seemed dark, with strange figures hovering overhead like ghosts in the air. In one painting there was a tidal wave with a boy, standing with just a bucket, facing the wall of water with fish being flung at him from the wave. In another there was a rainbow-colored fish, struggling on a hook, blood gushing from a gash in his throat, its eyes bursting from the head. The fish stared out of the painting, and seemed to be looking as if to ask some question.

Ben, noticing Laurel looking at the paintings, said, "I can't believe he hasn't gotten rid of these." He pointed to himself. "From my early fish period."

Martha fluttered around, puffing up pillows, saying things like, "I bet you guys are starved. Let me just stick some cheese puffs into the oven." But Harry said, "Com'on now, dear. Show them upstairs." Martha frowned, but obeyed, leading them up the staircase into the bedroom. The bedroom had an old brass bed which Laurel felt certain would squeak. "Just make yourself comfortable," Martha said, patting the crazy quilt. "You do want to be in the same room, don't you?"

Ben nodded and rolled his eyes. "Yes, we want to be in the same room." He winked at Laurel and she winked back but for a moment she thought it might be nice to be apart. Even though neither of them wanted to get involved, she found that they hadn't been apart, except for when he went to Wisconsin and she went to Europe, a single night. Lately her feelings for Ben had been muddled.

There were things about him she couldn't stand. His Hawaiian shirts, the punk haircuts he insisted upon, the way he left dishes in the sink and drank Ovaltine in the morning, that digital watch he was always setting. In the middle of an argument he'd set the clock and tell her how much more time she had to blow up. And his notion of true love, which was right out of a nineteenth-century novel—certainly not the kind of love people who live in a loft in lower Manhattan should be thinking about. He wanted that perfect mingling of the souls. He wanted two people to act as one.

Laurel acted at times like two people all by herself, Ben often commented. She'd thought about leaving him and occasionally told her sublettor to try and find something else. But in the end she'd stayed with him. She didn't know why. She couldn't explain it to him or to herself. It went beyond love. She knew that somewhere inside of them, they were alike. And, though she hated admitting this to anyone, let alone herself, she would be lost without him.

Harry and Martha uncorked a bottle of wine when Ben and Laurel came downstairs. Harry poured the wine and Martha ran in and out of the kitchen, checking the parsley potatoes, the rainbow trout. "I'll bet you caught it yourself, Dad," Ben said when he saw the fish frying in the kitchen.

"Naw," Harry said, rather shyly, "If you'd get here more often, maybe I'd catch my own."

Martha passed the cheese platter around. "Why don't you guys go off fishing. I'm sure the girls could amuse ourselves."

Laurel nodded. "I'm sure we could." But she couldn't imagine amusing herself while the men went off fishing.

To Laurel's surprise, dinner wasn't very good. The fish was overcooked. The potatoes uncooked. The spinach was too salty. "So," Harry turned to Ben, "You like running your own business?"

Ben had recently opened his own graphic design studio. "You know, I've got more clients than I can handle right now."

Harry nodded, listening carefully. "No more thoughts about painting again, huh?"

"I like what I'm doing," Ben replied, coldly.

"I don't blame you," Martha said. "I'd rather work with people around me any day.

Harry looked annoyed and said he was tired. "And you guys must be exhausted, no?" Everyone agreed that everyone was tired and right after the dishes, they headed upstairs.

Ben and Laurel crawled under the covers and Laurel said, "Will you hold me."

Ben yawned. "For a minute." They both tensed up. Laurel always wanted to be held longer than Ben wanted to hold her. But he reached out and pulled her close to him.

"I love you," Laurel whispered.

He kissed her on the forehead. "Me too." And he rolled over and went to sleep.

Laurel was up before Ben so she got dressed and went outside. When she got onto the beach, she saw Harry near the shore. He was dressed in fishing gear and on his hands and knees. In front of him were several boxes, filled with colored objects which Laurel saw as she approached. "Good morning," Laurel said to him. Then she stooped down and picked up a yellow plastic fish, something that looked like a bug with feathers. "What're these?"

"Oh, flies, lures. I thought I'd get my boxes ready, just in case."

"How come they're all different colors?"

Harry looked up at her slightly. "Well, each situation requires a different type of tackle. For instance, you don't catch a sturgeon with the same things you'd catch salmon with. You want to find the thing the fish thinks it knows. You fish with that." He explained to her how the flies looked like the bugs that come off the streams and how the lures look like the different fish. "In the lake you use lures. In the lake when you go out deep, you want something that'll shimmer like a minnow. You've gotta make the fish think you've got the real thing." Harry laughed. "You gotta fake the fish out. If you're gonna drag'em up from the deep, you've gotta get the right lure."

"Sounds pretty complicated," Laurel said. It did sound complicated to her.

"No, it's just common sense."

Later that morning Harry made one of his famous breakfasts—cranberry pancakes, crisp bacon, orange juice, scrambled eggs, a huge pot of coffee. Laurel groaned when she saw all the food. "I won't have room for turkey."

"Oh," Martha said, "We're having goose and you've got lots of time between now and dinner."

"Why don't you kids go for a long walk on the beach," Harry suggested.

Laurel took the plate heaped with pancakes as Harry passed it to her. "I've got an idea. Why don't I help Martha get dinner and you guys go for a walk?" Laurel saw Ben smile at her.

But Harry shook his head. "Now don't be silly. You're on vacation. You should relax."

Fifteen steps lead from the back of the Bancroft yard to the beach. Laurel and Ben climbed down slowly to walk on the sand. It was a cold, grey November day and they were bundled up. Ben held Laurel's hand as they walked. She felt a tension in his fingertips. "See what I mean? He just doesn't want to spend time with me. He'll find any excuse. He won't even take a walk."

"Well, you didn't really ask him, did you?"

Ben shook his head. "I don't have to ask him. I can tell. He'll always find excuses."

Laurel's ears were red and cold and she put her collar up. "Sounds like you're got your own set of excuses. Takes one to know one." Ben let go of her hand. He was irritated that she couldn't see the situation the way he saw it. He knew his father had been ignoring him for years. Laurel was also annoyed with Ben as she walked toward the water. Ben watched her walk away. Her auburn ponytail bobbed like a cork on the water. She was watching the gulls, skimming the surface of the water.

Ben caught up with her. "Mom used to love it here. She was crazy about the birds and the lake."

Laurel slipped her hand through Ben's arms. "I guess you miss her."

He wrapped his fingers around her fingers. "No," he spoke softly. "I miss him."

Later they sat down to Thanksgiving dinner. Martha had set the table with an old lace tablecloth and real silver. She cooked a tremendous goose. Laurel felt as if all she'd done since arriving was eat. She didn't know how she'd make it through this meal. "I just love Thanksgiving," Martha said, fluttering around the table. "Just think, Harry. It's been eighteen years we've been doing this together. I don't know where all the time went."

Harry was carving but his face suddenly seemed distracted. He looked up at the ceiling as if listening for an animal on the roof. "Is it really that long?"

Martha continued to move around the table. "So, everyone has what they want, right. You know, I can't remember when I cooked a goose last. Goose is fatty. You have to cook it slowly."

"Mom always made turkey, didn't she Dad?" Ben said.

His father thought for a moment. "I guess so. I guess she did make turkey."

"You don't like goose?" Martha asked Ben.

"Oh, I'm just used to having turkey, that's all."

"Well," Martha said, sitting down, "I thought we'd try something different for a change."

Ben shrugged. "I'm just not used to it."

Then Martha rose quickly and tossed her napkin down. "I forgot the cranberry jello." Her voice was shrill and everyone stared at her.

Harry kept his eyes on the napkin she tossed down. "What is it, dear?" Harry followed her into the kitchen.

Laurel looked at Ben. His face was flushed. "What's going on?" she whispered.

"She can't stand it," Ben whispered back. "She can't stand it even if
we mention her." But for some reason Laurel wasn't sure that that was
what was bothering Martha.

The next afternoon Ben, Laurel and Harry went to see Green Bay lose
to Cleveland. Laurel sat between Ben and Harry and she rooted for
Cleveland. They rooted for Green Bay. Laurel hadn't wanted to sit
between them, but that was the way they sat down on the bleachers.
Laurel went to the bathroom in the middle of the second quarter and
stayed away almost until halftime, but Ben and Harry didn't close the
space between them.

That evening after dinner, everyone drank cognac and sat around
the table. Ben played a fairly good ragtime and Harry did a few
numbers from the thirties. Then Ben played a medley of show tunes.
Martha poured more cognac and leaned on Ben's shoulder. When Ben
played, "Some Enchanted Evening," Martha sang into his ear, "You
may see a stranger across a crowded room . . ." Her voice was gravelly
and flat and she skimped on the high notes. She closed her eyes and let
her body swing.

Harry wrinkled his nose at Ben, but Martha opened her eyes in time
to see it. She stopped singing. "Is it that bad?" No one said a word.
"Tell me, if it's that bad, I don't have to sing at all."

"Dear, this isn't a competition." He waved his hand at her. "I'm
going to track down some more firewood." But when he went outside, Martha went upstairs. A little while later Harry came back in. His
face was red and a white cloud came from his mouth. "This should
make a nice fire." Then he looked around. "Where's Martha?" Ben
pointed upstairs and Harry said. "Damn." He went up and didn't
come back down again that evening.

When they got into bed later, Ben and Laurel had a fight. It was
their first real fight in a while. Normally they just sulked away from
each other, but tonight when they got into bed, Laurel felt as if she
just had to make love and she was certain Ben would not want to.

"Please, don't go to sleep. I need you." Laurel shook Ben, trying to convince him not to fall asleep.

"Not here. You can hear everything in this house. How about tomorrow night in New York?"

Laurel put her hand on his shoulders. "Please, please don't go to sleep. Please, I want to talk to you. Ben, I love you." Her fingers dug into his shoulders but she felt him drifting away from her, into that place where he could always hide.

He lay with his back to her. "Look, Laurel, I don't think this is what I want. Maybe you should move back to your apartment for a while."

"Then why did you bring me here. To sit at a football game between you and him. Is that all I'm here for?"

Ben groaned. "Would you please keep it down?"

"How can you possibly know what you want? You don't even try. You haven't even tried since I met you."

Suddenly Laurel was out of bed. She stood in her pink nightgown in the middle of a hooked rug in a patch of light, coming from the moon. She stood sobbing in that patch of light and Ben turned over onto his back.

She was crying and Ben just stared at her. He saw her standing there at the side of the bed, the light coming from the window through her pink nightgown. He saw her legs, her thighs, her breasts. He looked up at her hands, shielding her face and her disheveled hair, and she reminded him of another moment in his life, when he'd thought he'd seen his mother standing at the edge of his bed, just before she died. "Come here." He pulled the covers back and made a space for her to lie down. She was cold and shivering and he held her close. He kissed her gently on the forehead as she drifted to sleep.

But Ben couldn't sleep and after a little while he eased his way out of the bed. Leaving Laurel resting on the pillow, he slipped downstairs to get a drink of water. When he reached the first landing, he saw his father, sitting under a small lamp, reading from a journal on biochemistry. Ben wanted to go back into his room but his father had already seen him. "Hi there," Harry said. "Wanta beer?"

Ben said sure so Harry went and got two Heinekens. He popped them open and they sat down across from one another. "I had a fight with Laurel," Ben said, wondering why he said that.

Harry nodded. "The house isn't very soundproof." Harry took a long swig. "So, do you guys have plans?"

Ben was starting to feel uncomfortable. He felt as if he couldn't breathe and he wanted to go back upstairs. "No, we don't have plans. We fight too much."

"Nothing wrong with a good fight now and then. Martha and me, we fight sometimes, but I think it's better than keeping it all inside, the way your mother did."

The wind was howling ouside and the house suddenly seemed colder to Ben. His father looked odd under the light of the Tensor lamp. Finally Ben whispered, "But you and Mom, you were so happy."

Harry shrugged. "Oh, I loved your mother, but I never felt close to her. Martha, she's my friend. We don't have any secrets." He finished his beer. "It's not the same as with your mother, of course. But in some ways it's better." He paused, as if expecting Ben to say something, but Ben could think of nothing to say. "Hey," his father put his hand on his knee, "why don't you guys stay a few extra days and go fishing with me?"

Ben shook his head and yawned. "We've gotta get back. I guess I'd better get some sleep now." His whole body trembled. He didn't know what else to say. His father got up too, stretched, and they climbed the stairs together. When they reached the landing, they paused. His father touched him on the shoulder. "Don't say I didn't ask." Then they went into their separate rooms.

In the morning Laurel got up first. She looked out the window. It was a clear, cool day, good for flying. The room was chilly and she dressed quickly. Ben reached out and grabbed her while she was dressing. He pulled her to him and kissed her on the neck. "Hey," she said to him, "what's gotten into you?"

When Laurel went downstairs, she saw Martha sitting with a cup of coffee, staring down at the beach. "Look at that bird," Martha said. "It must be hurt."

Laurel looked out and saw the gull, running around in circles. Its head seemed connected to its wing and it kept twisting and turning. Then it would flop down exhausted on the sand. Then begin again. Something protruded from the wing, like a piece of bone, and it seemed to be sticking through. The gull turned and ran frantically, then sank back into the sand again.

Ben and Harry had come down by this time and they went out to the railing above the beach to look. "Its wing looks broken," Ben said.

But Laurel saw the thin, silver-blue fish protruding from under the wing, the wire wrapped around the body. "It's tangled up in something."

Ben leaned further over the railing. "You're right. It's all tangled up." Harry thought of the thick, green gardener's gloves and the wire cutters and he headed for the garage. Laurel and Ben went down to the beach together. They bent over the gull as it shook with pain, its wing hooked to its neck, the neck hooked to the mouth. It had three hooks in it and the blue-silver fish was the lure it had tried to take in its mouth. "Go tell my dad to hurry," Ben said.

Laurel ran up the steps. She wished she hadn't had any coffee on an empty stomach. She began to feel jittery and nauseous as she raced across the yard. She went into the house. "She's taken a lure," Laurel said to Martha.

"Oh, how awful," Martha replied, handing Laurel a warm sweater. "Put this on, dear." Laurel went into the garage, but Harry had already headed to the beach. She saw his head disappear as he descended the steps. She ran back to the railing to see if they needed anything from the house.

Ben and Harry had already put on the gardener's gloves and they were stooping over the bird. She watched from the railing above them while Ben held the gull as steadily as he could and his father, the doctor, snipped at the wires connecting the plastic sardine. After a few moments Harry tossed the sardine away. Ben and Harry, their hands entangled, worked on the hooks, squatting over the gull. In whispers they gave each other instructions. Laurel heard Ben say, "Dad, I can't get this one out of her wing." She heard Harry reply. "We'll have to give it a good yank." Then their voices faded and all Laurel could hear was the sound of the water.

Laurel was about to head down to join them when Martha, who had come to the railing, caught her by the arm. "They seem to be making out well," Martha said, as she led Laurel by the arm back toward the house and into the kitchen. The two women stood by the sink, cracking eggs, with their eyes to the window, watching the horizon. After a few minutes, they saw the gull rise from the beach and fly shakily to a distant rock. It landed on the rock and flapped its wings several times. They kept their eyes on it until it flew away.

Ben convinced Laurel to stay a little longer so that he and Harry could go fishing. They came back with enough lake trout for dinner. The trout had sleek, rainbow bodies and Harry commented on how it was rare this time of year to be able to catch this many because the water was already turning cold and the fish had gone down deep.

Joyce Carol Oates

SURF CITY

His number finally came up, his good luck number, published in the *Surf City Gazette* and announced over the radio, he'd won $1,150 in the state lottery in which a retired grocer from Camden won $1,726,092 and somebody else, a woman schoolteacher from upstate, won $628,530. About time, he thought. Maybe even a few years behind schedule.

His name was Harvey Kubeck, he was thirty-one years old, had a two-year-old son and another baby on the way. Both pregnancies hadn't been planned but weren't exactly accidents either. Except for the weeks when he was laid off from work he made good money at Republic Steel: when they laid him off he got part-time work driving a truck for a local construction outfit, part-time work as a security guard (not licensed to carry a gun) at the shopping mall, short-term jobs with a tree service his wife's uncle owned, whatever came along. He'd never gone downtown to collect unemployment, no one in his family did. For a long time it had seemed to him that luck was running against him. It wasn't just the things you could put your finger on, talk about, it was how you felt about yourself, the air you had to breathe. In fact it seemed to him that his bad luck was like dirty water, stinking sewage water splashing around his head, his face, it sickened him to think he'd get it in his mouth and swallow it. Months and months of things going against you until finally it's years, you're thirty, then you're thirty-one, not a kid any longer.

He'd gone to parochial school so he knew the Church's teaching on luck, it was supposed to be nothing but pagan superstition, it was supposed to be ignorant; good Catholics didn't put their faith in anything but God. But Harvey knew when his luck was bad and he was being cheated, it was just instinct to know. In any case he didn't believe in the Church any longer, hadn't been able to swallow that shit since he was fifteen, sixteen years old, he'd been a wise guy then and had actually told one of the priests at the high school to go screw, his buddies remembered that to this day. The priests had expelled him for a month, his father'd had to plead with them to take him back. Now he tried not to think about religion at all. He'd be angry if he did so he tried not to think about it, stayed away from arguing with his family or his in-laws. He had a bad temper and the thing about a bad temper, his father always said, the dangerous thing, is that you lose it at the wrong time, you get the wrong people.

His wife Marian went to mass most Sundays, low mass at 10 A.M. said by an older priest who never took more than a half-hour. Harvey made remarks, Harvey made jokes, why the hell did she bother when she didn't believe in most of that crap, and Marian said, flaring up at once, "A human being has got to believe in something, so keep your mouth to yourself." He thought it was funny, that's all. He just had to laugh, that's all, people believing crap being shoved at them year after year, it'd been going on for thousands of years in fact, he was only making the observation.

Still, he went along with the family, wanted to have his kids baptized, you never could tell about things like that—it was a way of betting after all. He didn't, he told his buddies, want to fuck up things for his kids if the Church was maybe right.

These past few months he'd been coiled tight as a spring, distracted, irritable, not really himself. He'd light a cigarette and put it down somewhere and forget it, then light another, coughing in a new harsh way that sounded angry, his little boy ducked away with his hands over his ears which Harvey didn't like to see. Marian complained that he had a habit of working his mouth like he was arguing with someone, she wished he'd cut it out. It's really weird, she said, you should see yourself. He wasn't arguing with anybody, he knew that, but he did a lot of thinking, how it was time for his luck to change, he'd been laid off at the plant and rehired and laid off again and again rehired and these days you only knew from week to week how long you'd be working, it burnt his ass, he said, no overtime for anybody not even the guys with thirty years seniority. There was a rumor also that the plant itself might close and relocate in Kentucky, or was it Tennessee, one of those shithead states, another rumor that the owners were stockpiling, keeping it all quiet, in case of a strike.

What's the point of a strike, Harvey went around saying in a voice heavy with sarcasm, why not fire bomb the dump instead?—it'd add up to the same thing.

It was hard for him to believe that he'd been there for almost six years now—he was still considered new, one of the younger men. He *was* new. Last time they laid him off with no clear promise of when he'd be called back Marian said, Honey just quit, tell them to go to hell, but he knew she didn't mean it, she'd worked before Paulie was born, waitressing mainly, salesclerking, she wasn't exactly eager to go back and now there was going to be another baby. Steel isn't the kind of job you walk away from, Harvey said. The pay scale was high. Also the benefits, the pension, all that, shit he'd have to be crazy to quit, he'd only wind up on unemployment and what then . . .?

Much of the time he wore ear guards on the job, especially when he was welding, they had the strange effect of eliminating the little noises you never notice and emphasizing the big ones, the vibrations, that is, the feel of the noises. It was really weird: he actually found himself listening, trying to figure out what he heard. For a while he monkeyed around with his Walkman to fix it so that he could listen to good loud rock music from the Surf City station, the ear phones under the ear guards, but it didn't work out, all the sounds came scrambled in together. After an hour his head buzzed and his jaws ached from clenching, he could get high, he thought, from wearing the ear guards themselves, then he'd go smoke a joint in the lavatory and everything would go floating, so weird there was no way to describe it.

Even at home he got into the habit of going around coiled tight, almost in a crouch, as if he was waiting for something to happen, some loud noise or surprise. His skin was hot and flushed, it was the blood beating inside, an artery throbbing in his forehead which was almost identical to an artery in his father's forehead he'd always hated since he was a young kid. His hair was a dark red clayey color bleaching out fair in the summer months, wavy, worn a little long, sideburns he kept trimmed. His shoulders and arms were muscular but there was a roll of fat around his waist Marian teased him about. He didn't know what his weight was, exactly, but he knew he couldn't be overweight, he wasn't the type.

He was good looking as he'd ever been, Marian said, except for that habit of his, working his mouth like he was talking to himself or arguing with someone. Curling his lip at people when he really meant to smile. "You're getting to be some kind of asshole, sometimes," Marian said, pouting as if she's been insulted. "Your mind's always off somewhere."

He'd take it light, wouldn't lose his temper, maybe make a joke or two like a t.v. comic with his timing down so perfect he doesn't even wait for laughs. But she just stared at him. Wouldn't smile, wouldn't give an inch. Pretending to be as dumb as one of her own asshole girlfriends who couldn't tell whether Harvey Kubeck was coming on to her or playing her for laughs.

When news came that he'd won $1,150 in the lottery Harvey didn't talk it up, went around acting as if he wasn't that surprised at winning, even that happy, at first, though he got happier when the shock wore off. He got a lot happier. The first night Marian looked at him and said, "How come you aren't more excited?—you didn't even call many people," and he shrugged, embarrassed, cigarette in his mouth, he said, "'Cause I figured it was coming." He said, his face burning, "I figured it's been coming for a fucking long time."

Next morning and the mornings that followed Harvey woke and before he even opened his eyes or wondered what time it was or what day of the week, did he have to work or not, he was thinking: This is more like it, Kubeck.

He said aloud, staring at his reflection in the bathroom mirror, the ruddy skin, the quizzical eyes, turning his head from side to side, slowly, pondering, admiring: This is the way it was meant to be.

Basically, he thinks, he's a happy contented person. Things have always gone well for him: he got through school, got through the National Guard, married the woman he wanted, has a baby boy he loves—in fact he's crazy about Paulie, really eats him up, when he has the time to concentrate. He isn't a loser, he isn't one of those poor bastards (he knows plenty, in his own family even) who fuck up everything they try. Just the past two or three years when his luck has been running against him. Or is it four years, five?—the steel business in trouble and trying to blame the union. Something in the air he breathes, the way the sky looks when he happens to glance up, the way food tastes, nothing you can put your finger on but you know it's there, you know you're being cheated. He'd look at himself in a mirror in some lavatory somewhere, late Saturday night in Surf City, he'd been drinking whiskey and beer and none of it had done much good, out with his buddies, Marian was home or over at her mother's house with Paulie, he'd take a look at that face and think, Who the hell's *that*, I don't want nothing to do with *that*.

But basically he's a happy person. His mother used to tell people what a sweet little boy he'd been, not crying much, making up games for himself, crap like that, Harvey doesn't remember any of it but he knows it's true. He knew when his luck was due to change even when he felt lousy with a morning hangover or when he was laid off again at the plant or when the telephone rang and he let Marian answer it because he felt too tired just then to answer it himself. (Who would it be? One of his in-laws maybe, or someone in his own family. Asking for a favor like all Harvey was was a strong arm, a back to carry out furniture or something. Or they'd be complaining. Wanting to commiserate with Marian, maybe. As if he wasn't right there in his own house trying not to listen. Sons of bitches, the fuckers, his blood beat hard and hot and heavy, he'd had enough of them all.) So when news came about the lottery he wasn't that surprised. Some of his family and in-laws came over to celebrate, they had a few beers, things to eat, his father took Polaroid pictures of Harvey holding up the check from the State of New Jersey Treasury, Harvey and Marian with their arms around each other, Harvey with little Paulie climbing in his lap, but it was like Harvey was really standing off to one side watching, thinking his own thoughts. So his luck had changed, well it was about time.

The sons of bitches.

Marian was expecting the baby in early November, now it was almost the end of the summer, the lottery money had come at the right time. The pregnancy hadn't been planned exactly but when Harvey got over his surprise he said he felt good about it, he felt right. Still, every few nights Marian would say, You aren't really happy about it, are you? and Harvey would say at once, What?—sure I'm happy. And Marian would say angrily, I know *you*, your mind's a thousand miles away. She'd rub her knuckles hard against his head until he stopped her. It's half your baby, isn't it, damn you, she'd say, and Harvey would say, kidding, Honey I can't vouch for *that*, and she'd get angrier, maybe try to slap him, they'd wrestled around for a while then go to bed, there he'd fit himself into her like a hand into a glove just tight enough, or maybe it was a shoehorn, a shoehorn and a satiny silky high-heeled shoe, she clutched at him and mashed her mouth against him as she usually did, it was clear sailing, Harvey thought, past a certain point, and then his mind floated clear, floated and floated, clear, a thousand no a million miles away.

The last time Harvey Kubeck had won anything it was $40 on the Sugar Ray Leonard–Thomas Hearns welterweight match, four years ago, just a bet with a guy at work and nothing to brag about but he'd felt good for weeks; it was something to focus his thoughts on when he was low. Then the memory faded and he had to make an effort to remember what it was that had felt so good. Sugar Ray Leonard giving lanky Thomas "Hit Man" Hearns the fight of his life, one great boxer humiliated by another.

The $40 hadn't lasted beyond the next day. What can you do with $40 after all?—it's chickenfeed.

(Years ago when Harvey was sixteen he'd gotten the idea he wanted to box. First the amateurs, then the professional league, why the hell not, give it a try. He fooled around at the Y, took lessons, went to all the local matches, told people he'd be trying out for the Golden Gloves sometime, welterweight division, the girls were impressed and Harvey's cousins were impressed but nothing came of it. His mind was quick enough but his fists were slow—he knew what he wanted to do but couldn't do it. He was always stumbling over his own feet. He never learned "defense"—got excited when he was popped and went a little crazy, then got popped again, then he'd find himself sitting on the canvas not knowing what the hell had hit him, then he couldn't make himself get up again to take more, some instinct in his gut kept him down, weak. The boxing coach liked Harvey, teased him saying he'd be known as "Iron Man" Kubeck once he got the knack, but a lot of the knack had to do with getting up after you've been hit and if you were hit by a punch you hadn't seen coming you didn't want to get up again and take more, just some goddamned instinct about it no matter how Harvey *wanted* to keep going. So that was that. He drifted away from the gym and nobody missed him or tried to get him to come back—he guessed he was better off anyway. Still he watched fights on television, admired top boxers like Leonard, Hagler, Durán. Christ he liked Roberto Durán—that hot spic!—the "Little Killer" Durán was called—but Harvey always felt something secret and satisfied when the best of them got beaten. Like Leonard out-boxed by Durán in their first match, Durán out-boxed by Leonard in the second, stymied, humiliated, hurt deep inside you could tell by the expression on his face. Now you know what it's like, Harvey would think. Now you fuckers know what it's like.)

This time he intended to concentrate more on the money he'd won—it surely wasn't chickenfeed. Maybe he'd divide it up: some for Marian—some for his parents—some for the loan company (Jesus he still owed at least half the list price on the Impala he'd bought three years ago)—some for himself—and some for a night on the town with his buddies. They'd drive up to Shore Acres Beach and work their way down, back to Surf City, he'd treat them all to oysters, pizza, corn on the cob, all the beer and drinks they wanted, what the hell. But also he wanted to surprise Marian and Paulie with a new color t.v., nineteen inches, console model, and with the trade-in on the old one that would still be how much?—$800 maybe, he'd have to check. Which was a lot of money. And there'd be the doctor and hospital bills for the new baby, and Marian was always complaining about the refrigerator, it's wearing out, it isn't big enough, and the linoleum in the kitchen looks like hell, and so on and so forth. It was starting to make him sick, thinking of all these things. It was starting to make him angry, that buzz in his head, something beating in his forehead, maybe he should just take the plunge and spend the money however he wanted. But then Marian would be mad. She'd be seriously mad. And he was frightened of her in one of those states especially now that she was pregnant again and if she came at him with her nails or fists, or kicking, kneeing, he couldn't even protect himself, the last time he'd tried, he'd slapped her twice, and Paulie had started bawling, and there was hell to pay for a solid week. She really made him eat shit, the woman knew how to do it. So he wanted to give her $500, let's say.

And $500 for his parents. They could use it, they were maybe even expecting it, he didn't want to disappoint them. So that was $1,000 right there: leaving him $150 which was nothing. Which would hardly pay for a night on the town. And there was the loan company. And there was—what else?

Those sons of bitches, he thought suddenly—they'd given him one of the little crap prizes instead of $1 million or $700,000 or even $50,000. Or $10,000. And being given one of the little crap prizes meant, what?—*he'd never get one of the big prizes now.*

Some days he felt so queer, so numb, it wasn't even himself, it was the way he'd felt at the National Guard camp where you just wanted to get drunk or stoned or stay in the shower running the water hot until it was all over and you could go back to real life. Other days, though, he felt good: people were still congratulating him, acting as if they envied him. He shrugged his shoulders, looked away, muttered something about not being one of the big prize winners, but nobody seemed to care. The point was he'd won, hadn't he. That was the point.

He realized it was an asshole idea to divide the money up as he'd planned. So one Friday evening after work he went to Sears like it was Christmas Eve and bought a refrigerator for Marian, avocado green, self-defrosting, and an eight-ounce bottle of Chanel No. 5 for Marian, and a red tricycle for Paulie, and he made a sizable down payment on a nineteen-inch t.v., a Westinghouse, top of the line the salesman said, with a carved mahogany cabinet. And Marian and Paulie were as happy as if it was Christmas. And Marian only said afterward, in bed, that she hoped he was going to save something, there'd be the hospital bills etcetera and they didn't have a whole lot in the bank, but she spoke almost shyly and didn't press the point when Harvey didn't respond. And when they went over to his parents' on Sunday Harvey took his dad off to the side and slipped him an envelope with a check for $350 in it. This is class, Harvey thought, keeping calm while his father thanked him, and then his mother, this is high style, Harvey thought, not showing off, just doing it as if it was something you did every Sunday just about.

And just as Marian assured him, the $350 meant as much to his parents as $500 would have meant. The idea was the gift. The sentiment behind it. They understood, didn't they, that Harvey had to be thinking of the new baby, that he owed on the car, etc., he wasn't a millionaire who could throw his money around. In fact Harvey's parents seemed pleased and surprised to get the check as if they hadn't been expecting anything from him at all.

"The point is, hon, you're generous to them," Marian said. "You're the best they have and they know it."

"Sure," Harvey said, frowning, embarrassed, "—*okay*," he said, cutting the discussion short. But he liked what Marian said and he knew it was true. He *was* generous. He wanted to be more generous yet, he wanted to show people how generous he really could be, suddenly he felt excited, a little dazed, it was like the sensation he had when he'd had a few beers somewhere then walked out into the cold, some winter night—left the smoky noisy barroom and walked outside with his jacket open, bareheaded, blinking with the surprise of the cold and the stillness, his breath beginning to steam. Eyes opening wide and clear. The way the cold air hits the lungs, slicing right in. The way it feels in the nostrils. Jesus Christ, Harvey thinks, blinking, wiping his mouth with the back of his hand, this is it, isn't it?— standing there smiling, dazed, squinting up at the stars.

He even sent a "floral display"—red and yellow roses, white carnations, mums of various colors, daisies—across town to his mother-in-law. Just for the hell of it. Just to give the old woman a thrill, and Marian a real surprise.

He was really himself now, he was really getting in stride.

Labor Day weekend, Harvey treated Marian and Paulie and Paulie's three-year-old cousin Ben (Harvey's older sister's kid) to a day at the beach: not Surf City which was getting tacky but Cohasset Bay where they could drive out to the old lighthouse. The lottery money was nearly gone, in fact it really was gone, but what the hell, it was a great day, the kids loved it, Marian said she felt like a kid again herself, lazing around all afternoon on a beach towel, listening to music, oiling herself, having a nap or two in the sun. She'd have preferred it that Harvey's sister came along but little Ben wasn't too much trouble, the boys were occupied in wading in the surf, chasing gulls, monkeying in the sand with their pails and shovels, the only problem for her, it wasn't really a problem, was that the wind blew so hard, you got tired walking into it or even standing up for long. . . . Harvey thought the wind was a good thing, it kept things healthy, the muggy air blown away. All afternoon he kept looking at Paulie, and he kept looking at Marian, he was feeling happy, sly, laughing to himself for no reason he knew, he *was* a generous man, people were probably talking about him. It was nothing for a millionaire to give away money: the whole thing, the context, was different for a man basically without a lot of money but with a generous spirit.

Marian had curly black hair, a skin that tanned olive-dark, on the beach she wore white-rimmed plastic sunglasses that made her look like some movie star, not twenty-nine years old but twenty at the most, her belly swollen just a little out, her breasts too looking swollen, held tight in the tiny bikini top with the thin straps. She'd shaved under her arms that morning and seemed to be lifting her arms more than usual, yawning, stretching luxuriously, Harvey remembered how in high school he'd stared secretly at the girls to see if they had hair under their arms or if they'd shaved it off, and he and the other boys would joke about it, also if a girl had begun to shave her legs, and if a girl hadn't, and you could see the hairs, you'd call out in a weird voice *Hair-ry legs!* and everybody would crack up while the girl wouldn't have a clue what the joke was; or, if she did, she'd be too ashamed to let on.

Marian noticed him looking at her, she didn't mind being stared at when she looked good and she knew she looked good today, she gave him a certain mock-smile, curling her lip in a way that was supposed to mimic him, she wriggled her shoulders, her ass, he was squatting down doing something with Paulie and he got vague with that he was doing, just looking at her, it was almost as if she wasn't his wife yet, they weren't married yet, just out on the beach for an afternoon, rock music on the transistor, his buddies and their girlfriends somewhere close by, beer in the cooler but the ice was melting, the sun was getting too hot or maybe wasn't hot enough, the sky was getting mottled, it looked like rain maybe, the sky bruising up to rain, except the wind was so rough it might blow the rain away: and there was Marian Boci looking at him, coming on to him, out here with all these people around, he knew what she was thinking and she knew he knew, he'd get hard just with staring at her, or not even staring at her but thinking about her, Marian Boci sticking her tongue in his mouth like it was a joke or a trick, giggling and shoving at him, drunk, or pretending to be drunk, all the guys thought she was just great, all the guys envied Harvey Kubeck and he said, Yeh, you better believe it, Marian's hot.

He'd thought too, off and on before they were married, before things got straightened out between them and she was still going around with other guys, he'd thought something might happen, something terrible but necessary, one night he'd lose control and drive his car into a bridge railing or something, Marian screaming next to him, or worst yet he'd just kill her: strangle her: he thought about it a lot.

There was an older guy who'd doused his girl with gasoline and lit a match to her, then doused himself and did the same thing—and Harvey thought about doing that too with Marian, not all the time but sometimes, when they quarreled or she wasn't talking to him on the telephone or he heard about her going out with another guy, it wasn't a serious thought like the other, and nothing came of any of it, she saw things his way eventually, she understood they were meant for each other and that was that.

What stayed with him from the Cohasset Bay beach, what really got to him, was the sand sculptures Paulie and Ben and some other little kids made. He hadn't even been paying all that much attention then Paulie led him over, and here was this fish, they said it was a dolphin, maybe five feet long, one foot high, the goddamdest lifelike thing, with fins and gills and eyes and a mouth, and all around it they'd made little hard-packed things of sand from turning sand pails upside down, it just hit Harvey that this was a work of art, he got the camera and took some pictures, the kids clowning around but really proud, Paulie's daddy looming over them.

He said to Marian, who was impressed too, that it was a shame to leave the thing behind on the beach, nobody else'd appreciate it. Big kids would probably trample it down. "Well," Marian said, yawning a little, raising her arms to stretch, "—Paulie's like you, hon, he's got a real imagination."

Next weekend, Saturday night, he treated his buddies like he'd been saying he would, though the lottery money was all gone and in fact he had to borrow a little back from his father, it was a secret between him and the old man and nobody else was going to know. Marian especially who was acting worried about what she called the "future."

They got a late start, 9 P.M., supper at the Lobster Shanty then over to Gill's for a few beers, then down to the Windjammer where there was a punk rock band none of the guys liked, then they drove across the bay to Lenape Sound where there was a tavern run by some guy they knew, and as soon as Harvey stepped inside he felt at home, he felt great, it wasn't cause he'd been drinking all night, it was just a feeling you had, the right kind of atmosphere, even the noise the right level, some friendly place where things were lively too and your interest would be kept up. It was Stan and Jacky and Fritz and Pete. And Harvey. Who insisted upon treating. Round after round. They had whiskey, they had draft beer, they had tequilas. Marian said to telephone her around twelve, so she'd know he was okay, and when was he coming home, but he kept putting it off, then he couldn't find the telephone the bartender directed him to, then when he found it it

was out of order or something, his two dimes just kept being returned. Fishing them out Harvey thought something was weird, then
he thought, he realized, he wasn't angry at the telephone as he would
have been most nights, some other night he might have tried to rip it
from the wall, no he just felt it was all some kind of joke, he'd ride with
the joke, he was feeling so good, riding so high, he wasn't about to let
some fucking out-of-order telephone get him down. The point is, he
thought, his 20¢ was returned—little things like that were part of his
new good luck.

He weaved a little coming back into the bar but he wasn't drunk, he
didn't have any trouble finding his buddies though the place was
crowded. There were Jacky and Pete in some kind of discussion with a
big heavy guy in a t-shirt, *Harley-Davidson Sarasota Florida* on the
back, nobody Harvey knew, he was maybe thirty-five years old wearing his hair in a ponytail, going to fat, the shoulders, the small of the
back, even the neck, weighed two hundred twenty pounds at least, a
girl next to him maybe eighteen years old, hair like broom sage and
wearing sunglasses in the bar, leaning against his big arm. Harvey
came over ready to buy them all another round, ready to be introduced, the big guy's name was Terry and Jacky seemed to know him,
but it turned out it wasn't any kind of friendly discussion, it was
actually an argument, about somebody Terry knew that Jacky also
knew, ran a gas station in Atlantic City, maybe, Harvey couldn't
follow it except he knew right away that Terry was the kind of asshole
he'd like to smash with his fists, you'd just like to see a wise guy fucker
like that laid out somewhere dead, wipe the grin off his face, put some
respect in his eyes, the fear of the Lord as Harvey's father said.

The argument continued for a while, Terry was calling Jacky fuckface, and Harvey said to Terry go fuck yourself, and the bartender
who was listening who seemed to be a friend of Fritz's or maybe a
cousin, Harvey'd been introduced when they first came in but hadn't
exactly heard, he came over and told them to keep it down please, he
said to Terry maybe he'd better move on, there's lots of places on the

strip and it was still early. So Terry and his girl left after a few minutes, Terry told them all to go to hell, go fuck themselves, bunch of assholes etc. but he kept on moving, the girl had to hurry after him in her high heeled shoes and she looked scared.

So that happened, but again it was weird, Harvey didn't feel angry he felt instead like it was all part of his life now, him being out with his buddies, everybody having a good time, the way he'd planned it in his head almost from the first hour when the news came about the lottery, thinking of a place like this, maybe not in Lenape Sound cause he wasn't familiar with it like he was with Surf City, but a place like this, him and his buddies, Pete and Stan and Jacky and Fritz, then there was Gary who couldn't make it cause they were going out of town or something, he felt bad that Gary wasn't with them but just for a second or a half-second, already the thought floated away and his good happy feeling returned, Jacky was making them all crack up with what he was saying about the guy with the ponytail, Harvey decided on another tequila and the bartender smiled at him, said, Harv this is on me, okay? and he felt that kick of something special, something just right, meant only for him, some kind of secret. Nah, he said, I can pay for it, but the bartender insisted, so he gave in, then they were all eating oysters, the second time that night, then Harvey was having trouble with the cigarette machine, laughing cause his coins weren't being returned this time, but a little pissed-off too, starting to punch at the machine, a few kicks, one of his buddies pulled him away saying forget it: Harv could bum a cigarette from him anytime he wanted.

They left that bar, drove a mile or two down the Bay Road to another place, big parking lot practically in the dunes, music inside, somebody else was driving Harvey's Impala now which irritated him a little but he didn't intend to get in a fight right now, he'd make his point later when they drove back to Surf City. This place, the atmosphere took getting used to, too many customers pushing around the bar, too many women maybe, couples trying to dance and getting bumped into, a lot of noise, but Harvey felt good after his first draft beer or two, his buddies were flying high just like him, lots of wise guy stuff and laughing, almost choking with laughter, Fritz telling them how Harv had told Father Donahue to go screw, they'd heard it a hundred times already but it always cracked them up. Harvey thought he saw the big guy with the ponytail, he thought he saw him and the girl on the other side of the room, but then he lost them, forgot about them, he was bumming cigarettes which he'd light and drop on the floor, once he burnt his fingers with somebody's lighter, how the fuck it happened he couldn't figure out, those things were safety proof. Harvey was thinking he liked this bar as well as the other one, maybe better. He felt at peace. But well he felt excited too. It was hard to put your finger on—things going the way they were supposed to go. The way they were meant. Like the satisfaction seeing a river or something running along, or even raindrops rolling down a windshield, it could fascinate you, it was hard to say why. Harvey saw the sky bunching up over the Surf City beach and the first raindrops pelting and the thunder sounding and there's that good clean fresh air, that almost surprising air, just before a storm, and he and the other kids ran like hell down the beach, yelling and laughing, trying to outrace the storm, the raindrops hitting like bullets, older people scrambling around putting away their beach crap, gathering up their kids, assholes acting like lightning was going to strike them the next minute.

He saw then that that guy with the ponytail *was* there in the bar, the girl with him, but they hadn't noticed Harvey and his friends. Actually they were on their way out, the girl had her sunglasses slid atop her head, pressing close against him with her arm through his, the guy gave a look around the room, a last look, but he still didn't see Harvey and his friends. The son of a bitch, Harvey thought. Who are you calling fuckface, fuckface?—you're dead, Harvey thought, putting down his glass of draft beer.

The girl wasn't any eighteen either, probably Marian's age, heavy makeup on her face and black stuff on her eyes, her ass wriggling in some kind of a silky play suit, really short shorts, bare legs and those high heeled shoes: a real slut.

Harvey poked his buddies and said Look, and they looked, and he said Want to get him? and they were sort of indecisive and Harvey said Let's go, and they paid up at the bar, and followed the two out into the parking lot, it was good luck, Harvey thought, the bastard's motorcycle was parked way down at the end, way down, almost in the dunes. Harvey started in trotting, he wasn't even going to wait for his buddies, he felt so good, the whole night had been moving toward this, weeks and weeks, half his life, like a river running fast, his heart fast too, he knew enough not to call out any kind of warning, not even to bother calling the bastard a name, the trainer at the Y had said don't waste that rush you get, that good strong feeling, that's some kind of chemical or hormone, adrenaline, now you're going to need it and now you think maybe you're scared but remember you're *not*, you're just getting ready to fight. When it hits them there's lots of guys that panic or start talking too fast but don't you ever make that mistake, just ride with the feeling, okay?—just ride with it, let it carry you along, that good strong feeling, someday maybe it's going to save your life.

And when you're in the ring don't ever feel sorry for your opponent cause why the hell should you, he's your opponent and he's out for your ass.

So Harvey got first to the guy, just started swinging, the girl screamed, the guy shouted something and tried to block Harvey's fist but Harvey got him square in the face, left cheekbone, so hard his knuckles felt like they were broken but the hurt just faded away at once. Now the bastard was backing away crouched, now Harvey could see the sick pleading look in his eyes, Harvey got him next in the gut, that big soft fat gut, a real belly blow that doubled him over, any referee that saw that the fucking fight would be over right now and Kubeck through for the season, but there wasn't any referee, just Harvey and the guy with the ponytail, trying to use his fists, trying even to use a knee, he swung clumsily at Harvey and Harvey just danced aside, knowing to do some quick peppery jabbing with his left, a hard uppercut with his right, shit it felt like his whole hand was broken now but he didn't give a damn, didn't have time to worry, the guy stumbled backward, fell to his knees, Harvey used his knee to get him in the face, there was blood streaming out of his nose and mouth, now Fritz and Pete were trying to pull Harvey away but he just shrugged them off, nobody was going to stop him, it was between him and his opponent and nobody was going to stop him, How d'you like it now, fuckface, Harvey said, okay you motherfucker, Harvey was saying, the air felt so good from the ocean, the wind so fresh and clean in his lungs, he was just getting higher and higher like his heart could burst with wanting to laugh, nobody was going to stop him now after so long.

The guy had fallen, even in the half-light from the parking lot Harvey could see he was bleeding pretty bad, the pavement and the sand were going dark by his head, then there were some headlights, then they heard a car door slam, Fritz said, Harv come *on*, but whoever it was wasn't coming any closer, they just weren't about to see what was going on by the dunes and Harvey knew ahead of time that that was how it was: he just knew. So he said Here's one for the road, sucker, bringing his fist down hard on the back of the guy's neck like he was doing karate and wanted to break it. One of his buddies was keeping the girl quiet, the others were trying to stop him, he felt so weird, so certain of himself, he just kept punching, kicking, he kicked anywhere he could, the guy's head, the guy's fat belly, he was laughing saying How's it feel now you son of a bitch, wiping his mouth with his forearm, How's it feel now you cocksucker, something jumped in his mind and he was thinking for a second he had on steel-toed shoes like at work but of course he hadn't, these were just his regular shoes, summer shoes, loafers Marian had made him get, they were oyster-white and pretty stylish, supposed to be Italian but not expensive like the real kind, he'd bought them at the mall back in

June before he ever guessed that his luck would be changing and his whole life would be turned around.

There was some confusion about getting back home, who was going to drive who, they'd come in two cars, Harvey's and Pete's, but finally he got home, it was 3:20 A.M. and there was Marian watching television, dressed for bed and barefoot, her face oily with cream. He could tell she was angry but she was frightened too which made him feel better toward her, he shrugged her off when she came over, asking right away about his hand though he was hiding it, asking if he'd been in a fight, he went past her into the kitchen and got a beer from the refrigerator, pulled off the ring and tossed it somewhere, Marian was pulling at his arm, saying he was drunk, saying he was cockeyed drunk and not to wake Paulie, her voice was low and flat and accusing but he could tell she was scared. He just shoved her out of the way and went into the bathroom.

He was in there a while, five minutes, ten, he heard the telephone ringing but it was only his head, a good loud buzzing like Quāāludes but he couldn't remember having taken any that night, unless it was back at that place before the last place where the bartender gave him a drink on the house, hell of a nice guy, that was a place he intended to go back to, some cousin or somebody of Fritz's, but mainly he thought it must be just what he'd drunk and how good he felt from messing up that son of a bitch with the ponytail, Harley-Davidson t-shirt, big black bike, the works, and the girl gone crazy thinking her boyfriend was dead which anybody could see he wasn't: not crawling around like he was and making noises like he was, puking into the sand, puke and blood, the son of a bitch.

When he came out of the bathroom Marian said in that low voice, "Barbara just called," meaning Pete's wife, and Harvey didn't bother replying, got his shoes off with a grunt, pulled his shirt off over his head without taking time to unbutton it, his fingers were getting too numb to work the buttons, he was suddenly very tired and ready for bed, and Marian pulled at his arm, Marian said, "She says there was some trouble tonight," but he just pushed her away, not hard, just out of his way. She said, "Was there?"

He was rubbing his face with the shirt. Waves of exhaustion like he'd been working overtime, two hours overtime, could hardly keep from keeling over, but there were waves of something else too, short quick stabbing waves, excitement, elation, the knowledge of some-thing secret. He could smell Marian's hair and the stale powdery scent of her underarms. The special rayony smell of that shortie nightgown of hers with the lace top. Her mouth was close to his ear, her breath was hot and acusing, she said again, "Was there? Harvey? Was there?" and he said, "Was there what?" She was so close, he hadn't expected her so close, he reached around and grabbed hold of her ass, she gave him a slap, told him again not to wake Paulie, did he know what time it was, he could feel himself getting hard though he was almost too tired to keep his eyes open, stumbling to the bed and hauling Marian with him, she gave him a real slap on the side of the face so that his ear stung, he fell laughing onto the bed not giving a damn if the bed-springs broke, "C'mon shut up an' get to bed," he said, it really turned him on that Marian was always pushing him, seeing how far she could go with him, he wouldn't want some wife like his brother had or his brother-in-law or half the guys he knew, scared to death they were going to get it in the face, too scared even to cry, Marian *was* scared but she kept at him, her eyes showing white the way they did, "Look Harvey, was there trouble?—I want to know," she asked, and he said, "No there was not."

She said something he didn't catch, then she was drawing off her bathrobe, he had to watch her through his fingers because of the light that hurt his eyes, he liked that nightgown of hers that was a queer translucent aqua color, wide lacy straps like something a little girl might wear, lace bodice you could see through in the right light, he knew suddenly that the baby was going to be a girl and he knew that was right, that balanced things out, there would be Paulie and there would be Paulie's baby sister, that was the way it would work out, he'd bet a thousand dollars, his luck was going to hold.

The nightgown clung with static electricity to Marian's belly and buttocks, and seeing his face, his eyes, she turned slightly away, intimidated, maybe, or embarrassed. She could see things in his face, Harvey knew, he could never see himself.

In the dark he went for her, wordless. Marian resisted, then gave in, murmuring something he couldn't make out, she had to lift her hips, she had to help him get inside her, they were both breathing hard, then Harvey was pumping himself into her, his jaws clenched, his eyes shut tight, he hadn't known he was so hot, so urgent, his heartbeat so fast. Marian held his sides tight with her knees as she sometimes did, holding him back, trying to hold him back, so in his plunge he wouldn't squeeze her belly and breasts, wouldn't hurt her. She was whispering something, she closed her fingers in his hair but he paid no attention, he was panting, grunting, then suddenly it was over—that flame coursing through his groin and belly that always astonished him, it was so strong, so powerful, it was familiar but it always astonished him, knocked the breath out of him as if he'd been kicked. Then he was lying by himself in the damp sheets and Marian was in the bathroom, a narrow sliver of light, water running in the distance, or maybe it was the surf, the waves breaking, a waterfall, a cascade of water sparkling in the sun, suddenly he is sinking in a slow turn, weightless, wordless, a deep deep turning, now he hardly needs to breathe because it is all being done for him, he is turning slow into a dark pool of water secret beneath the crashing waterfall, this is his place, this is his secret, deep beyond dreaming, floating free, and here, here suddenly he is.

Tim O'Brien

THE THINGS THEY CARRIED

First Lieutenant Jimmy Cross carried letters from a girl named Martha, a junior at Mount Sebastian College in New Jersey. They were not love letters, but Lieutenant Cross was hoping, so he kept them folded in plastic at the bottom of his rucksack. In the late afternoon, after a day's march, he would dig his foxhole, wash his hands under a canteen, unwrap the letters, hold them with the tips of his fingers, and spend the last hour of light pretending. He would imagine romantic camping trips into the White Mountains in New Hampshire. He would sometimes taste the envelope flaps, knowing her tongue had been there. More than anything, he wanted Martha to love him as he loved her, but the letters were mostly chatty, elusive on the matter of love. She was a virgin, he was almost sure. She was an English major at Mount Sebastian, and she wrote beautifully about her professors and roommates and mid-term exams, about her respect for Chaucer and her great affection for Virginia Woolf. She often quoted lines of poetry; she never mentioned the war, except to say, Jimmy, take care of yourself. The letters weighed 10 ounces. They were signed Love, Martha, but Lieutenant Cross understood that Love was only a way of signing and did not mean what he sometimes pretended it meant. At dusk, he would carefully return the letters to his rucksack. Slowly, a bit distracted, he would get up and move among his men, checking the perimeter, then at full dark he would return to his hole and watch the night and wonder if Martha was a virgin.

The things they carried were largely determined by necessity. Among the necessities or near-necessities were P-38 can openers, pocket knives, heat tabs, wristwatches, dogtags, mosquito repellent, chewing gum, candy, cigarettes, salt tablets, packets of Kool-Aid, lighters, matches, sewing kits, Military Payment Certificates, C rations, and two or three canteens of water. Together, these items weighed between 15 and 20 pounds, depending upon a man's habits or rate of metabolism. Henry Dobbins, who was a big man, carried extra rations; he was especially fond of canned peaches in heavy syrup over pound cake. Dave Jensen, who practiced field hygiene, carried a toothbrush, dental floss, and several hotel-sized bars of soap he'd stolen on R&R in Sydney, Australia. Ted Lavender, who was scared, carried tranquilizers until he was shot in the head outside the village of Than Khe in mid-April. By necessity, and because it was SOP, they all carried steel helmets that weighed 5 pounds including the liner and camouflage cover. They carried the standard fatigue jackets and trousers. Very few carried underwear. On their feet they carried jungle boots—2.1 pounds—and Dave Jensen carried three pairs of socks and a can of Dr. Scholl's foot powder as a precaution against trench foot. Until he was shot, Ted Lavender carried 6 or 7 ounces of premium dope, which for him was a necessity. Mitchell Sanders, the RTO, carried condoms. Norman Bowker carried a diary. Rat Kiley carried comic books. Kiowa, a devout Baptist, carried an illustrated New Testament that had been presented to him by his father, who taught Sunday school in Oklahoma City, Oklahoma. As a hedge against bad times, however, Kiowa also carried his grandmother's distrust of the white man, his grandfather's old hunting hatchet. Necessity dictated. Because the land was mined and booby-trapped, it was SOP for each man to carry a steel-centered, nylon-covered flak jacket, which weighed 6.7 pounds, but which on hot days seemed much heavier. Because you could die so quickly, each man carried at least one large compress bandage, usually in the helmet-band for easy access. Because the nights were cold, and because the monsoons were wet, each carried a green plastic poncho that could be used as a raincoat or groundsheet or makeshift tent. With its quilted liner, the poncho weighed almost 2 pounds, but it was worth every ounce. In April, for instance, when Ted Lavender was shot, they used his poncho to wrap him up, then to carry him across the paddy, then to lift him into the chopper that took him away.

They were called legs or grunts.

To carry something was to hump it, as when Lieutenant Jimmy Cross humped his love for Martha up the hills and through the swamps. In its intransitive form, to hump meant to walk, or to march, but it implied burdens far beyond the intransitive.

Almost everyone humped photographs. In his wallet, Lieutenant Cross carried two photographs of Martha. The first was a Kodachrome snapshot signed Love, though he knew better. She stood against a brick wall. Her eyes were gray and neutral, her lips slightly open as she stared straight-on at the camera. At night, sometimes, Lieutenant Cross wondered who had taken the picture, because he knew she had boyfriends, because he loved her so much, and because he could see the shadow of the picture-taker spreading out against the brick wall. The second photograph had been clipped from the 1968 Mount Sebastian Yearbook. It was an action shot—women's volleyball—and Martha was bent horizontal to the floor, reaching, the palms of her hands in sharp focus, the tongue taut, the expression frank and competitive. There was no visible sweat. She wore white gym shorts. Her legs, he thought, were almost certainly the legs of a virgin, dry and without hair, the left knee cocked and carrying her entire weight, which was just over one hundred pounds. Lieutenant Cross remembered touching that left knee. A dark theater, he remembered, and the movie was *Bonnie and Clyde*, and Martha wore a tweed skirt, and during the final scene, when he touched her knee, she turned and looked at him in a sad, sober way that made him pull his hand back, but he would always remember the feel of the tweed skirt and the knee beneath it and the sound of the gunfire that killed Bonnie and Clyde, how embarassing it was, how slow and oppressive. He remembered kissing her good night at the dorm door. Right then, he thought, he should've done something brave. He should've carried her up the stairs to her room and tied her to the bed and touched that left knee all night long. He should've risked it. Whenever he looked at the photographs, he thought of new things he should've done.

What they carried was partly a function of rank, partly of field specialty.

As a first lieutenant and platoon leader, Jimmy Cross carried a compass, maps, code books, binoculars, and a .45-caliber pistol that weighed 2.9 pounds fully loaded. He carried a strobe light and the responsibility for the lives of his men.

As an RTO, Mitchell Sanders carried the PRC-25 radio, a killer, 26 pounds with its battery.

As a medic, Rat Kiley carried a canvas satchel filled with morphine and plasma and malaria tablets and surgical tape and comic books and all the things a medic must carry, including M&Ms for especially bad wounds, for a total weight of nearly 20 pounds.

As a big man, therefore a machine gunner, Henry Dobbins carried the M-60, which weighed 23 pounds unloaded, but which was almost always loaded. In addition, Dobbins carried between 10 and 15 pounds of ammunition draped in belts across his chest and shoulders.

As PFCs or Spec 4s, most of them were common grunts and carried the standard M-16 gas-operated assault rifle. The weapon weighed 7.5 pounds unloaded, 8.2 pounds with its full 20-round magazine. Depending on numerous factors, such as topography and psychology, the riflemen carried anywhere from 12 to 20 magazines, usually in cloth bandoliers, adding on another 8.4 pounds at minimum, 14 pounds at maximum. When it was available, they also carried M-16 maintenance gear—rods and steel brushes and swabs and tubes of

LSA oil—all of which weighed about a pound. Among the grunts, some carried the M-79 grenade launcher, 5.9 pounds unloaded, a reasonably light weapon except for the ammunition, which was heavy. A single round weighed 10 ounces. The typical load was 25 rounds. But Ted Lavender, who was scared, carried 34 rounds when he was shot and killed outside Than Khe, and he went down under an exceptional burden, more than 20 pounds of ammunition, plus the flak jacket and helmet and rations and water and toilet paper and tranquilizers and all the rest, plus the unweighed fear. He was dead weight. There was no twitching or flopping. Kiowa, who saw it happen, said it was like watching a rock fall, or a big sandbag or something—just boom, then down—not like the movies where the dead guy rolls around and does fancy spins and goes ass over teaket-tle—not like that, Kiowa said, the poor bastard just flat-fuck fell. Boom. Down. Nothing else. It was a bright morning in mid-April. Lieutenant Cross felt the pain. He blamed himself. They stripped off Lavender's canteens and ammo, all the heavy things, and Rat Kiley said the obvious, the guy's dead, and Mitchell Sanders used his radio to report one U.S. KIA and to request a chopper. Then they wrapped Lavender in his poncho. They carried him out to a dry paddy, estab-lished security, and sat smoking the dead man's dope until the chop-per came. Lieutenant Cross kept to himself. He pictured Martha's smooth young face, thinking he loved her more than anything, more than his men, and now Ted Lavender was dead because he loved her so much and could not stop thinking about her. When the dustoff arrived, they carried Lavender aboard. Afterward they burned Than Khe. They marched until dusk, then dug their holes, and that night Kiowa kept explaining how you had to be there, how fast it was, how the poor guy just dropped like so much concrete. Boom-down, he said. Like cement.

In addition to the three standard weapons—the M-60, M-16, and M-79—they carried whatever presented itself, or whatever seemed appropriate as a means of killing or staying alive. They carried catch-as-catch-can. At various times, in various situations, they carried M-14s and CAR-15s and Swedish Ks and grease guns and captured AK-47s and Chi-Coms and RPGs and Simonov carbines and black market Uzis and .38-caliber Smith and Wesson handguns and 66mm LAWs and shotguns and silencers and blackjacks and bayonets and C-4 plastic explosives. Lee Strunk carried a slingshot; a weapon of last resort, he called it. Mitchell Sanders carried brass knuckles. Kiowa carried his grandfather's feathered hatchet. Every third or fourth man carried a Claymore antipersonnel mine—3.5 pounds with its firing device. They all carried fragmentation grenades—14 ounces each. They all carried at least one M-18 colored smoke grenade—24 ounces. Some carried C-S or tear gas grenades. Some carried white phosphorus grenades. They carried all they could bear, and then some, including a silent awe for the terrible power of the things they carried.

In the first week of April, before Lavender died, Lieutenant Jimmy Cross received a good-luck charm from Martha. It was a simple pebble, an ounce at most. Smooth to the touch, it was a milky white color with flecks of orange and violet, oval shaped, like a miniature egg. In the accompanying letter, Martha wrote that she had found the pebble on the Jersey shoreline, precisely where the land touched water at high tide, where things came together but also separated. It was this separate-but-together quality, she wrote, that had inspired her to pick up the pebble and to carry it in her breast pocket for several days, where it seemed weightless, and then to send it through the mail, by air, as a token of her truest feelings for him. Lieutenant Cross found this romantic. But he wondered what her truest feelings were, exactly, and what she meant by separate-but-together. He wondered how the tides and waves had come into play on that afternoon along the Jersey shoreline when Martha saw the pebble and bent down to rescue it from geology. He imagined bare feet. Martha was a poet, with the poet's sensibilities, and her feet would be brown and bare, the toenails unpainted, the eyes chilly and somber like the ocean in March, and though it was painful, he wondered who had been with her that afternoon. He imagined a pair of shadows moving along the strip of sand where things came together but also separated. It was phantom jealousy, he knew, but he couldn't help himself. He loved her so much. On the march, through the hot days of early April, he carried the pebble in his mouth, turning it with his tongue, tasting sea salts and moisture. His mind wandered. He had difficulty keeping his attention on the war. On occasion he would yell at his men to spread out the column, to keep their eyes open, but then he would slip away into daydreams, just pretending, walking barefoot along the Jersey shore, with Martha, carrying nothing. He would feel himself rising. Sun and waves and gentle winds, all love and lightness.

What they carried varied by mission.

When a mission took them to the mountains, they carried mosquito netting, machetes, canvas tarps, and extra bug juice.

If a mission seemed especially hazardous, or if it involved a place they knew to be bad, they carried everything they could. In certain heavily mined AOs, where the land was dense with Toe Poppers and Bouncing Betties, they took turns humping a 28-pound mine detector. With its headphones and big sensing plate, the equipment was a stress on the lower back and shoulders, awkward to handle, often useless because of the shrapnel in the earth, but they carried it anyway, partly for safety, partly for the illusion of safety.

On ambush, or other night missions, they carried peculiar little odds and ends. Kiowa always took along his New Testament and a pair of moccasins for silence. Dave Jensen carried night-sight vitamins high in carotin. Lee Strunk carried his slingshot; ammo, he claimed, would never be a problem. Rat Kiley carried brandy and M&Ms. Until he was shot, Ted Lavender carried the starlight scope, which weighed 6.3 pounds with its aluminum carrying case. Henry Dobbins carried his girlfriend's panty hose wrapped around his neck as a comforter. They all carried ghosts. When dark came, they would move out single file across the meadows and paddies to their ambush coordinates, where they would quietly set up the Claymores and lie down and spend the night waiting.

Other missions were more complicated and required special equipment. In mid-April, it was their mission to search out and destroy the elaborate tunnel complexes in the Than Khe area south of Chu Lai. To blow the tunnels, they carried 1-pound blocks of pentrite high explosives, 4 blocks to a man, 68 pounds in all. They carried wiring, detonators, and battery-powered clackers. Dave Jensen carried ear-plugs. Most often, before blowing the tunnels, they were ordered by higher command to search them, which was considered bad news, but by and large they just shrugged and carried out orders. Because he was a big man, Henry Dobbins was excused from tunnel duty. The others would draw numbers. Before Lavender died there were 17 men in the platoon, and whoever drew the number 17 would strip off his gear and crawl in headfirst with a flashlight and Lieutenant Cross's .45-caliber pistol. The rest of them would fan out as security. They would sit down or kneel, not facing the hole, listening to the ground beneath them, imagining cobwebs and ghosts, whatever was down there—the tunnel walls squeezing in—how the flashlight seemed impossibly heavy in the hand and how it was tunnel vision in the very strictest sense, compression in all ways, even time, and how you had to wiggle in—ass and elbows—a swallowed-up feeling—and how you found yourself worrying about odd things—will your flashlight go dead?—do rats carry rabies?—do you hear the shot that gets you?—if you screamed, how far would the sound carry?—would your buddies hear it?—would they have the courage to drag you out? In some respects, though not many, the waiting was worse than the tunnel itself. Imagaination was a killer.

On April 16, when Lee Strunk drew the number 17, he laughed and muttered something and went down quickly. The morning was hot and very still. Not good, Kiowa said. He looked at the tunnel opening, then out across a dry paddy toward the village of Than Khe. Nothing moved. No clouds or birds or people. As they waited, the men smoked and drank Kool-Aid, not talking much, feeling sympathy for Lee Strunk but also feeling the luck of the draw. You win some, you lose some, said Mitchell Sanders, and sometimes you settle for a rain check. It was a tired line and no one laughed.

Henry Dobbins ate a tropical chocolate bar. Ted Lavender popped a tranquilizer and went off to pee.

After five minutes, Lieutenant Jimmy Cross moved to the tunnel, leaned down, and examined the darkness. Trouble, he thought—a cave-in maybe. And then suddenly, without willing it, he was thinking about Martha. The stresses and fractures, the quick collapse, the two of them buried alive under all that weight. Dense, crushing love. Kneeling, watching the hole, he tried to concentrate on Lee Strunk and the war, all the dangers, but his love was too much for him, he felt paralyzed, he wanted to sleep inside her lungs and breathe her blood and be smothered. He wanted her to be a virgin and not a virgin, all at once. He wanted to know her. Intimate secrets—why poetry? Why so sad? Why that grayness in her eyes? Why so alone? Not lonely, just alone—riding her bike across campus or sitting off by herself in the cafeteria—even dancing, she danced alone—and it was the aloneness that filled him with love. He remembered telling her that one evening. How she nodded and looked away. And how, later, when he kissed her, she received the kiss without returning it, her eyes wide-open, not afraid, not a virgin's eyes, just flat and uninvolved.

Lieutenant Cross gazed at the tunnel. But he was not there. He was buried with Martha under the white sand at the Jersey shore. They were pressed together, tight and bonded, and the pebble in his mouth was her tongue. He was smiling. Vaguely, he was aware of how quiet the day was, the sullen paddies, yet he could not bring himself to worry about matters of security. He was beyond that. He was just a kid at war, in love. He was twenty-two years old. He couldn't help it.

A few moments later Lee Strunk crawled out of the tunnel. He came up grinning, filthy but alive. Lieutenant Cross nodded and closed his eyes while the others clapped Strunk on the back and made jokes about rising from the dead.

Worms, Rat Kiley said. Right out of the grave. Fuckin' zombie.

The men laughed. They all felt great relief.

Spook City, said Mitchell Sanders.

Lee Strunk made a funny ghost sound, a kind of moaning, yet very happy, and right then, when Strunk made that high happy moaning sound, when he went *Ahhooooo*, right then Ted Lavender was shot in the head on his way back from peeing. He lay with his mouth open. The teeth were broken. There was a swollen black bruise under his left eye. The cheekbone was gone. Oh shit, Rat Kiley said, the guy's dead. The guy's dead, he kept saying, which seemed profound—the guy's dead. I mean really.

The things they carried were determined to some extent by superstition. Lieutenant Cross carried his good-luck pebble. Dave Jensen carried a rabbit's foot. Norman Bowker, otherwise a very gentle person, carried a thumb that had been presented to him as a gift by Mitchell Sanders. The thumb was dark brown, rubbery to the touch, and weighed 4 ounces at most. It had been cut from a VC corpse, a boy of fifteen or sixteen. They'd found him at the bottom of an irrigation ditch, badly burned, flies in his mouth and eyes. The boy wore black shorts and sandals. At the time of his death he had been carrying a pouch of rice, a rifle, and three magazines of ammunition.

You want my opinion, Mitchell Sanders said, there's a definite moral here.

He put his hand on the dead boy's wrist. He was quiet for a time, as if counting a pulse, then he patted the stomach, almost affectionately, and used Kiowa's hunting hatchet to remove the thumb.

Henry Dobbins asked what the moral was.

Moral?

You know. *Moral*.

Sanders wrapped the thumb in toilet paper and handed it across to Norman Bowker. There was no blood. Smiling, he kicked the boy's head, watched the flies scatter, and said, It's like with that old TV show—Paladin. Have gun, will travel.

Henry Dobbins thought about it.

Yeah, well, he finally said. I don't see no moral.

There it *is*, man.

Fuck off.

They carried USO stationery and pencils and pens. They carried Sterno, safety pins, trip flares, signal flares, spools of wire, razor blades, chewing tobacco, liberated joss sticks and statuettes of the smiling Buddha, candles, grease pencils, the *Stars and Stripes*, fingernail clippers, Psy-Ops leaflets, bush hats, bolos, and much more. Twice a week, when the resupply choppers came in, they carried hot chow in green mermite cans and large canvas bags filled with iced beer and soda pop. They carried plastic water containers, each with a 2-gallon capacity. Mitchell Sanders carried a set of starched tiger fatigues for special occasions. Henry Dobbins carried Black Flag insecticide. Dave Jensen carried empty sandbags that could be filled at night for added protection. Lee Strunk carried tanning lotion. Some things they carried in common. Taking turns, they carried the big PRC-77 scrambler radio, which weighed 30 pounds with its battery. They shared the weight of memory. They took up what others could no longer bear. Often, they carried each other, the wounded or weak. They carried infections. They carried chess sets, basketballs, Vietnamese-English dictionaries, insignia of rank, Bronze Stars and Purple Hearts, plastic cards imprinted with the Code of Conduct. They carried diseases, among them malaria and dysentery. They carried lice and ringworm and leeches and paddy algae and various rots and molds. They carried the land itself—Vietnam, the place, the soil—a powdery orange-red dust that covered their boots and fatigues and faces. They carried the sky. The whole atmosphere, they carried it, the humidity, the monsoons, the stink of fungus and decay, all of it, they carried gravity. They moved like mules. By daylight they took sniper fire, at night they were mortared, but it was not battle, it was just the endless march, village to village, without purpose, nothing won or lost. They marched for the sake of the march. They plodded along slowly, dumbly, leaning forward against the heat, unthinking, all blood and bone, simple grunts, soldiering with their legs, toiling up the hills and down into the paddies and across the rivers and up again and down, just humping, one step and then the next and then another, but no volition, no will, because it was automatic, it was anatomy, and the war was entirely a matter of posture and carriage, the hump was everything, a kind of inertia, a kind of emptiness, a dullness of desire and intellect and conscience and hope and human sensibility. Their principles were in their feet. Their calculations were biological. They had no sense of strategy or mission. They searched the villages without knowing what to look for, not caring, kicking over jars of rice, frisking children and old men, blowing tunnels, sometimes setting fires and sometimes not, then forming up and moving on to the next village, then other villages, where it would always be the same. They carried their own lives. The pressures were enormous. In the heat of early afternoon, they would remove their helmets and flak jackets, walking bare, which was dangerous but which helped ease the strain. They would often discard things along the route of march. Purely for comfort, they would throw away rations, blow their Claymores and grenades, no matter, because by nightfall the resupply chopper would arrive with more of the same, then a day or two later still more—fresh watermelons and crates of ammunition and sunglasses and woolen sweaters—the resources were stunning—sparklers for the Fourth of July, colored eggs for Easter—it was the great American war chest—the fruits of science, the smokestacks, the canneries, the arsenals at Hartford, the Minnesota forests, the machine shops, the vast fields of corn and wheat—they carried like freight trains—they carried it on their backs and shoulders—and for all the ambiguities of Vietnam, all the mysteries and unknowns, there was at least the single abiding certainty that they would never be at a loss for things to carry.

After the chopper took Lavender away, Lieutenant Jimmy Cross led his men into the village of Than Khe. They burned everything. They shot chickens and dogs, they trashed the village well, they called in artillery and watched the wreckage, then they marched for several hours through the hot afternoon, and then at dusk, while Kiowa explained how Lavender died, Lieutenant Cross found himself trembling.

He tried not to cry. With his entrenching tool, which weighed 5 pounds, he began digging a hole in the earth.

He felt shame. He hated himself. He had loved Martha more than his men, and as a consequence Lavender was now dead, and this was something he would have to carry like a stone in his stomach for the rest of the war.

All he could do was dig. He used his entrenching tool like an axe, slashing, feeling both love and hate, and then later, when it was full dark, he sat at the bottom of his foxhole and wept. It went on for a long while. In part, he was grieving for Ted Lavender, but mostly it was for Martha, and for himself, because she belonged to another world, which was not quite real, and because she was a junior at Mount Sebastian College in New Jersey, a poet and a virgin and uninvolved, and because he realized she did not love him and never would.

Like cement, Kiowa whispered in the dark. I swear to God—boom, down. Not a word.

I've heard this, said Norman Bowker.

A pisser, you know? Still zipping himself up. Zapped while zipping.

All right fine. That's enough.

Yeah, but you had to see it, the guy just—

I *heard*, man. Cement. So why not shut the fuck *up?*

Kiowa shook his head sadly and glanced over at the hole where Lieutenant Jimmy Cross sat watching the night. The air was thick and wet. A warm dense fog had settled over the paddies and there was the stillness that precedes rain.

After a time Kiowa sighed.

One thing for sure, he said. The Lieutenant's in some deep hurt. I mean that crying jag—the way he was carrying on—it wasn't fake or anything, it was real heavy-duty hurt. The man cares.

Sure, Norman Bowker said.

Say what you want, the man does care.

We all got problems.

Not Lavender.

No, I guess not, Bowker said. Do me a favor, though.

Shut up?

That's a smart Indian. Shut up.

Shrugging, Kiowa pulled off his boots. He wanted to say more, just to lighten up his sleep, but instead he opened his New Testament and arranged it beneath his head as a pillow. The fog made things seem hollow and unattached. He tried not to think about Ted Lavender, but then he was thinking how fast it was, no drama, down and dead, and how it was hard to feel anything except surprise. It seemed unChristian. He wished he could find some great sadness, or even anger, but the emotion wasn't there and he couldn't make it happen. Mostly he felt pleased to be alive. He liked the smell of the New Testament under his cheek, the leather and ink and paper and glue, whatever the chemicals were. He liked hearing the sounds of night. Even his fatigue, it felt fine, the stiff muscles and the prickly awareness of his own body, a floating feeling. He enjoyed not being dead. Lying there, Kiowa admired Lieutenant Jimmy Cross's capacity for grief. He wanted to share the man's pain, he wanted to care as Jimmy Cross cared. And yet when he closed his eyes, all he could think was

Boom-down, and all he could feel was the pleasure of having his boots off and the fog curling in around him and the damp soil and the Bible smells and the plush comfort of the night.

After a moment Norman Bowker sat up in the dark.

What the hell, he said. You want to talk, *talk*. Tell it to me.

Forget it.

No man, go on. One thing I hate, it's a silent Indian.

For the most part they carried themselves with poise, a kind of dignity. Now and then, however, there were times of panic, when they squealed or wanted to squeal but couldn't, when they twitched and made moaning sounds and covered their heads and said Dear Jesus and flopped around on the earth and fired their weapons blindly and cringed and sobbed and begged for the noise to stop and went wild and made stupid promises to themselves and to God and to their mothers and fathers, hoping not to die. In different ways, it happened to all of them. Afterward, when the firing ended, they would blink and peek up. They would touch their bodies, feeling shame, then quickly hiding it. They would force themselves to stand. As if in slow-motion, frame by frame, the world would take on the old logic—absolute silence, then the wind, then sunlight, then voices. It was the burden of being alive. Awkwardly, the men would reassemble themselves, first in private, then in groups, becoming soldiers again. They would repair the leaks in their eyes. They would check for casualties, call in dustoffs, light cigarettes, try to smile, clear their throats and spit and begin cleaning their weapons. After a time someone would shake his head and say, No lie, I almost shit my pants, and someone else would laugh, which meant it was bad, yes, but the guy had obviously not shit his pants, it wasn't that bad, and in any case nobody would ever do such a thing and then go ahead and talk about it. They would squint into the dense, oppressive sunlight. For a few moments, perhaps, they would fall silent, lighting a joint and tracking its passage from man to man, inhaling, holding in the humiliation. Scary stuff, one of them might say. But then someone else would grin or flick his eyebrows and say, Roger-dodger, almost cut me a new asshole, *almost*.

There were numerous such poses. Some carried themselves with a sort of wistful resignation, others with pride or stiff soldierly discipline or good humor or macho zeal. They were afraid of dying but they were even more afraid to show it.

They found jokes to tell.

They used a hard vocabularly to contain the terrible softness. *Greased* they'd say. *Offed, lit up, zapped while zipping*. It wasn't cruelty, just stage presence. They were actors and the war came at them in 3-D. When someone died, it wasn't quite dying, because in a curious way it seemed scripted, and because they had their lines mostly memorized, irony mixed with tragedy, and because they called it by other names, as if to encyst and destroy the reality of death itself. They kicked corpses. They cut off thumbs. They talked grunt lingo. They told stories about Ted Lavender's supply of tranquilizers, how the poor guy didn't feel a thing, how incredibly tranquil he was.

There's a moral here, said Mitchell Sanders.

They were waiting for Lavender's chopper, smoking the dead man's dope.

The moral's pretty obvious, Sanders said, and winked. Stay away from drugs. No joke, they'll ruin your day every time.

Cute, said Henry Dobbins.

Mind blower, get it? Talk about wiggy—nothing left, just blood and brains.

They made themselves laugh.

There it is, they'd say, over and over, as if the repetition itself were an act of poise, a balance between crazy and almost crazy, knowing without going, There it is, which meant be cool, let it ride, because Oh yeah, man, you can't change what can't be changed, there it is, there it absolutely and positively and fucking well *is*.

They were tough.

They carried all the emotional baggage of men who might die. Grief, terror, love, longing—these were intangibles, but the intangibles had their own mass and specific gravity, they had tangible weight. They carried shameful memories. They carried the common secret of cowardice barely restrained, the instinct to run or freeze or hide, and in many respects this was the heaviest burden of all, for it could never be put down, it required perfect balance and perfect posture. They carried their reputations. They carried the soldier's greatest fear, which was the fear of blushing. Men killed, and died, because they were embarassed not to. It was what had brought them to the war in the first place, nothing positive, no dreams of glory or honor, just to avoid the blush of dishonor. They died so as not to die of embarassment. They crawled into tunnels and walked point and advanced under fire. Each morning, despite the unkowns, they made their legs move. They endured. They kept humping. The did not submit to the obvious alternative, which was simply to close the eyes and fall. So easy, really. Go limp and tumble to the ground and let the muscles unwind and not speak and not budge until your buddies picked you up and lifted you into the chopper that would roar and dip its nose and carry you off to the world. A mere matter of falling, yet no one ever fell. It was not courage, exactly; the object was not valor. Rather, they were too frightened to be cowards.

By and large they carried these things inside, maintaining the masks of composure. They sneered at sick call. They spoke bitterly about guys who had found release by shooting off their own toes or fingers. Pussies, they'd say. Candyasses. It was fierce, mocking talk, with only a trace of envy or awe, but even so the image played itself out behind their eyes.

They imagined the muzzle against flesh. They imagined the quick, sweet pain, then the evacuation to Japan, and a hospital with warm beds and cute geisha nurses.

They dreamed of freedom birds.

At night, on guard, staring into the dark, they were carried away by jumbo jets. They felt the rush of takeoff. *Gone!* they yelled. And then velocity—wings and engines—a smiling stewardess—but it was more than a plane, it was a real bird, a big sleek silver bird with feathers and talons and high screeching. They were flying. The weights fell off, there was nothing to bear. They laughed and held on tight, feeling the cold slap of wind and altitude, soaring, thinking *It's over, I'm gone*— they were naked, they were light and free—it was all lightness, bright and fast and buoyant, light as light, a helium buzz in the brain, a giddy bubbling in the lungs as they were taken up over the clouds and the war, beyond duty, beyond gravity and mortification and global entanglements—*Sin loi!* they yelled, *I'm sorry, motherfuckers, but I'm out of it, I'm goofed, I'm on a space cruise, I'm gone!*—and it was a restful, disencumbered sensation, just riding the light waves, sailing that big silver freedom bird over the mountains and oceans, over America, over the farms and great sleeping cities and cemeteries and highways and the golden arches of McDonald's, it was flight, a kind of fleeing, a kind of falling, falling higher and higher, spinning off the edge of the earth and beyond the sun and through the vast, silent vacuum where there were no burdens and where everything weighed exactly nothing—*Gone!* they screamed, *I'm sorry but I'm gone!*—and so at night, not quite dreaming, they gave themselves over to lightness, they were carried, they were purely borne.

On the morning after Ted Lavender died, First Lieutenant Jimmy Cross crouched at the bottom of his foxhole and burned Martha's letters. Then he burned the two photographs. There was a steady rain falling, which made it difficult, but he used heat tabs and Sterno to build a small fire, screening it with his body, holding the photographs over the tight blue flame with the tips of his fingers.

He realized it was only a gesture. Stupid, he thought. Sentimental, too, but mostly just stupid.

Lavender was dead. You couldn't burn the blame.

Besides, the letters were in his head. And even now, without photographs, Lieutenant Cross could see Martha playing volleyball in her white gym shorts and yellow T-shirt. He could see her moving in the rain.

When the fire died out, Lieutenant Cross pulled his poncho over his shoulders and ate breakfast from a can.

There was no great mystery, he decided.

In those burned letters Martha had never mentioned the war, except to say, Jimmy, take care of yourself. She wasn't involved. She signed the letters Love, but it wasn't love, and all the fine lines and technicalities did not matter.

The morning came up wet and blurry. Everything seemed part of everything else, the fog and Martha and the deepening rain.

It was a war, after all.

Half smiling, Lieutenant Jimmy Cross took out his maps. He shook his head hard, as if to clear it, then bent forward and began planning the day's march. In ten minutes, maybe twenty, he would rouse the men and they would pack up and head west, where the maps showed the country to be green and inviting. They would do what they had always done. The rain might add some weight, but otherwise it would be one more day layered upon all the other days.

He was realistic about it. There was that new hardness in his stomach.

No more fantasies, he told himself.

Henceforth, when he thought about Martha, it would be only to think that she belonged elsewhere. He would shut down the day-dreams. This was not Mount Sebastian, it was another world, where there were no pretty poems or mid-terms exams, a place where men died because of carelessness and gross stupidity. Kiowa was right. Boom-down, and you were dead, never partly dead.

Briefly, in the rain, Lieutenant Cross saw Martha's gray eyes gazing back at him.

He understood.

It was very sad, he thought. The things men carried inside. The things men did or felt they had to do.

He almost nodded at her, but didn't.

Instead he went back to his maps. He was now determined to perform his duties firmly and without negligence. It wouldn't help Lavender, he knew that, but from this point on he would comport himself as a soldier. He would dispose of his good-luck pebble. Swallow it, maybe, or use Lee Strunk's slingshot, or just drop it along the trail. On the march he would impose strict field discipline. He would be careful to send out flank security, to prevent straggling or bunching up, to keep his troops moving at the proper pace and at the proper interval. He would insist on clean weapons. He would confiscate the remainder of Lavender's dope. Later in the day, perhaps, he would call the men together and speak to them plainly. He would accept the blame for what had happened to Ted Lavender. He would be man about it. He would look them in the eyes, keeping his chin level, and he would issue the new SOPs in a calm, impersonal tone of voice, an officer's voice, leaving no room for argument or discussion. Commencing immediately, he'd tell them, they would no longer abandon equipment along the route of march. They would police up their acts. They would get their shit together, and keep it together, and maintain it neatly and in good working order.

He would not tolerate laxity. He would show strength, distancing himself.

Among the men there would be grumbling, of course, and maybe worse, because their days would seem longer and their loads heavier, but Lieutenant Cross reminded himself that his obligation was not be loved but to lead. He would dispense with love; it was not now a factor. And if anyone quarreled or complained, he would simply tighten his lips and arrange his shoulders in the correct command posture. He might give a curt little nod. Or he might not. He might just shrug and say, Carry on, then they would saddle up and form into a column and move out toward the villages west of Than Khe.

THE SHAWL

Stella, cold, cold, the coldness of hell. How they walked on the roads together, Rosa with Magda curled up between sore breasts, Magda wound up in the shawl. Sometimes Stella carried Magda. But she was jealous of Magda. A thin girl of fourteen, too small, with thin breasts of her own, Stella wanted to be wrapped in a shawl, hidden away, asleep, rocked by the march, a baby, a round infant in arms. Magda took Rosa's nipple, and Rosa never stopped walking, a walking cradle. There was not enough milk; sometimes Magda sucked air; then she screamed. Stella was ravenous. Her knees were tumors on sticks, her elbows chicken bones.

Rosa did not feel hunger; she felt light, not like someone walking but like someone in a faint, in trance, arrested in a fit, someone who is already a floating angel, alert and seeing everything, but in the air, not there, not touching the road. As if teetering on the tips of her fingernails. She looked into Magda's face through a gap in the shawl: a squirrel in a nest, safe, no one could reach her inside the little house of the shawl's windings. The face, very round, a pocket mirror of a face: but it was not Rosa's bleak complexion, dark like cholera, it was another kind of face altogether, eyes blue as air, smooth feathers of hair nearly as yellow as the Star sewn into Rosa's coat. You could think she was one of *their* babies.

Rosa, floating, dreamed of giving Magda away in one of the villages. She could leave the line for a minute and push Magda into the hands of any woman on the side of the road. But if she moved out of line they might shoot. And even if she fled the line for half a second and pushed the shawl-bundle at a stranger, would the woman take it? She might be surprised, or afraid; she might drop the shawl, and Magda would fall out and strike her head and die. The little round head. Such a good child, she gave up screaming, and sucked now only for the taste of the drying nipple itself. The neat grip of the tiny gums. One mite of a tooth tip sticking up in the bottom gum, how shining, an elfin tombstone of white marble gleaming there. Without complaining, Magda relinquished Rosa's teats, first the left, then the right; both were cracked, not a sniff of milk. The duct crevice extinct, a dead volcano, blind eye, chill hole, so Magda took the corner of the shawl and milked it instead. She sucked and sucked, flooding the threads with wetness. The shawl's good flavor, milk of linen.

It was a magic shawl, it could nourish an infant for three days and three nights. Magda did not die, she stayed alive, although very quiet. A peculiar smell, of cinnamon and almonds, lifted out of her mouth. She held her eyes open every moment, forgetting how to blink or nap, and Rosa and sometimes Stella studied their blueness. On the road they raised one burden of a leg after another and studied Magda's face. "Aryan," Stella said, in a voice grown as thin as a string; and Rosa thought how Stella gazed at Magda like a young cannibal. And the time that Stella said "Aryan," it sounded to Rosa as if Stella had really said "Let us devour her."

But Magda lived to walk. She lived that long, but she did not walk very well, partly because she was only fifteen months old, and partly because the spindles of her legs could not hold up her fat belly. It was fat with air, full and round. Rosa gave almost all her food to Magda, Stella gave nothing; Stella was ravenous, a growing child herself, but not growing much. Stella did not menstruate. Rosa did not menstruate. Rosa was ravenous, but also not; she learned from Magda how to drink the taste of a finger in one's mouth. They were in a place without pity, all pity was annihilated in Rosa, she looked at Stella's bones without pity. She was sure that Stella was waiting for Magda to die so she could put her teeth into the little thighs.

Rosa knew Magda was going to die very soon; she should have been dead already, but she had been buried away deep inside the magic shawl, mistaken there for the shivering mound of Rosa's breasts; Rosa clung to the shawl as if it covered only herself. No one took it away from her. Magda was mute. She never cried. Rosa hid her in the barracks, under the shawl, but she knew that one day someone would inform; or one day someone, not even Stella, would steal Magda to eat her. When Magda began to walk Rosa knew that Magda was going to die very soon, something would happen. She was afraid to fall asleep; she slept with the weight of her thigh on Magda's body; she was afraid she would smother Magda under her thigh. The weight of Rosa was becoming less and less; Rosa and Stella were slowly turning into air.

Magda was quiet, but her eyes were horribly alive, like blue tigers. She watched. Sometimes she laughed—it seemed a laugh, but how could it be? Magda had never seen anyone laugh. Still, Magda laughed at her shawl when the wind blew its corners, the bad wind with pieces of black in it, that made Stella's and Rosa's eyes tear. Magda's eyes were always clear and tearless. She watched like a tiger. She guarded her shawl. No one could touch it; only Rosa could touch it. Stella was not allowed. The shawl was Magda's own baby, her pet, her little sister. She tangled herself up in it and sucked on one of the corners when she wanted to be very still.

Then Stella took the shawl away and made Magda die.

Afterward Stella said: "I was cold."

And afterward she was always cold, always. The cold went into her heart: Rosa saw that Stella's heart was cold. Magda flopped onward with her little pencil legs scribbling this way and that, in search of the shawl; the pencils faltered at the barracks opening, where the light began. Rosa saw and pursued. But already Magda was in the square outside the barracks, in the jolly light. It was the roll-call arena. Every morning Rosa had to conceal Magda under the shawl against a wall of the barracks and go out and stand in the arena with Stella and hundreds of others, sometimes for hours, and Magda, deserted, was quiet under the shawl, sucking on her corner. Every day Magda was silent, and so she did not die. Rosa saw that today Magda was going to die, and at the same time a fearful joy ran in Rosa's two palms, her fingers were on fire, she was astonished, febrile: Magda, in the sunlight, swaying on her pencil legs, was howling. Ever since the drying up of Rosa's nipples, ever since Magda's last scream on the road, Magda had been devoid of any syllable; Magda was a mute. Rosa believed that something had gone wrong with her vocal cords, with her windpipe, with the cave of her larynx; Magda was defective, without a voice; perhaps she was deaf; there might be something amiss with her intelligence; Magda was dumb. Even the laugh that came when the ash-stippled wind made a clown out of Magda's shawl was only the air-blown showing of her teeth. Even when the lice, head lice and body lice, crazed her so that she became as wild as one of the big rats that plundered the barracks at daybreak looking for carrion, she rubbed and scratched and kicked and bit and rolled without a whimper. But now Magda's mouth was spilling a long viscous rope of clamor.

"Maaaa—"

It was the first noise Magda had ever sent out from her throat since the drying up of Rosa's nipples.

"Maaaa . . . aaa!"

Again! Magda was wavering in the perilous sunlight of the arena, scribbling on such pitiful little bent shins. Rosa saw. She saw that Magda was grieving for the loss of her shawl, she saw that Magda was going to die. A tide of commands hammered in Rosa's nipples: Fetch, get, bring! But she did not know which to go after first, Magda or the shawl. If she jumped out into the arena to snatch Magda up, the howling would not stop, because Magda would still not have the shawl; but if she ran back into the barracks to find the shawl, and if she found it, and if she came after Magda holding it and shaking it, then she would get Magda back, Magda would put the shawl in her mouth and turn dumb again.

Rosa entered the dark. It was easy to discover the shawl. Stella was heaped under it, asleep in her thin bones. Rosa tore the shawl free and flew—she could fly, she was only air—into the arena. The sunheat murmured of another life, of butterflies in summer. The light was placid, mellow. On the other side of the steel fence, far away, there were green meadows speckled with dandelions and deep-colored violets; beyond them, even farther, innocent tiger lilies, tall, lifting their orange bonnets. In the barracks they spoke of "flowers," of "rain": excrement, thick turd-braids, and the slow stinking maroon waterfall that slunk down from the upper bunks, the stink mixed with a bitter fatty floating smoke that greased Rosa's skin. She stood for an instant at the margin of the arena. Sometimes the electricity inside the fence would seem to hum; even Stella said it was only an imagining, but Rosa heard real sounds in the wire: grainy sad voices. The farther she was from the fence, the more clearly the voices crowded at her. The lamenting voices strummed so convincingly, so passionately, it was impossible to suspect them of being phantoms. The voices told her to hold up the shawl, high; the voices told her to shake it, to whip with it, to unfurl it like a flag. Rosa lifted, shook, whipped, unfurled. Far off, very far, Magda leaned across her air-fed belly, reaching out with the rods of her arms. She was high up, elevated, riding someone's shoulder. But the shoulder that carried Magda was not coming toward Rosa and the shawl, it was drifting away, the speck of Magda was moving more and more into the smoky distance. Above the shoulder a helmet glinted. The light tapped the helmet and sparkled it into a goblet. Below the helmet a black body like a domino and a pair of black boots hurled themselves in the direction of the electri- fied fence. The electric voices began to chatter wildly. "Maamaa, maaamaaa," they all hummed together. How far Magda was from Rosa now, across the whole square, past a dozen barracks, all the way on the other side! She was no bigger than a moth.

All at once Magda was swimming through the air. The whole of Magda traveled through loftiness. She looked like a butterfly touching a silver vine. And the moment Magda's feathered round head and her pencil legs and balloonish belly and zigzag arms splashed against the fence, the steel voices went mad in their growling, urging Rosa to run and run to the spot where Magda had fallen from her flight against the electrified fence; but of course Rosa did not obey them. She only stood, because if she ran they would shoot, and if she tried to pick up the sticks of Magda's body they would shoot, and if she let the wolf's screech ascending now through the ladder of her skeleton break out, they would shoot; so she took Magda's shawl and filled her own mouth with it, stuffed it in and stuffed it in, until she was swallowing up the wolf's screech and tasting the cinnamon and almond depth of Magda's saliva; and Rosa drank Magda's shawl until it dried.

OTHER LIVES

Climbing up with a handful of star decals to paste on the bathroom ceiling, Claire sees a suspect-looking shampoo bottle on the cluttered top shelf. When she opens it, the whole room smells like a subway corridor where bums have been pissing for generations. She thinks back a few days to when Miranda and Poppy were playing in here with the door shut. She puts down the stars and yells for the girls with such urgency they come running before she's finished emptying it into the sink.

From the doorway, Poppy and her best friend Miranda look at Claire, then at each other. "Mom," says Poppy. "You threw it *out?*"

Claire wants to ask why they're saving their urine in bottles. But sitting on the edge of the tub has lowered her eye level and she's struck speechless by the beauty of their kneecaps, their long suntanned legs. How strong and shaky and elegant they are! Like newborn giraffes! By now she can't bring herself to ask, so she tells them not to do it again and is left with the rest of the morning to wonder what they had in mind.

She thinks it has something to do with alchemy and with faith, with those moments when children are playing with such pure concentration that anything is possible and the rest of the world drops away and becomes no more real than one of their 3-D Viewmaster slides. She remembers when she was Poppy's age, playing with her own best friend Evelyn. Evelyn's father had been dead several years, but his medical office in a separate wing of their house was untouched, as if office hours might begin any minute. In his chilly consulting room, smelling of carpet dust and furniture polish and more faintly of gauze and sterilizing pans, Claire and Evelyn played their peculiar version of doctor. Claire would come in and from behind the desk Evelyn would give her some imaginary pills. Then Claire would fall down dead and Evelyn would kneel and listen to her heart and say, "I'm sorry, it's too late."

But what Claire remembers best is the framed engraving on Evelyn's father's desk. It was one of those trompe l'oeil pieces you see sometimes in cheap art stores. From one angle, it looked like two Gibson girls at a table sipping ice cream sodas through straws. From another, it looked like a skull. Years later, when Claire learned that Evelyn's father had actually died in jail where he'd been sent for performing illegal abortions, she'd thought what an odd picture to have on an abortionist's desk. But at the time, it had just seemed marvelous. She used to unfocus her eyes and tilt her head so that it flipped back and forth. Skull, ladies. Skull, ladies. Skull.

Dottie's new hairdo, a wide corolla of pale blond curls, makes her look even more like a sunflower—spindly, graceful, rather precariously balanced. At one, when Dottie comes to pick up Miranda, Claire decides not to tell her about the shampoo bottle.

Lately, Dottie's had her mind on higher things. For the past few months, she's been driving down to the New Consciousness Academy in Bennington where she takes courses with titles like "Listening to the Inner Silence" and "Weeds for Your Needs." Claire blames this on one of Dottie's friends, an electrician named Jeanette. Once at a party, Claire overheard Jeanette telling someone how she and her boyfriend practice birth control based on lunar astrology and massive doses of wintergreen tea.

"Coffee?" says Claire, tentatively. It's hard to keep track of what substances Dottie's given up. Sometimes, most often in winter when

Joey and Raymond are working and the girls are at school, Dottie and Claire get together for lunch. Walking into Dottie's house and smelling woodsmoke and wine and fresh-baked bread, seeing the table set with blue bowls and hothouse anemones and a soup thick with sausage, potatoes, tomatoes put up from the fall, Claire used to feel that she must be living her whole life right. All summer, she's been praying that Dottie won't give up meat.

Now Dottie says, "Have you got any herbal tea?" and Claire says, "Are you kidding?" "All right, coffee," says Dottie. "Just this once."

As Claire pours the coffee, Dottie fishes around in her enormous parachute-silk purse. Recently, Dottie's been bringing Claire reading material. She'd started off with Krishnamurti, Rajneesh, the songs of Milarepa; Claire tried but she just couldn't, she'd returned them unread. A few weeks back, she'd brought something by Dashiell Hammett about a man named Flitcraft who's walking to lunch one day and a beam falls down from a construction site and just misses him, and he just keeps walking and never goes to his job or back to his wife and family again.

When Claire read that, she wanted to call Dottie up and make her promise not to do something similar. But she didn't. The last time she and Dottie discussed the Academy, Dottie described a technique she'd learned for closing her eyes and pressing on her eyelids just hard enough to see thousands of pinpricks of light. Each one of those dots represents a past life, and if you know how to look, you can see it. In this way, Dottie learned that she'd spent a former life as a footsoldier in Napoleon's army on the killing march to Moscow. That's why she so hates the cold. Somehow Claire hadn't known that Dottie hated the winter, but really, it follows: a half-starved, half-frozen soldier cooking inspired sausage soup three lives later.

"I meant to bring you a book," says Dottie. Then she says, "A crazy thing happened this morning. I was working in front of the house, digging up those irises by the side of the road so I could divide them. I didn't hear anything but I must have had a sense because I turned around and there was this old lady—coiffed, polyestered, dressed for church, it looked like. She told me she'd come over from Montpelier with some friends for a picnic and got separated. Now she was lost and *so* upset.

"I said, Well, okay, I'll drive you back to Montpelier. We got as far as Barre when suddenly her whole story started coming apart and I realized: She hadn't been in Montpelier for twenty years. She was from that Good Shepherd House, that old folks' home up the road from us. I drove her back to the Good Shepherd, what else could I do? The manager thanked me, he was very embarassed she'd escaped. Then just as I was pulling out, the old lady pointed up at the sky and gave me the most hateful triumphant smile, and I looked up through the windshield and there was this flock of geese heading south." Dottie catches her breath, then says, "You know what? It's August. I'd forgotten."

What Claire can't quite forget is that years ago, the first time she and Joey met Dottie and Raymond, afterwards Joey said, "They don't call her dotty for nothing." It took them both a while to see that what looked at first like dottiness was really an overflow of the same generosity which makes Dottie cook elegant warming meals and drive senile old ladies fifty miles out of her way to Montpelier. On Tuesdays and Thursdays, when Dottie goes down to the Academy, she's a volunteer chauffeur service, picking up classmates—including Jeanette the electrician—from all over central Vermont. Even Joey's come around to liking her, though Claire's noticed that he's usually someplace else when Dottie's around.

Now he's in the garden, tying up some tomatoes which fell last night in the wind. Finding them this morning—perfect red tomatoes smashed on top of each other—had sent her straight to the bathroom with her handful of star decals. That's the difference between me and Joey, Claire thinks. Thank God there's someone to save what's left of the vines.

Joey doesn't see Claire watching him but Dottie does and starts to flutter, as if she's overstayed. She calls up to Miranda, and just when it begins to seem as if they might not have heard, the girls drag them-selves downstairs.

"Why does Miranda have to go?" says Poppy.

"Because it's fifteen miles and Miranda's mom isn't driving fifteen miles back and forth all day," says Claire.

"But I don't want to go," says Miranda.

They stand there, deadlocked, until Poppy says, "I've got an idea. I'll go home with Miranda and tonight her mom and dad can come to dinner and bring us both back and then Miranda can sleep over."

"That's fine with me," says Claire.

"Are you sure?" says Dottie.

Claire's sure. As Dottie leans down to kiss her good-bye, Claire thinks once more of sunflowers, specifically of the ones she and Joey and Poppy plant every summer on a steep slope so you can stand underneath and look up and the sunflowers look forty feet tall.

Washing his hands at the sink, Joey says, "One day she's going to show up in saffron robes with a begging bowl and her hair shaved down to one skanky topknot and then what?"

Claire thinks: Well, then we'll cook up some gluey brown rice and put a big glob in Dottie's bowl. But this sounds like something they'd say at the New Consciousness Academy, some dreadful homily about adaptation and making do. All she can think of is, "I cried because I had no shoes until I met a man who had no feet," and that's not it.

One night, not long after Dottie started attending the Academy, they were all sitting outside and Dottie looked up and said, "Some-times I feel as if my whole life is that last minute of the planetarium show when they start showing off—that is, showing off what their projector can do—and the moon and planets and stars and even those distant galaxies begin spinning like crazy while they tell you the coming attractions and what time the next show begins. I just want to find someplace where it's not rushing past me so fast. Or where, if it is, I don't care."

"I hope you find it," Joey said. "I really do." Later that night, he told

Claire that he knew what Dottie meant. "Still," he said, "it was creepy. The whole conversation was like talking to someone who still thinks *El Topo* is the greatest movie ever made."

Joey had gone through his own spiritual phase: acid, Castenada, long Sunday afternoons in front of the tonkas in the Staten Island Tibetan museum. All this was before he met Claire. He feels that his having grown out of it fifteen years ago gives him the right to criticize. Though actually, he's not mocking Dottie so much as protecting her husband Raymond, his best friend. Remote as the possibility seems, no one wants Dottie to follow in Flitcraft's footsteps.

Now Claire says, "I don't think she'd get her hair permed if she was planning to shave it." Then she steels herself, and in the tone of someone expecting bad news asks if any tomatoes are left. Joey says, "We'll be up to our *ears* in tomatoes," and Claire thinks: He'd say that no matter what.

One thing she loves about Joey is his optimism. If he's ever discontent, she doesn't know it. Once he'd wanted to be on stage, then he'd worked for a while as a landscaper, now he's a junior-high science teacher—a job which he says requires the combined talents of an actor and a gardener. His real passion is for the names of things: trees, animals, stars. But he's not one of those people who use such knowledge to make you feel small. It's why he's a popular teacher and why Poppy so loves to take walks with him, naming the wildflowers in the fields. Claire knows how rare it is for children to want to learn anything from their parents.

When Claire met Joey, she'd just moved up to Vermont with a semi-alcoholic independently wealthy photographer named Dell. Dell hired Joey to clear a half-acre around their cabin so they could have a garden and lawn. Upstairs there's a photo Dell took of them at the time and later sent as a wedding present to prove there were no hard feelings. It shows Claire and Joey leaning against Joey's rented backhoe; an uprooted acacia tree is spilling out of the bucket. Joey and

Claire look cocky and hard in the face, like teen-age killers, Charlie Starkweather and his girl. Claire can hardly remember Dell's face. He always had something in front of it—a can of beer, a camera. If he had only put it down and looked, he'd have seen what was going on. Anyone would have. In the photo, it's early spring, the woods are full of musical names: trillium, marsh marigold, jack in the pulpit.

On the day they learned Claire was pregnant and went straight from the doctor's to the marriage license bureau in Burlington, Joey pulled off the road on the way home and took Claire's face in his hands and told her which animals mated for life. Whooping cranes, snow geese, macaws, she's forgotten the rest. Now they no longer talk this way, or maybe it goes without saying. Claire's stopped imagining other lives; if she could, she'd live this one forever. Though she knows it's supposed to be dangerous to get too comfortable, she feels it would take a catastrophe to tear the weave of their daily routine. They've weathered arguments, and those treacherous, tense, dull periods when they sneak past each other as if they're in constant danger of sneezing in each other's faces. Claire knows to hold on and wait for the day when what interests her most is what Joey will have to say about it.

Some things get better. Claire used to hate thinking about the lovers they'd had before; now all that seems as indistinct as Dell's face. Though they've had eight years to get used to the fact of Poppy's existence, they're still susceptible to attacks of amazement that they've created a new human being. And often when they're doing something together—cooking, gardening, making love—Claire comes as close as she has ever come to those moments of pure alchemy, that communion Poppy and Miranda must share if they're storing their pee in bottles.

Soon they'll get up and mix some marinade for the chickens they'll grill outside later for Dottie and Raymond. But now Joey pours himself some coffee and they sit at the table, not talking. It is precisely the silence they used to dream of when Poppy was little and just having her around was like always having the bath water running or something about to boil over on the stove.

First the back doors fly open and the girls jump out of the car and run up to Poppy's room. Then Dottie gets out, then Raymond. From the beginning, Raymond's reminded Claire of the tin woodsman in *The Wizard of Oz*, and often he'll stop in the middle of things as if waiting for someone to come along with the oil can. He goes around to the trunk and takes out a tripod and something wrapped in a blanket which looks at first like a rifle and turns out to be a telescope.

"Guess what!" When Raymond shouts like that, you can see how snaggletoothed he is. "There's a meteor shower tonight. The largest concentration of shooting stars all year."

The telescope is one of the toys Raymond's bought since his paintings started selling. Raymond's success surprises them all, including Raymond. His last two shows were large paintings of ordinary garden vegetables with skinny legs and big feet in rather stereotypical dance situations. It still surprises Claire that the New York art world would open its heart—would have a heart to open—to work bordering on the cartoonish and sentimental. But there's something undeniably mysterious and moving about those black daikon radishes doing the tango, those little cauliflowers in pink tutus on points before an audience of sleek and rather parental-looking green peppers. And there's no arguing with Raymond's draftmanship or the luminosity of his color; it's as if Memling lived through the sixties and took too many drugs. What's less surprising is that there are so many rich people who for one reason or another want to eat breakfast beneath a painting of dancing vegetables.

Claire has a crush on Raymond; at least that's what she thinks it is. It's not especially intense or very troublesome; it's been going on a long time and she doesn't expect it to change. If anything did change, it would probably disappear. She doesn't want to live with Raymond and now, as always when he hugs her hello, their bones grate; it's not particularly sexual.

She just likes him, that's all. When it's Raymond coming to dinner, she cooks and dresses with a little more care than she otherwise might, and spends the day remembering things to tell him which she promptly forgets. Of course, she's excited when Dottie or anyone is coming over. The difference is: With Dottie, Claire enjoys her food. With Raymond, she often forgets to eat.

Barbecued chicken, tomatoes with basil and mozzarella, pasta with chanterelles Joey's found in the woods—it all goes right by her. Luckily, everyone else is eating, the girls trekking back and forth from the table to the TV. The television noise makes it hard to talk. It's like family dinner, they can just eat. Anyway, conversation's been strained since Dottie started at the Academy. Claire fears that Joey might make some semi-sarcastic remark which will hurt Raymond more than Dottie. Raymond's protective of her; they seem mated for life. It's occurred to them all that Dottie is the original dancing vegetable.

What does get said is that the meteor shower isn't supposed to pick up till around midnight. But they'll set up the telescope earlier so the girls can have a look before they're too tired to see.

Joey and Raymond and the girls go outside while Dottie and Claire put the dishes in the sink. Claire asks if Poppy was any trouble that afternoon and Dottie says, "Oh, no. They played in the bathroom so quiet, I had to keep yelling up to make sure they were breathing. Later they told me they'd been making vanishing cream from that liquidy soap at the bottom of the soap dish. I said, You're eight years old, what do you need with vanishing cream? They said, to vanish. I told them they'd better not use it till they had something to bring them back from wherever they vanished to, and they said, yeah, they'd already thought of that."

"Where did they *hear* about vanishing cream?" says Claire. She feels she ought to tell Dottie—feels disloyal for not telling her—to watch for suspicious-looking shampoo bottles on the upper shelves. But she doesn't. It's almost as if she's saving it for something.

"Speaking of vanishing," says Dottie. She hands Claire the book she'd forgotten that afternoon. It's Calvino's *The Baron in the Trees.* Claire's read it before, and it seems like the right moment to ask, so she says, "Does this mean that you're going to get up from the table one night and climb up in the trees and never come down again?"

Dottie just looks at her. "Me in the trees?" she says. "With *my* allergies?"

They're amazed by how dark it is when they go outside. "I told you," says Dottie. "It's August."

The grass is damp and cool against their ankles as they walk across the lawn to where Miranda and Poppy are taking turns at the telescope. "Daddy," Claire hears Poppy say. "What's that?"

Joey crouches down and looks over her shoulder. Claire wonders what they see. Scorpio? Andromeda? Orion? Joey's told her a thousand times but she can never remember what's in the sky when.

Before Joey can answer, Raymond pulls Poppy away from the telescope and kneels and puts one arm around her and the other around Miranda. "That one?" he says, pointing. "That one's the Bad Baby. And it's lying in the Big Bassinet."

"Where?" cry the girls, and then they say, "Yes, I see!"

"And that one there's the Celestial Dog Dish. And that"—he traces his finger in a wavy circle—"is the Silver Dollar Pancake."

"What's that one?" says Miranda.

"Remember *Superman II?*" Raymond's the one who takes the girls to movies no one else wants to see. "That's what's left of the villains after they get turned to glass and smashed to smithereens."

"Oh, no," say the girls, and hide their faces against Raymond's long legs.

Claire's tensed, as if Raymond's infringed on Joey's right to name things, or worse, is making fun of him. But Joey's laughing, he likes Raymond's names as much as the real ones. Claire steps up to the telescope and aims it at the thin crescent moon, at that landscape of chalk mountains and craters like just-burst bubbles. But all she sees is the same flat white she can see with her naked eye. Something's wrong with the telescope, or with her. The feeling she gets reminds her of waking up knowing the day's already gone wrong but not yet why, of mornings when Poppy's been sick in the night, or last summer when Joey's father was dying.

By now the others have all lain down on the hillside to look for shooting stars. There aren't any, not yet. Claire wonders if Dottie is listening to the inner silence or thinking of past lives, if Raymond is inventing more constellations. She can't imagine what Joey's thinking. She herself can't get her mind off Jeanette the electrician and her boyfriend, drinking penny-royal tea and checking that sliver of moon to see if this is a safe night for love.

On the way in, Joey says, "Lying out there, I remembered this magazine article I haven't thought of in years, about Jean Genet at the '68 Democratic convention in Chicago. The whole time, he kept staring at the dashboard of the car they were driving him around in. And afterwards, when they asked him what he thought of it—the riots, the beatings and so forth—he just shrugged and said, 'What can you expect from a country that would make a car named Galaxy?'"

Over coffee, the conversation degenerates into stories they've told before, tales of how the children tyrannize and abuse them, have kept them prisoner in their own homes for years at a time. The reason they can talk like this is that they all know: The children are the light of their lives. A good part of why they stay here is that Vermont seems like an easy place to raise kids. Even their children have visionary names: Poppy, Miranda. O brave new world!

When Claire first moved here with Dell, she commuted to New York, where she was working as a free-lance costume designer. She likes to tell people that the high point of her career was making a holster and fringed vest and chaps for a chicken to wear on "Hee

Haw." Later she got to see it on TV, the chicken panicky and humiliated in its cowboy suit, flapping in circles while Grandpa Jones fired blanks at its feet and yelled, "Dance!" Soon it will be Halloween and Claire will sew Poppy a costume. So far she's been a jar of peanut butter, an anteater with pockets full of velveteen ants, Rapunzel. Last fall Claire made her a caterpillar suit with a back which unzipped and reversed out into butterfly wings. Poppy's already told her that this year she wants to be a New Wave, so all Claire will have to do is rip up a T-shirt and buy tights and wraparound shades and blue spray-on washable hair dye.

Dottie is telling about the girls making vanishing cream when Joey pretends to hear something in the garden and excuses himself and goes out. Dottie says she wants to stay up for the meteor shower but is feeling tired so she'll lie down awhile on the living-room couch.

Claire and Raymond are left alone at the table. It takes them so long to start talking, Claire's glad her crush on Raymond will never be anything more; if they had to spend a day in each other's company, they'd run out of things to say. Still it's exciting. Raymond seems nervous, too.

Finally he asks how her day was, and Claire's surprised to hear herself say, "Pretty awful." She hadn't meant to complain, nor had she thought her day was so awful. Now she thinks maybe it was. "Nothing really," she says. "One little thing after another. Have you ever had days when you pick up a pen and the phone rings and when you get off, you can't find the pen?"

"Me?" says Raymond. "I've had decades like that."

Claire says, "I woke up thinking I'd be nice and cook Poppy some French toast. So I open the egg carton and poke my finger through one of those stuck-on leaky eggs. When I got through cleaning the egg off the refrigerator, the milk turned out to be sour. I figured, Well, I'll make her scrambled eggs with coriander, she likes that. I went out to the garden for coriander and all the tomatoes were lying on the ground. The awful part was that most of them looked fine from on top, you had to turn them over to see they were smashed. You know: first you think it's all right and then it isn't all right."

"I almost never think it's all right," says Raymond. "That's how I take care of that."

"Know how *I* took care of it?" says Claire. "I went crying to Joey. Then I went upstairs and got out these star decals I'd been saving, I thought it would make me feel better. I'd been planning to paste them on the ceiling over the tub so I could take a shower with all the lights out and the stars glowing up above and even in winter it would be like taking a shower outside." Suddenly Claire is embarrassed by this vision of herself naked in the warm steamy blackness under the faint stars. She wonders if Dottie is listening from the other room and is almost glad the next part is about finding the shampoo bottle.

"That's life," says Raymond. "Reach for the stars and wind up with a bottle of piss."

"That's what I thought," says Claire. "But listen." She tells him about calling the girls in and when she says, "Like newborn giraffes," she really does feel awful, as if she's serving her daughter up so Raymond will see her as a complicated person with a daily life rich in similes and astonishing spiritual reverses. Now she understands why she hadn't mentioned the incident to Dottie or Joey. She was saving it for Raymond so it wouldn't be just a story she'd told before. But Raymond's already saying, "I know. Sometimes one second can turn the whole thing around."

"One winter," he says, "Miranda was around two, we were living in Roxbury, freezing to death. We decided it was all or nothing. We sold everything, got rid of the apartment, bought tickets to some dinky Caribbean island where somebody told us you could live on fish and mangoes and coconuts off the trees. I thought, I'll paint shells, sell them to the tourists. But when we got there, it wasn't mango season, the fish weren't running, and the capital city was one giant cinderblock motel. There was a housing shortage, food shortage, an everything shortage.

"So we took a bus across the island, thinking we'd get off at the first tropical paradise, but no place seemed very friendly and by then Miranda was running another fever. We would up in the second-biggest city, which looked pretty much like a bad neighborhood in L.A. We were supposed to be glad that our hotel room had a balcony facing main street. Dottie put Miranda to bed, then crawled in and pulled the covers over her head and said she wasn't coming out except to fly back to Boston.

"At that moment, we heard a brass band, some drums. By the time I wrestled the balcony shutters open, a parade was coming by. It was the tail end of carnival, I think. The whole island was there, painted and feathered and glittered to the teeth, marching formations of guys in ruffly Carmen Miranda shirts with marimbas, little girls done up like bumblebees with antennae bobbing on their heads. Fever or no fever, we lifted Miranda up to see. And maybe it was what she'd needed all along. Because by the time the last marcher went by, her fever was gone.

"Miranda fell asleep, then Dottie. I went for a walk. On the corner, a guy was selling telescopes. Japanese-made, not like that one out there, but good. They must have been stolen off some boat, they were selling for practically nothing. So I bought one and went down to the beach. The beach was deserted. I stayed there I don't know how long. It was the first time I ever looked through a telescope. It was something."

For the second time that day, Claire's struck speechless. Only this time, what's astonishing is, she's in pain. She feels she's led her whole life wrong. What did she think she was doing? If only she could have been on that beach with Raymond looking through a telescope for the first time, or even at the hotel when he came back. Suddenly her own memories seem two-dimensional, like photographs, like worn-out duplicate baseball cards she'd trade all at once for that one of Raymond's. She tells herself that if she'd married Raymond, she might be like Dottie now, confused and restless and wanting only to believe that somewhere there is a weed for her need. She remembers the end of the Hammett story: After Flitcraft's brush with death, he goes to Seattle and marries a woman exactly like the wife he left on the other side of that beam. There's no guarantee that another life will be better or even different from your own, and Claire knows that. But it doesn't help at all.

There's a silence. Claire can't look at Raymond. At last he says, "If I could paint what I saw through that telescope that night, do you think I'd ever paint another dancing vegetable in my whole fucking life?"

For all Raymond's intensity, it's kind of a funny question, and Claire laughs, mostly from relief that the moment is over. Then she notices that Dottie has come in. Dottie looks a little travel-worn, as if she might actually have crossed the steppes from Moscow to Paris. She seems happy to be back. As it turns out, she's been closer than that. Because what she says is, "Suppose I'd believed that old lady and dropped her off in the middle of Montpelier? What would have happened then?"

Claire wants to say something fast before Raymond starts inventing adventures for a crazy old lady alone in Montpelier. Just then, Joey reappears. Apparently, he's come back in and gone upstairs without their hearing; he's got the girls ready for bed, scrubbed and shiny, dressed in long white cotton nightgowns like slender Edwardian angels. Claire looks at the children and the two sets of parents and thinks a stranger walking in would have trouble telling: Which one paints dancing vegetables? Which one's lived before as a Napoleonic solider? Which ones have mated for life? She thinks they are like constellations, or like that engraving on Evelyn's father's desk, or like sunflowers seen from below. Depending on how you look, they could be anything.

Then Raymond says, "It's almost midnight," and they all troop outside. On the way out, Raymond hangs back and when Claire catches up with him, he leans down so his lips are grazing her ear and says, "I hope this doesn't turn out to be another Comet Kohoutek."

Outside, Claire loses sight of them, except for the girls, whose white nightgowns glow in the dark like phosphorescent stars. She lays down on the grass. She's thinking about Kohoutek and about that first winter she and Joey lived together. How excited he was at the prospect of seeing a comet, and later, how disappointed! She remembers that the Museum of Natural History set up a dial-in Comet News Hot-line which was supposed to announce new sightings and wound up just giving data about Kohoutek's history and origins. Still Joey kept calling long distance and letting the message run through several times. Mostly he did it when Claire was out of the house, but not always. Now, as Claire tries not to blink, to stretch her field of vision wide enough for even the most peripheral shooting star, she keeps seeing how Joey looked in those days when she'd come home and stamp the snow off her boots and see him—his back to her, his ear to the phone, listening. And now, as always, it's just when she's thinking of something else that she spots it—that ribbon of light streaking by her so fast she can never be sure if she's really seen it or not.

Lynne Sharon Schwartz

THE PAINTERS

The pair of children looked Asian, two or three years old, their glossy heads like lacquered bowls bobbing in the sunlight. Kneeling at the wide-open window, they pulled white tissues from a box and sent them wafting down on the breeze. A flimsy-looking iron gate reached to their stomachs, but every few seconds they popped up to lean out over it, clapping their hands as the tissues caught on the branches of trees, wrapped around a lamp post, and fluttered leisurely to the concrete below like great snowflakes.

Not a soul in sight. Della watched from across the street, a floor above them—the fifth; they would not see her if she waved. If she called out, the sound could startle them, make them lose their balance. She shut her eyes and curled her hands into fists as one child leaned way out, the tops of the bars pressing into his legs. The police? It was her first day here; she didn't even know the opposite building's address. And the time it would take, the heavy footsteps clattering up the stairs. . . . Meanwhile they would fall and she would relive this moment all the years to come, remembering herself watching at the window of the empty bedroom in her new apartment, her new life, thinking about how she would remember herself at the window, watching. . . .

Just then a dark-haired woman appeared from the invisible spaces of the apartment across the street, plucked each child from the windowsill, and snatched up the box of tissues. Shut the window, thought Della, but the woman receded into the invisible spaces.

Della turned to savor the emptiness that surrounded her, mute and undemanding. The apartment was a stroke of luck, found quickly by an acquaintance who was good at such things—inexpensive, airy, and, apart from dark walls enclosing an aura of shabbiness, sound. Devoid of identity, but not for long. The moving truck would be arriving any minute, bearing half the contents of her former home. Once Ezra had told her, those rooms had felt like the scene of something unsavory, a parody of the life she thought she was living. Della had packed feverishly, all thought suffocated by the radio tuned to the most raucous station she could find. This irritated Ezra, who was an announcer for a classical music station, but in his guilt and confusion he had dared not complain, only hovered nearby looking pained, clearly uncertain whether it was more urbane to offer help or not. Are you sure you don't want to keep it? he had urged. It would give you some stability. It doesn't seem fair for you to be the one moving out. Della had answered, No, you keep it. Live in it with her. Look where stability has gotten me.

Numbed by the heat, Della sank down to the floor, leaning against a mud-colored wall, and ran her fingers along the floorboards: good hardwood floors, and recently scraped. She ran her fingers down her bare leg: good long legs, recently suntanned over the July 4 weekend, before Ezra told her. In her youth she had been a ballet dancer—faceless in the corps but swift and exhilarated, fulfilled; her enduring fringe benefits were a litheness of movement and a knack for twisting up her hair in sleek knots. Good legs, she thought, yet they hadn't counted in the long run. For all she knew the new woman was drab and stumpy.

When the movers left hours later, it was as if Della stepped out of a dream. With the old chest of drawers, the washing machine (Ezra had insisted), the armchairs, desk, and stereo surrounding her, it was plain to see that she would have to live here. Her life, whatever that meant, her flesh's short span of animation, would trudge forward in time, in the unending cycles of light and darkness, its own cycles and wants felt within these walls.

She slipped the new keys into her pocket and walked out onto the hushed and darkening street. Perhaps she would be mugged, even killed. Only the first moments would be dreadful, and then the rest of her life effortlessly taken from her. But she passed no one menacing, only a heavy old woman in Bermuda shorts inching her way forward with a walker. On the lively avenue she sat at a small plastic table and ate two slices of pizza, and on her way home took note of a Chinese restaurant, a delicatessen, and a barbecued ribs place.

She felt very little conviction about trudging forward. Nevertheless tomorrow, once her telephone was installed, she would find painters; the landlord, snarling, had refused any repairs— "You're getting a bargain as it is!"—but it was not possible to live, with convictions or not, between these dark green and mud-colored walls. She unrolled a narrow futon, bought to replace the double bed where she had slept in an illusion, stretched out on her stomach, and fell into a deep sleep.

Three days later the painters appeared promptly at nine, recommended by the same able acquaintance who had found the apartment. They were not really painters, she had told Della, but artists. Of course they were as good as or better than real painters, but cheaper. And they spoke English, they could understand instructions, which many real painters didn't these days, and in addition could do carpentry and practically anything else Della might want done. In short, a find.

Della was accustomed to painters in white overalls arriving with surly mumbles, laden with supplies. These painters, in jeans and navy-blue T-shirts and backpacks, arrived empty-handed, greeted her and introduced themselves as if it were a social occasion. The man's name was Paolo and he looked intimidating: stocky, strong, and dark, with longish straight black hair, sharp assessing eyes, and a cigarette dropping from his lips. The woman, Margie, who did more of the talking, had an efficient, calming manner, something like a neophyte nurse or a schoolteacher. She was an inch or two taller than Paolo and was fresh-faced and blue-eyed, with very white teeth and hair so blonde it was almost white, cut like a man's except for wisps of bangs brushing her eyelids. At once Della wondered whether they were a couple, if they lived and slept together as well as painted together. Probably not. Paolo, whose few words were spoken in a slight Spanish accent, was too forbidding for Margie, and she seemed too ingenuous for him.

"Okay, where is the paint?" he said after a tour of the four large rooms.

"Oh, I didn't know—I guess I thought you would take care of all that." She felt foolish—had she expected an ambulance corps, a vehicle equipped for any contingency?

Paolo shrugged. "We'll go out for the paint. Do you have brushes, rollers, a ladder?"

Della shook her head. No expression altered his face—only a formidable neutrality.

"No problem," Margie said cheerily. "We'll put it all in the truck."

"Oh, do you have a truck?"

"Brand new. Our pride and joy." Margie darted to the window to point out a dilapidated maroon pickup parked across the street, its back piled with an assortment of wood and metal. "Now we don't have to lug our stuff through the streets. Paolo does very large pieces."

Della glanced up at the building opposite. The babies, thank goodness, were sitting sedately at the windowsill, dipping wands into a bowl set between them and blowing bubbles through the iron bars. The bubbles caught the summer sunlight in patches as they drifted radiantly upwards.

"This job could take a while," Paolo said. "It's going to need a lot of plastering. Whoever did it last time painted right over the cracks." He came to the window to crush his cigarette on the bricks outside, glanced below at the small flower garden, and put the butt in his pocket. "It could be slapped on in three days, but we don't do that kind of work."

"You also may need two or even three coats to cover up these weird colors," said Margie. "What colors did you have in mind?"

"White. All white. As much as it takes." Suddenly she felt light and happy and protected in their presence. Even Paolo's gruffness was soothing: no smooth promises. "I've got the time. I took a month off from work to move in and fix the place up." Della worked for a publishing firm, designing books and book jackets. Her vacation money would pay these strange painters who fit in no ready category. In her old life, the painters sent by the landlord had been gray-haired men or teen-agers who spoke Greek and nodded enigmatically to whatever she said and left their cigarette butts on the floor.

"Are you going to be here the whole time, then?" asked Margie.

"Yes, I'm going to paint with you."

The first day, Della painted a closet in the room where Paolo was scraping and plastering the ceiling. It was a room she intended to use as a studio in case she did any free-lance work, or as an extra bedroom in case her son Frank came to stay. Frank was in the Peace Corps in Costa Rica, building a school or a hospital, she had forgotten which, but that would not last forever. Paolo worked in silence, standing bare-chested on the ladder he had borrowed from the super, a cigarette pasted to his bottom lip. Della had given him a saucer for an ashtray, which was balanced on the top rung.

His voice startled her. "Are you going to live here alone?"

"Yes."

"It's a nice place. Light."

That seemed to be all. From the living room came pounding music. Margie, pulling a radio from her backpack, had asked if Della would object to the rock music of WAPP. Della would object to nothing except Ezra's creamy tones.

"Where do you live?" she ventured from the closet, in Paolo's direction.

"We have a loft in SoHo. Ancient, but big enough so we can both work. My work needs a lot of space."

"I used to live not far from there, on Bleecker Street. Then we lived in Chelsea, but I moved here because my husband took up with a younger woman." She shocked herself a bit, with that. But why not? She no longer had a rooted social position, she could say anything she pleased. Even "took up with."

"That's too bad. How young?"

"Thirty-three. Precisely ten years younger than I am."

"That's the age Margie is. I'm thirty-five."

"Really? I thought you were both younger. I thought you were kids."

Paolo smiled, making the cigarette tremble precariously. "We thought you were younger too. These things are rough, I know. Margie's husband left her for a man. They were married five years and he discovered, or decided, he was gay."

"She seems very innocent, for that." Paolo said nothing, kept plastering. "Where are you from?"

"Argentina."

"But Paolo is Italian, isn't it?"

He gave her a sideways glance. "There are many Italians in Argentina. Some less now, in my family."

"Do you mean. . . ?" For her work Della had read a book about the military regime in Argentina, she told him. She had designed the jacket. "Is that why you came?"

"I had to. First they killed my father. My uncle and my brother-in-law disappeared—my sister was left with two babies. I was next. I got here nine years ago, practically crawling up two continents."

"That's terrible. Did you have anybody here, family, friends?"

"A friend of my father's, yes, otherwise I'd still be living underground. After I got the green card I worked in the flower market. That's where I met Margie—she came in to buy a plant. She helped me get back to making sculptures." He stopped abruptly and climbed down from the ladder. "Time for lunch."

"I wish I had something to offer you, but—" She waved vaguely at the emptiness and suddenly felt very hungry herself.

"Margie brought sandwiches. She made a ham last night. There's plenty for you too. Anything around to drink, though? Beer, maybe?"

Della flushed with pleasure at the invitation. Stepping out of the closet, she took off her painter's hat and shook out her hair. "I'll run around the corner and get some. It'll just take a minute."

He peered past her. "Beautiful closet, Della. High-class work. If you keep this up we'll let you prime the bathroom."

They settled on the floor in the living room, where the two chairs and the stereo were shrouded in plastic dropcloths. Margie, snapping open a can of beer, said, "Paolo told me what happened. For what it's worth, it gets better in time. I thought I would never recover but I did, pretty much." With the white painter's hat hiding her cropped hair, with her paint-spattered shorts and bare feet, Margie looked like a twelve-year-old boy.

"This is a wonderful sandwich," said Della gravely. "It may be the best sandwich I've ever had. I'm not trying to recover. I'm just trying to get the apartment painted. I may keep painting it over and over, even after you both leave. I'll get fired from my job and go on unemployment and just stay home and paint, till the walls meet each other."

"Please don't paint over our work, Della," said Paolo. "Who knows, someday you may be able to say, These walls are the work of Paolo and Margie."

Della laughed faintly and sipped some beer. She had never been a beer drinker but it seemed suitable now, in her new life, sharing an indoor picnic with strangers after working in the sultry heat.

"I know how you're feeling, to talk that way. Can you imagine how I felt, with Bill, when I realized that for five years, every time we were together, my body was not . . . That maybe he was wishing or imagining I was something else? God knows what went through his head. And I thought he liked it. I thought that was how men acted when they were liking it. You know?"

"Please," said Della, hugging her knees tight. "I do know. But I don't want to think about any of that. Maybe ever again."

"Margie has learned to say everything aloud for her health. Her shrink taught her. She wants me to go too, for my anger." Paolo gave a grunting laugh. "Maybe to have it removed, like a wart."

Margie moved closer to him, till their shoulders were touching. "I wish I could make you see," she said softly. Then to Della, "Paolo is an extraordinary artist. Everything he does is huge and powerful and . . . larger than life. But there are still some things he refuses to understand. I grew up on a farm in Montana. I drove a tractor and pulled turkeys in out of the rain. I hardly knew, when I got married, about people like Bill. But how could I go so long and not see what was right in front of me? I have to understand."

"But I understand perfectly what happened to me," Paolo said sullenly. "Only I don't make peace with it, like you do. It's not a private thing. I don't want to make peace with it."

She had been right at the start, Della thought. They were too different, and the difference made her uneasy. She wanted the new apartment pure and free of conflict. "How about another beer?" They sat silent, like petulant children. "Does either of you know anything about wiring? I have a lamp I'd like to hang in that spare room."

"Why not?" Paolo shrugged again. "I'll bring the manual along tomorrow, just in case. I can also hook up the washing machine that sits there idle."

The telephone woke Della out of thick sleep the next morning. She reached out but found nothing; when she reached to nudge Ezra there was only a grainy wall. She opened her eyes: new apartment, new life. Telephone on the floor, six feet away.

"Hi. I want to know what's going on. You haven't written in weeks and Dad said you moved out."

She had forgotten all about Frank, or at least about telling Frank. On the day Ezra pronounced their marriage over, Della had said he didn't have to know yet, far off as he was in Costa Rica. On that day Costa Rica had seemed an imaginary place and Frank an imaginary son. Now his voice restored him to physical existence. She recalled stuffing his body into snowsuits and grabbing him away from open windows, but with more alacrity than the woman across the street.

"Don't worry, we're both fine. We're living separately, that's all."

In his relentless way, Frank questioned her until she told him how Ezra had decided that their marriage was stunting his personal growth, whereas with his new woman he explored undreamed of depths and heights. There was a silence; she wondered if they had been disconnected.

"I don't know what to say. Maybe it's just a phase."

"I doubt it. For me it's no phase. I have a wonderful new apartment—" and new painters, she almost added. "Never mind. Tell me how you're doing. How is the hospital coming along?"

It was a school after all. "I have some good news, at least I hope you'll think so. I'm going to bring Milagros back with me at the end of the two years. We're going to get married. We've been—"

"Milagros?" It sounded like a man's name.

"I wrote you about her in my last two letters, remember?" She's one of the architectural students assigned to our project." He paused and Della scanned her memory. "Don't you read my letters?"

"I'm sorry. It's just that I was sleeping soundly. That's . . . wonderful."

"You're not bothered that she's Costa Rican, I hope? Part Indian, actually. I mean, people can think they're very sophisticated, but when—"

"Oh, she's Costa Rican?"

"I wrote you! She speaks very good English, though."

"No, that doesn't bother me. Only a Nazi would bother me. But they've mostly gone to Argentina, haven't they?"

"Mom, go back to sleep. I've got to go anyway, they're calling me. Give me your new address. But I won't be able to write for a while—

we're going on a field trip. I wish you and Dad could work things out. That's really some shock.''

Milagros, thought Della as she hung up. She remembered dimly the lightweight airletters lying on the hall table. Yes, two had arrived after the day Ezra came into the kitchen where she was measuring out coffee and told her that their marriage had been a gross error of long duration, that he needed an entirely different kind of woman, only he hadn't known it till a few months ago, when she materialized in the studio. Della tried to remember what she had done about the coffee. She tried to remember reading Frank's letters, but could retrieve nothing at all since that day except finding the apartment and packing. Not even a movie, though she had liked movies, in her old life. Nor could she recall anything happening in the world. No information from the past three weeks seemed to have adhered, except for the facts about Paolo and Margie: Argentina, the sister left with two children, crawling up two continents, the flower market; Montana, turkeys in the rain, Bill the homosexual.

With those exceptions, thought Della, she had become like H.M. She had read about the case of H.M. a while ago at work, in a book about brain malfunctioning for which she had designed the jacket. H.M. had undergone brain surgery to control epilepsy and afterward was incapable of learning anything new. Whatever part of him kept new information had been sliced out. H.M. could remember everything he had known before his lobotomy, and he could still understand what was said to him, but could not retain it for more than a minute. He was told that his father had died, but immediately forgot it. Well, there was no danger of that happening to her; her father had been dead for many years and she knew it. H.M. had to be reminded again and again. And so it was with every single thing. He could not remember a new face, a new room, a new tune, a movie, or even what had occurred in the movie five minutes earlier. He could not grow past the moment they cut out parts of his brain. That was quite different from Ezra's lamenting his stunted growth—Ezra was capable of learning new things, he was learning them right now, every day and every night. Only she was stuck in the moment when he told her their long mistake was ending, the nerves linking them were being snipped. Della had designed a very successful jacket for that book: a pane of shattered glass against the bars of a luminous rainbow. Every crack and filigree in the shattered pane was clearly delineated. Light from the colors behind the glass bled through in glimmers. The border of the design was black as night.

She rose and walked to the window. Ah yes, the babies—that she remembered well. They were at it again, stretching their bodies over the iron bars and opening their hands to send tissues skimming on the wind. The tissues looked like a regatta of sailboats seen from far off. Della shielded her eyes and shivered in the heat. She felt she could not bear her life or the terror that the babies would fall to their death as she watched. When she looked again the dark-haired woman appeared, pulled them from the windowsill and lowered the window half way. The doorbell rang—Paolo and Margie, come to continue painting.

While Margie finished the ceiling in the spare room, Paolo hooked up the washing machine and Della did a load of wash. Paolo hung the lamp: they all exclaimed on how sinister the color of the walls—gun metal—seemed in the artificial light, then cheered as Della applied the first stroke of chastening white. Paolo scraped and plastered in the bedroom and Margie began spraying the metal cabinets white. They worked steadily till amost three o'clock, when Della went out for barbecued ribs which they gnawed lazily on the living room floor, listening to the rock music on Margie's radio, punctuated by weather reports. Ninety-six degrees.

"Too hot to work," said Della. "Let's call it a day."

"I want to be air-conditioned," Margie said, rolling a beer can on her forehead. "Let's go to a movie."

They took turns in the shower, where Della had not yet hung a shower curtain. As Paolo emerged with his hair slicked back, apologizing for taking so long—he had had to mop up the whole floor—

Della was reminded of the men in her life, Ezra and Frank, her former life, who also flung themselves about in the shower. Neither she nor Margie had that problem, but Margie emerged saying she would be glad to install a new shower head; a sharper, more tingly flow would do wonder for Della's skin and spirit. They laughed at two Marx Brothers films at a revival house, then Paolo and Margie drove Della home in the pickup and she fell quickly into a deep, long sleep.

Painting in the kitchen the next day, while Paolo was out at the hardware store, Della said, "You always talk about Paolo's work, how big and powerful it is, what wonderful compositions he makes out of junk. What about yours? What's it like?"

"Well, it's small and I guess you would say delicate, in comparison to Paolo's. But then most things are. I work with light. How light hits surfaces and refracts. I build things, little models, and when they're set in various kinds of light, the light and shadows become part of the piece. It changes according to where it's put."

"But when do you get a chance to do it, if you do this kind of work all day?"

"We only do this about half the year, the warm months usually, because, you know, people like to keep the windows open. The rest of the year we mostly do our own work. Sometimes we hang shows for galleries downtown, for extra money. Paolo can work at night but I'm too tired after a day of this, and anyway, I need daylight. I work on Sundays. That's when he sleeps."

"Do you think you'll go on this way indefinitely, or—" Della didn't know what she wanted to say after "or." Simply, the life Margie described did not sound like a life she could imagine living except for a short period, before embarking on "real" life. Like Frank in the Peace Corps, or herself dancing in the corps of the Joffrey at nineteen. Yet why on earth not? Thousands lived such lives, and no doubt had done so all the years she spent with Ezra.

"Well, I know what you mean, sure. I think I'd like to be married again, even after what happened with Bill. Maybe have a baby. More than maybe. I mean, I'm not going to be able to do that forever. And we've been together four years. But Paolo's not ready, he says. You've heard about the new man, afraid of commitment and all that garbage."

"He seems already committed."

"That's exactly what I tell him, but . . ."

"Isn't that a very American syndrome?"

"He picks things up fast."

They heard the key in the door. Paolo returned with magnets so the kitchen cabinet doors would close properly, and a special bit for his drill so that he could put up standards for bookshelves. Margie, turning on her radio, suggested that when Della finished the kitchen door she might prepare all the windows to be painted. Mesmerized by the heat and remote blank contentment, Della moved slowly from room to room, dusting the window frames and sills and sticking masking tape around the edges of every pane, until Paolo shouted to them with excitement—come see what he had unearthed in the bathroom. She had to laugh as she confronted the bizarre mottled walls. Dismally faded browns and blues and grays lay bared: bulbous masses assembling for a thunderstorm, strata of history in the form of successive paint jobs.

"Found art!" he cried. "This should be preserved for posterity. It's almost like a de Kooning, if only the colors would be brighter."

Margie gave her clever chuckle. "Beyond New Wave. But you didn't have to scrape down that far. I mean, Della is paying for this."

"I wouldn't charge for anything in the service of art! Even the degree of scraping is a creative act. You should put it under glass, Della. It's a statement about the past, the juxtaposition of eras, like archeology. You could charge admission. One wall at least."

"Come off it. It's so ugly it hurts," said Della.

"So straight! Where's your nerve? Wait—we have to add something contemporary." He grabbed the can of white spray paint from Margie's hand and sprayed a small heart on the wall above the bathtub.

Inside the heart he sprayed the letters "P" and "M," linked by curlicues. "There!"

"Don't mind him," said Margie. "It must be the heat."

Della went back to taping windowpanes, grateful that the babies
across the street were nowhere in sight. Dreamily she mused about the
near future, when Paolo would outgrow this childish phase and marry
Margie and they would have the baby she craved. Margie would stay
home and not work so hard, and Paolo would . . . Get a job, she almost
continued. But that was absurd—she was molding them into something other than they were. Paolo would be discovered and sell his
work to rich collectors. Margie would work too, when she wasn't
taking care of the baby, and maybe she would be famous, with her
smaller and more delicate pieces. It was a naïve fantasy, Della knew; it
might even be objectionable. Yet it made her happy.

Later that afternoon Margie went out for pizza and beer, and as
they ate on the living room floor Della asked Paolo to tell her
something about Costa Rica.

"What does that mean, 'something' about Costa Rica? It's an entire
country. What parts do you want to know about?"

"I'm not sure. You could start with the government, like they used
to do in school, then the products and resources, the mountains and
rivers, remember? Well, maybe you didn't do that. Anyway, start. I'll
remember what's important to me."

With a mild jab at the insularity of North Americans, Paolo
obliged, and what Della remembered mostly, after he and Margie left
for the weekend, was that Costa Rica was one of the few Latin
American countries with a democratic government and not under the
rule of the military. Actually, Frank must have mentioned that; the
fact did not strike her as entirely new. Costa Rica did not even possess
a standing army, Paolo said. The United States, however, which
considered Costa Rica little more than a satellite, had recently pro-
posed to send military advisers there as part of the effort to aid
Nicaraguan contras. Paolo was surprised Della knew nothing about

this, nor about Costa Rica's enormous national debt, since both had been in the papers, but she explained how she had not been reading the papers much since the day Ezra declared the past twenty-odd years a detour in his personal development, and how even if she had been, she would probably have forgotten what she read. Paolo had looked confused by her explanation, but Margie understood and said all of that would pass in time.

Della spent the weekend sleeping and wandering dazedly through the baking streets. On Monday morning, Margie carried in a large shopping bag packed with mounds of tissue paper. "I brought one of my pieces to show you. But we have to be very careful with it. It's fragile." She and Paolo unwrapped it on the washing machine. It was a construction of wood and masonite about a foot and a half high, finished in gradations of white and gray and suggesting an architect's miniature model. Yet not quite a building; rather, a mélange of possible parts of buildings, a structure of fable. Looking closely, Della saw that Margie had painted a range of shadows here and there, making it tricky to tell which grays were painted and which were a response to the light. Studying the piece was almost like a game, a brainteaser.

"How wonderful. So complex." Indeed, it was more subtle than she had expected, its profusion of planes and angles and crannies, all neatly trimmed and lucid, giving the illusion of a simplicity just out of reach.

"Let me take it over to the light," Paolo said. "You can't really appreciate it here." He brought it into the bedroom, where the morning sun beamed in. Standing at the window, he held it high and revolved it in his hands. As light struck the piece, its patterns shifted; flashes of rainbow appeared, shadows disappeared. "*Ay Dios mío*, those babies! They'll fall out! Where is their mother?"

"Hey, don't drop it!" Margie took the piece from him and set it down in a corner.

"Oh, not again," moaned Della. "Every other day I think they're about to die."

"One day they will. *Oyé, chiquillos!*" he called loudly.

"No, no!" Della grabbed his arm. "Don't shout! They could lose their balance. Just do nothing. Don't look."

"I can't not look. Let's call the police."

The woman appeared from the invisible spaces of the apartment and pulled the children off the windowsill. She left the window open.

"*Señora, por favor!*" Paolo shouted something in Spanish.

"But they're Chinese. Or Korean," said Della. "She wouldn't understand Spanish."

Paolo called again but the woman had vanished. "They looked like Latinos to me."

Della's shoulders sagged in exhaustion. She saw Margie, pale and still, sitting on the floor next to her sculpture. In the shadowy corner it had lost its verve; its interest had become purely geometrical and barren. Again Della praised it but the moment was spoiled. Margie said she would go wrap it up so no one tripped over it.

"Oh, Della, I forgot to mention on Friday . . ." Paolo said. "I pulled up a piece of that ridiculous wavy linoleum—behind the stove, don't worry—and there's a good surface underneath. I could put down tiles if you like—the kitchen would look a lot better. A domestic metamorphosis."

"Ha! I'm not sure I want to go that far. Is the linoleum so bad?"

He gave a loud laugh. "Well, it's not that I'm dying to rip up a floor in this heat."

"Let me think about it." Climbing up the ladder in the bathtub to paint the ceiling, Della began figuring rapidly. The plastering was all done. The spare room was finished, the living room and bedroom close to it. It might be only a few days till . . . The telephone rang rooms away, its first ring since Frank's call from Costa Rica. "Paolo, Margie, would someone get it, please?"

Paolo, who had been painting the bedroom window frame, handed her the receiver with a comic flourish, whispering, "*Un hombre.*"

"Della? Hello, Della?"

"Who is this?"

"It's me, Ezra. What's the matter?"

"Nothing."

"Didn't you recognize my voice?"

"What do you want?"

"I had to get your number from Information."

"Well?"

"Who was that answering the phone?"

"The painter."

"He didn't sound like a painter."

"How should a painter sound?"

"I meant he sounded too educated to be a painter. All the painters we've ever had didn't speak much English."

"Well, this one speaks excellent English." She turned towards Paolo and grinned. He grinned back.

"Okay, it's not my business, I realize. I was calling about Frank. This girl he says he wants to marry, Della, may be a very nice girl, but he's far too young for such a big commitment. I don't think it's something we ought to encourage. He may come to regret it."

"You mean marry in haste, repent at leisure?" Della had been pregnant when she and Ezra married. They had also been in love.

"You could put it that way. Then, of course, Costa Rica. It's quite a different culture."

"Are you familiar with Costa Rica? Costa Rica may be the only nation in the Americas without a standing army. One of the few, certainly. And yet now this government—"

"I don't see what that . . . Della, is everything all right? Are you managing?"

"Fine. I have to go now, the painter needs me."

"That's not very funny. I'm writing to Frank to try to explain things. Would you write too?"

"This place is so upside down at the moment, I don't even think I could find a piece of paper." Della hung up.

"The husband?" Paolo asked.

She nodded.

"He has a voice like a radio announcer."

"That's because he is one."

"Maybe he is one because he has that voice."

"You have a point there."

"He's getting lonely, eh? Wants to reconsider?"

"Nope, nothing like that. By the way, you might as well rip up that kitchen floor."

"Are you sure? Do you want to price some tiles first?"

"No, that's okay. Also, about the bookshelves—if I got the wood this week could you help me sand and stain it?"

Paolo gave his usual neutral shrug. "All right, why not?"

She drifted into the living room, where the ceiling and two walls already gleamed white against the old forest green color. Margie's roller was attached to a long stick. As she saw Della she smiled and jiggled it in time to the music, doing a bouncy little dance. Della envisioned the entire room white and glistening, its accumulated gloom sealed into oblivion, with sunlight filtering in through pale wooden slatted shades. "That looks great, Margie. Do you think, if I bought some window shades for the whole place, you might put them up?"

"No problem. I'll check out the window frames and see what kind of brackets you'll need."

Late in the afternoon Paolo went out for Chinese food and beer. When all the containers were empty, Margie reached across the living room floor for her huge shopping bag and pulled out a game, Trivial Pursuit, which she announced would distract Della from her troubles and prove that her memory was basically intact. Oh no, Della said, she had lost the competitive instinct, and Paolo groaned with disdain. But in the end they gave in.

The game turned out to be like Go to the Head of the Class, which Della had played as a girl and also played with Frank when he was small. She was soon winning, for many of the questions were about people and events in the news before Paolo's and Margie's era: FDR, Neville Chamberlain, Billie Holiday, the Lindbergh kidnapping, Jesse Owens, the abdication of Edward VI. They were before her own era as well, she realized, yet she knew about them. Paolo and Margie could answer questions about Greek and Roman mythology, about the Medici popes, and about the French Revolution, but didn't seem to know much that had happened in the twentieth century before 1960. On the other hand, Margie was very good with questions about art and music and, unexpectedly, baseball. Paolo was better than either of them at geography—he was spectacular at geography, Della noted—but his downfall was questions about American popular culture, particularly that segment of it promulgated on television—he did not know the name of Fred Flintstone's wife, or what "Bonanza" was, or how many children were in the Brady bunch—and about American heroes familiar to all schoolchildren, such as Patrick Henry and John Paul Jones. He was reduced to muttering curses in Spanish, or possibly Italian, when asked the name of Perry Mason's secretary and loyal sidekick.

Della laughed. "I could never forget that—Della Street. My parents were apparently great Perry Mason fans." She had to explain the curious mass appeal of Perry Mason; they had neither read the books nor seen the television series. "I always wondered why. There was nothing memorable about her. She just filled a necessary role. Maybe they liked the sound of it."

"Why didn't you ask them?" said Paolo.

"Well . . . they were drowned in a sailing accident when I was four."

Margie gasped. "You never told us!"

"It never came up. I've only known you less than two weeks."

"Still. So who took care of you? Did you grow up in an orphanage?"

"No. I stayed with an aunt and uncle. I was lucky. To have them, I mean."

"But do you still remember your parents? Can you see them in your mind?" Margie seemed intrigued by the news.

"Oh yes. My father more than my mother, strangely enough. He was a very big man, with very big gestures. He didn't know his own strength, my aunt used to say. I think she blamed him for the accident. I remember this game we used to play. He would sit in a certain chair with his arms outstretched and I would run to him. He caught me and locked me in with his legs, I was his prisoner, then he pushed me away and I ran backwards, then back to him again, over and over, and laughing all the way through. One time he pushed me away so hard I toppled backwards right into the French windows and cut my arm on the broken glass." Della paused. She felt a bit light-headed. "I can still feel the thrill of that game, being captured and enfolded, all warm and safe, and then pushed away. It was only pretend, the pushing away part. It never really felt dangerous. I still have the scar." The memory was pulsing in her brain like a blip on a radar screen. She held out her arm to show them the small white circle near her wrist.

"My father never went in much for games. He has Alzheimer's now," Margie said. "Last time I saw him, when my mother died, I had to keep introducing myself. He couldn't keep it in his head from one minute to the next." She poured a long swig of beer down her throat. "I almost think I'd rather be an orphan like you two."

"Orphan! I think at a certain age, my age anyway, it no longer applies. Though maybe it should. Was your mother also . . . political?" she asked Paolo.

"My mother died of a cerebral hemorrhage. Even under a *junta* some people manage to die of natural causes. It's much less glamorous, I know."

"Okay! You don't have to make it an international incident. What ever happened to your sister? The one who was left with the two small children."

"Ah, my sister. A few years after her husband disappeared my sister met a man, very nice, very decent. Also a radio announcer, it happens.

But she keeps thinking maybe her husband is still alive somewhere. She won't get married—she is afraid of being a bigamist."

"But they emptied the prisons long ago, I read. Surely he's not going to turn up after all this time?"

"No. But she's a religious woman. God could send him back. I'm not sure if it would be a reward or a punishment at this point."

Margie finished her third can of beer. She grazed Paolo's bare foot with her own, then crossed her ankle over his. "She should see my therapist. She's terrific with endings. I mean, like a special talent. Scrapes you up off the floor and puts you back into shape for the next bout."

"Maybe you should find someone who does middles," Della suggested.

"There never seem to be any middles, just beginnings and endings. And everyone can handle beginnings. They're the fun part. Endings are the real challenge, don't you think? I mean, they're costing me a fortune. That's money I ought to be using to visit my father in Butte."

Paolo turned to Della, his eyes large with injury, entreating. "But I'm not ending anything! I'm right here with her. I don't know why she keep talking that way. Too much beer, that's what."

"You're right. I'm talking nonsense." Margie put the beer down. She squeezed Paolo's hand, then kissed it. "Let's get it together here. Your turn, champ."

In a week the apartment was finished. Like new, Della thought. Light filtered through the slatted shades, striping the fresh walls. The kitchen floor was metamorphosed by white tiles. Paolo had hung a pegboard for pots and pans, and screwed the magnets into the latches of the cabinets. The bookshelves, stained and in place, awaited their books, still packed in cartons. In the bedroom, Margie had hung a full-length mirror Della got at the Salvation Army store, and in the bathroom, once Della put up a shower curtain, she had installed a more invigorating shower head. On the final day she hooked up the stereo system and speakers. Then they had cleaned up the debris and left. But they must get together very soon, they all vowed. Della must come down to the studio to see their work, and they would go to dinner in Little Italy or in Chinatown. And Paolo and Margie must come back for a real dinner, sitting around a table, as soon as Della got her dishes unpacked and got a table.

She returned to work. It took enormous effort to get herself dressed and presentable for the office each day and do the projects assigned her. She tried to reestablish a routine of shopping on the way home and preparing dinner, as she had done for most of her adult life—programmed like a machine, she had often thought. But she couldn't seem to break the newer habit of dropping in at the pizzeria, the Chinese restaurant, or the delicatessen. Unlike H.M., she had succeeded in learning something new, not to cook dinner. In the evenings she listened to records on the stereo and sent change of address cards to magazines, to her bank and her credit card accounts. When writing to Frank, she remembered to ask how Milagros was, and remembered it was a school he was building, not a hospital. She unpacked dishes and books, and bought items like wastebaskets and ice cube trays, which she had forgotten to take from the old apartment.

Out all day, she naturally didn't see the babies at the window across the street. But when they didn't appear over the weekend, she decided the family must have gone away on vacation. To the country or the seashore, where the buildings were low.

Often she thought about calling Paolo and Margie, but a cloud of uncertainties, like gnats, surrounded her. Perhaps they had only felt sorry for her. Perhaps it was the custom in their generation or in their circles for people thrown together by circumstance to become intimate at first sight, then to forget each other as easily when circumstances changed. But could an instinct like friendship change from one generation to the next, or in different circles? Surely not, yet customs could be more powerful than feelings, and among these new customs Della was at a loss, like a foreigner, or Rip Van Winkle.

Perhaps Paolo and Margie made friends with all their employers, for fun and profit. Yet hadn't Margie confided that they had never had such a good time on any job? Often they couldn't wait to leave. Paolo, she said, usually felt uncomfortable with new people. Constrained. Why, at their previous job he hadn't even been permitted to smoke indoors and had to go out on the fire escape. Literally fuming, she recalled with her chuckle. Neither had they been taking advantage of her, Della knew, for their meticulous records of hours worked and expenses at the hardware store tallied with her own: they had not charged for the many hours spent sitting on the floor eating and playing games or telling stories, nor for the whimsical excavation of the bathroom walls. Still . . .

Della tried to brush doubt from her mind, tried to trust. She would call at precisely the right moment—too soon would appear dependent and clinging, too late could find her drifted to the gray recesses of memory. She chose one early evening twelve days after they had left. The sunlight in the apartment was declining, but still rich and gold. Paolo answered on the first ring.

"Della! It's good to hear you! How're you doing?" He sounded truly pleased. With an awkard haste, Della invited him and Margie to come for dinner on Friday or Saturday night.

"I hate to tell you this, but—"

Her chest felt rammed in. Don't say it, she thought. But he already had. She was gone. "But why? What happened?"

"I don't understand it myself. One of those things."

"Of course you understand. She wanted to get married and have a baby."

"That was part of it. But there were other things too. She's . . . Oh, it's too involved. We wanted to call you, Della, but things were really rough for a while. I'm okay now. I'll come Friday, or would you rather go out somewhere? Or else come down here and I'll show you my stuff."

"Oh no," whispered Della. Her heart was racing, she was feeling sick, she wanted only not to talk any more. "No I couldn't do that."

"I don't get it. Why not?"

"I wanted to see the both of you."

"But . . . You sound like a child, Della."

"I can't help it."

"Oh. Was it just that we were a cute couple? Was that all? The hired help? The spic and his chick?"

"No, no, stop. You don't understand at all. Please, just forget it. I'm sorry."

"Do you want the number where Margie's staying?" he asked coldly.

"Another time, maybe."

She knew they would be there, even before she looked. They were leaning far out, waving at a flock of birds overhead. Back from vacation, or perhaps they had never gone; yes, that was another fantasy. The babies flung their arms about and shouted, so for the first time Della could hear their voices. The syllables were foreign, though at this distance she couldn't tell whether they were Chinese or Spanish or baby talk. As always, they looked about to topple out—she should be used to it by now. But she would never be used to it. It took only one time. She wished they would fall right away, if they were going to, and get it over with. Where was their mother? Where was their father, for that matter? How would she live the rest of her life here?

She turned and walked slowly through the fresh, chaste rooms. Soon the weather would change; the windows would be closed. They would get older, they would grow up. She could only wait.

John Updike

POKER NIGHT

The plant has been working late, with the retailers hustling to get their inventories up for Christmas even though this is only August, so I grabbed a bite on the way to the doctor's and planned to go straight from there to poker. The wife in fact likes my not coming home now and then; it gives her a chance to skip dinner and give her weight problem a little knock.

The doctor has moved from his old office over on Poplar to one of these new medical centers, located right behind the mall, where for years there was a field where I can remember as a kid the Italians growing runner beans on miles and miles of this heavy brown string. The new center is all recessed ceiling lighting and there's moss-colored carpet everywhere and Muzak piped into the waiting room but if you look at their doors you could put a fist through them easily and you can hear the other doctors and patients through the walls, everything they say, including the breathing.

What mine said to me wasn't good. In fact, every time I tried to get a better grip on it it seemed to get worse.

He provided a lot of cheerful energetic talk about the treatments they have now, the chemotherapy and then cobalt and even something they can do with platinum, but at my age I've seen enough people die to know there's no real stopping it, just a lot of torment on the way. If it wasn't for company insurance and Medicaid you wonder how many of these expensive hospitals would still be in business.

I said at least I was glad it hadn't been just my imagination. I asked if he thought it could have been anything to do with any of the chemicals they have to use over at the plant and he said all prim-mouthed he really couldn't venture any opinion about that.

He was thinking lawsuit, but I had been just curious. Me, I've always figured if it isn't going to be one thing it'll be another; in this day and age you can stand out on a street corner waiting for the light to change and inhale enough poison to snuff out a rat.

We made our future appointments and he gave me a wad of prescriptions to get filled. Closing the door I felt somebody could have put a fist through me pretty easily too.

But drug stores are cheerful bright places, and while waiting I had a Milky Way and leafed through a *People*, and by the time the girl behind the counter had the medicine ready you could tell from her smile and the way the yellow Bic-click stuck out of her smock pocket that nothing too bad was going to happen to me, ever. At least at a certain level of my mind this seemed the case.

Moths were thick as gnats under the street lights and there was that old summer happiness in the sticky swish of car tires on tar and the teen-agers inside the cars calling out even to people they didn't know. I got into my own car and after some thinking drove in the Heights direction to poker.

I wanted to be sharing this with the wife but then they were counting on me to be the sixth and a few hours couldn't make much difference. Bad news keeps: Isn't that what the old people used to say?

The group has been meeting every other Wednesday for over thirty years, with some comings and goings, people moving away and coming back. We've even had some deaths, but up to now none of the regulars, just substitutes—brother-in-laws or neighbors called in to round out the table for that one night.

It was at Bob's tonight. Bob's a framer, in his own shop downtown: it's amazing what those guys get now, maybe forty, fifty bucks for just a little watercolor somebody's aunt did and they've just inherited, or some kid's high school diploma.

Jerry does mechanical engineering for an outfit beyond the new mall, Ted's a partner in a downtown fruit store, Greg manages the plumbing business his father founded way back, Rick's a high school guidance counselor believe it or not, and Arthur is in sales for Doerner's Paints. Arthur had to be on the road tonight, which is why they needed me to make six.

It all began when we were newlyweds more or less starting up our families in the neighborhood between Poplar and Forrest, on the side of the avenue away from what used to be the wallpaper factory, before they broke it up into little commercial rental units. One April night I got this call from Greg, a guy I hardly knew except everybody knew his old man's truck.

I thought Alma would make resistance, both Jimmy and Grace must have been under two at the time and Alma was still trying to give piano lessons in the evenings. But she said go ahead, I'd been working pretty hard and she thought I could use the relaxation.

Now none of us live in the neighborhood except me and Ted, and he talks about moving to a condo now that the kids are out of the house, except he hates the idea of fighting the traffic into town every day. From where it is now he can walk to the fruit store in a blizzard if he has to, and that crazy Josie of his never did learn how to drive.

For years Arthur has been over on the Heights too, about three of these curving streets away from Bob's place, and Rick is over on the other side of town toward the lake, and Jerry has gone and bought himself a run-down old dairy farm to the south; he's fixing up the barn as a rental property, doing most of the work himself on weekends. Also over the years there have been some changes as to wives and business situations.

But the stakes haven't changed, and with inflation and our moving more or less up in the world the dimes and quarters and even the dollar bills look like chips, flipping back and forth. It really *is* pretty much relaxation now, with winning more a matter of feeling good than the actual cash.

I arrived maybe ten minutes late because of the wait in the drugstore. The little paper bags in the pocket rattled when I threw my jacket on the sofa and the sound turned my stomach, reminding me of my secret.

Did you ever have the strong feeling that something *has* to be a dream, and that tomorrow you'll wake up safe? It used to come to me all the time as a kid, whenever I'd be in trouble.

I got a beer and settled in at the table between Ted and Rick. The five faces, all lit up with beer already and the flow of the cards, looked like balloons, bright pink balloons in that overhead light Bob has rigged up in his den, a naked 100-watt bulb on an extension cord propped up there among the exposed two-by-eights.

He's been working on his den for years, bringing down the ceiling and the walls in for better insulation. But the framing business keeps him downtown Saturdays as well as evenings, and the plasterboard sheets and two-by-fours and rolls of insulation have been leaning around so long in this den it always gives us something to rib him about.

I thought, *I might never see this room finished*. The thought hit me like lead in the stomach; but I figured if I sat perfectly quiet and drank the first beer fast the balloons of their faces would slowly take me up with them, to where I could forget my insides.

And it worked, pretty well. The cards began to come to me, under the bright lights, the aces and deuces and the queens with their beautiful cold faces, and I really only made two mistakes that night.

The one was, I hung on with two pair, jacks and eights, all the way into the dollar-raise stage of a game of seven-card high-low when Jerry had four cards of a straight showing and only two of the nines, the card he needed, were accounted for. But I figured he would *have* to bet as if he had it whether he did or not; as it turned out, he did have it, and I wasn't even second-best, since Greg had been sitting there sandbagging with three kings.

The other was, in the last round, when the pots really build, I folded a little full house, fives and treys, in a game of Twin Beds because so many pairs were already out there on the board I figured somebody had to have me beat. I was wrong: Rick won it with an Ace-high heart flush.

Can you imagine, winning Twin Beds with a flush? It's in my character to feel worse about folding a winner than betting a loser; it seems less of a sin against God or nature or whatever.

Maybe my concentration was off; it did seem silly, at moments, sitting here with these beered-up guys (it gets pretty loud toward the end) playing a game like kids killing a rainy Sunday afternoon when I'd just been told my number was up. The cards at these moments looked incredibly thin: a kind of silver foil beaten to just enough thickness to hide this huge ball of lead that was under everything.

My cards as it happened were generally pretty dull, so I had time to look around. The guys' faces looked like pink balloons but their hands as they reached on the table were another story entirely: they were old guys' hands, withered long spotted white claws with blackened finger-nails and gray hair and blue veins.

We had grown old together. We were all drawing near to death, and I guess that was the comfort of it, the rising up with them.

Ted spilled his beer as he tends to do as the evening wears on, reaching for some cards or the popcorn basket or his bifocals (it's an awkward length: you can see your own cards fine with the short vision but the cards in the middle tend to blur, and vice versa) and everybody howled and kidded as they were waiting to do, and my throat began to go rough, they were all so damn sweet, and I'd known them so damn long, without ever saying much of anything except this clowning around and whose deal it was; maybe that was the sweetness. Their faces blurred and came up in starry points like that out-of-focus thing they do with television cameras now—, the false teeth and glasses and the high foreheads where hair had been—and the crazy thought came to me that I wouldn't mind which it was so much, Heaven or Hell, as long as there was some kind of company.

Ted has these slightly swollen-looking hands, nicked around the fingers and fat at the sides of the palms, from handling the crates I suppose, and you would think, deft as he much have to be every day in the fruit store, picking out plums and tomatoes for the fancy lady customers, he would be the last one of us to be knocking his beer glass over. But he's always the one, just like Rick is the one to hang in there with junk and Bob the one to catch that one cased card in the deck he needs.

I wound up about five dollars down. If I'd had the guts to stay with that little full house I might have been fifteen dollars ahead.

I put on my jacket and the rustling in the pockets reminded me of the prescriptions and the doctor. Horse around all you want, reality is there in the end, waiting.

The wife wasn't up. I didn't expect her to be, at a quarter to twelve.

But she wasn't asleep, either. She asked me from the bed in the dark how I did.

I said I broke about even. She asked me what the doctor had said.

I asked her if she'd like to come down to the kitchen and talk. I don't know exactly why I didn't want anything said in the bedroom, but I didn't.

She said she'd love to, she had skipped supper tonight and was starving. There was some leftover lasagna in the fridge she could warm in the micro-oven in a minute; she'd been lying there in the dark thinking about it.

Alma isn't fat exactly; solid is more how I think of it. When you're with her in bed, you can feel she still has a waist, and ins and outs.

We went downstairs and turned on the light and she in her bathrobe heated the Pyrex dish half full of lasagna and I thought about one more beer and decided against it. Then the lasagna was so hot—amazing, how those microwaves do it; from the inside out, they say, vibrating the molecules—I went and got the beer just to soothe my mouth.

I told her everything as much like the doctor has told me as I could.

His exact words, his tone of voice as if it wasn't him saying this but a kind of prerecorded announcement; the look of the recessed lights about his examining table and his powder-blue steel desk and of his fake wood-grained wainscoting all revived in me as if I'd just come from there, as if I hadn't been to poker at all.

Alma did and said all the right things, of course. She cried but not so much I'd panic and came up with a lot of sensible talk about second opinions and mysterious remissions and how we'd take it a day at a time and had to have faith.

But she wasn't me. I was me.

While we were talking across the kitchen table there was a barrier suddenly that I was on one side of and she was on the other, over-weight and over fifty as she was, a middle-aged tired woman up after midnight in a powder-blue bathrobe but with these terribly alive dark eyes, suddenly. I had handed her this terrible edge.

You could see it in her face, her mind working. She was considering what she had been dealt; she was thinking how to play her cards.

Nancy Willard

HOW POETRY CAME INTO THE WORLD
AND WHY GOD DOESN'T WRITE IT

Several months ago I walked into a bookshop determined not to buy a book and saw, among the remainders, a small volume called *The Lost Books of Eden*. It beckoned to me like the serpent poised at the Tree of Knowledge. I considered the price. I considered my purse. I said to myself, "Opening that book could be dangerous to my economy," and I went out. Instead of leaving the scene of temptation, I walked around the block. When the bookshop came into view, I remembered the parable: the kingdom of heaven is like unto a man seeking goodly pearls who, when he had found one pearl of great price, went and sold all that he had and bought it. Also, wisdom is better than rubies, knowledge is better than gold, etc. Nothing makes us more vulnerable to temptation than ignorance. I had to know what was in that book.

Alas! When I looked for the book, it was gone. The clerk was sorry. *The Lost Books of Eden* had just been sold. Since that time I have speculated on what it might have contained. I have nearly reconstructed the lost books of Eden in my head. My reconstruction goes light on doctrine and heavy on losses. I see myself as an insurance salesman. Adam and Eve have found their way to my office. They draw up two vinyl-covered chairs and tell me their tragedy. They have lost everything through an act of God.

"Can you be more specific?" I say, shuffling through my papers for the right forms. "Exactly what did you lose?"

"Eternal life," says Adam.

"The roses I'd just planted in the western bower," said Eve.

"My free time," says Adam.

"My animals," says Eve. "Even the hummingbirds were eating out of my hand."

"Poetry," says Adam.

"Poetry," says Eve.

"Poetry?" I exclaim. "Well, that's the first thing you've mentioned that *can* be replaced. There's plenty of poetry outside of Eden."

"But it's not the same here as it was there," says Adam. "Poetry was invented in Eden. There was a well in the garden. Any time you put your ear to it, you heard a poem. Anytime you drank from it, you spoke poems. Poetry was so easy. No waiting, no revising, no dry spells."

"Where does the Bible tell how God invented poetry?" I ask.

"God didn't invent it," says Adam. "I did."

"I did too," says Eve. "Remember me?"

"Where does it say so in the Bible?" I demand.

"In the books that were lost," says Adam. "The lost books of Eden. You don't believe me?"

"I don't know what to believe," I answer.

"Look, pretend you're in Eden," says Eve. "God has just spent six days inventing the animals and the birds and the plants, and He's exhausted. He hasn't invented poems; there are some things only humans can make. Unless you want to call the sun and the moon and the birds and the beasts God's poems. Unless you want to call Adam His first reader. The one who's entertained and instructed."

"When God made me in His own image, He made me a creator too," says Adam. "And let me tell you, this creation business interested me a good deal. Especially after God let me name everything. The plants weren't too hard, except there were so many of them. I'd look at a plant and say the first sound that came into my head. And that sound would write itself in letters of gold on the air. Sycamore.

Turnip. Gingko. Parsley. Later, in the cool of the evening, God stopped by to see how things were going.

'Did you name them all? You didn't forget any of my weeds?'

'Not a one,' I told him.

'Nice work, Adam,' said God. 'Now I want you to name the animals.'

One by one, the animals filed by me and waited to see what I would call them. A low beast with pointed ears and long whiskers came by, softly, softly. I said the first sound that came into my head.

'Cat.'

And the name wrote itself on the air in letters of gold: C-A-T.

'That's what you think,' said the cat. 'That's what you call me. But it's not what I call myself.'

'What do you call yourself?' I asked.

'I am he who counteracts the powers of darkness with my electrical skin and glaring eyes,' announced the cat.

The cat's name for himself also appeared on the air in letters of gold.

'To me you're a cat,' I tell him. 'Next!'

Another small beast hopped up. A beast with long ears and a brief tail. And again I said the first sound that came into my head.

'Hare.'

The name hung in the air for a moment before it floated down to the grass. Nice, short, easy to say.

'That's my first name,' said the little beast, 'but not my last.'

'What is your last name?'

'Which one?' asked the hare. 'There's jumper and racer, there's hug-the-ground and frisky legs, there's long lugs, grass-biter, dew-hammer, race-the-wind, jig-foot—'

'Wait!' I exclaimed.

'There's creep-along, sitter-still, shake-the-heart, fern-sitter, hedge-squatter—'

The names were writing themselves in the air like crazy.

'You're *hare* to me,' I said.

The animals took their names politely but they kept their own, and they let me know that those were their real names. At the end of the day, names sparkled in heaps on the grass; the garden was littered with them. I gathered them up and threw them in the well under the Tree of Knowledge. But they didn't sink out of sight. They stuck together, they made new names, they told each other secrets. I could see that Creation was no simple matter.

So one day I said to God,

'Show me how You made some of this stuff. That snake, for example.'

'No,' says God. 'Trade secret. I don't give away my trade secrets.'

'How about one little secret? A blade of grass, for example. Or that cat sitting in the grass.'

God considered the cat. He considered it all at once, eternally, from its alpha to its omega.

'It's a funny thing,' said God, 'but I don't thrill to it anymore. Except when you do, Adam. What good is creation if nobody enjoys it?'

'I enjoy it.'

'Tell me about it,' said God.

I thought hard. What could I tell God about the grass? I sat at the well and poked around for that word to see what happened to it.

'Grass!' I called hopefully.

To my surprise, the word *grass* swam right up like a fish and stayed there, shimmering. I took a big drink from the well. And that evening when God came by to see how things were, I opened my mouth and the well-words rolled out. Words about the grass.

'A child said *What is the grass?* fetching it to me with full hands,

How could I answer the child? I do not know what it is any more than he.

I guess it must be the flag of my disposition, out of hopeful green stuff woven.

Or I guess it is the handkerchief of the Lord,
A scented gift and remembrancer designedly dropt,
Bearing the owner's name someway in the corners, that we
may see and remark, and say *Whose?*

'Nice,' says God. 'That's awfully nice.'

'You mean the grass?' I said.

'No, the questions. They make me forget I know all the answers.
Can you make them work on something else?'

And God went away. The next evening I looked around the garden
and spied a tyger lounging under the Tree of Knowledge. I looked
into the well. There, lazing on the surface of the water, gleamed my
questions about the grass. I stirred them back down and I leaned close
to the water.

'Tyger,' I said.

The word TYGER swam right up, and I took a drink from the well.
And that evening God came by to see how I was doing.

'I've got some questions for you, God. Questions about the tyger.'

'Let's hear them,' says God.

So I opened my mouth and the well-words rolled out. Words about
the tyger.

Tyger! Tyger! burning bright
in the forests of the night,
What immortal hand or eye
could frame thy fearful symmetry?

In what distant deeps or skies
Burnt the fire of thine eyes?
On what wings dare he aspire?
What the hand dare seize the fire?

And what shoulder, and what art,
Could twist the sinews of thy heart?
And when thy heart began to beat,
What dread hand? and what dread feet?

What the hammer? what the chain?
In what furnace was thy brain?
What the anvil? What dread grasp
Dare its deadly terrors clasp?

When the stars threw down their spears,
And water'd heaven with their tears,
Did he smile his work to see?
Did he who made the Lamb make thee?

Tyger! Tyger! burning bright
in the forests of the night,
What immortal hand or eye,
Dare frame thy fearful symmetry?

'I like it,' says God.

The tyger liked it too. Said the questions made him seem mysterious and important. For awhile everything in the garden wanted me to say questions about it. I made questions about the lion and the rose and the wren and the snake and the lamb, I made questions for all of them. It was 'Little lamb who made thee' and 'Little rose who made thee,' and all the creatures in the garden were happy. And every time I said my questions to God, He nodded.

'Nice,' He'd say.

But I could see that God was getting bored. After all, didn't He make everything? Didn't He know it all from the beginning? So I decided to try something new. I'd let God ask the questions. I'd think of something and give Him a couple of clues, and I'd wrap it in images like a gift in a box. And when God guessed what I was thinking of, the box would open.

For my first gift, I'd start with the well itself.

The next evening when God came by to see how I was doing, I said,

As round as an apple,
As deep as a cup,
And all God's horses
Cannot pull it up.

'What are you talking about?' said God.

'This well,' I said.

'Say it again,' said God.

I said it again.

'Nice,' said God, and He looked all pleased. 'The way you made me see it. The way you made it part apple and part cup. The way you made it important. What do you call this thing?'

I said the first name that came into my head.

'Riddle.'

For days I went around creation riddling this and riddling that. Leaves, flowers, birds, a stone, an egg. I even riddled an egg.

> 'In marble walls as white as milk,
> lined with a skin as soft as silk
> within a fountain crystal clear
> a golden apple doth appear,
> No doors are there to this stronghold
> Yet thieves break and steal the gold.'

I could see the hen was pleased but God was getting a trifle bored. Enough riddles already, I thought. I'll try something else. God liked the way I made the well part apple and part cup, and He liked the way I made the egg part marble and silk, part gold and milk, and part crystal. What was the point of making Him say, 'It's an egg' or 'It's a well'? I could just give Him the part He liked: the part where I linked the egg and the well with other things.

I murmered "egg" over the well, and up swam the word. There in the depths of the well twinkled my questions about the tyger and the lamb and the lion and the rose and the snake, and they were tangled up with my riddles about the well and the egg and the stone and the leaves and the birds; you could hardly tell where one started and the other left off. The word 'egg' had got so mixed up with other words that I hardly recognized it. It looked as if a dream had rocked it for seven nights running.

Nevertheless, I took a long cool drink.

That evening when God found me in the garden, I said,

'You remember the riddle about the egg.'

'Which one?' asked God. 'Weren't there several?'

'The one where it turned into marble walls as white as milk.'

'Oh, yes,' said God. 'That was nice.'

'Well, I've got another egg for you. But you don't have to find it. You just have to believe it.'

'I'm listening,' said God.

So I opened my mouth and the well-words rolled out.

> 'In this kingdom
> the sun never sets;
> under the pale oval
> of the sky
> there seems no way in
> or out,
> and though there is a sea here
> there is no tide.
>
> For the egg itself
> is a moon
> glowing faintly
> in the galaxy of the barn,
> safe but for the spoon's
> ominous thunder,
> the first delicate crack
> of lightning.'

'You just told me the egg is a moon and I believed you,' said God. 'I, Who made the egg and Who made the moon. It's a lie. It's like the lies angels tell.'

'What other lies are there?' I asked.

'Never mind,' said God. 'What do you call it?'

I said the first name that came into my head.
'Metaphor.'

And for a long while I was happy. But man cannot live by metaphor alone, or questions, or riddles, or even the names of things. And one evening when God stopped by the garden to see how things were going, I said,
    'God, I'm depressed. I have this wonderful life in the lovely garden and I'm depressed.'
    God looked at me for a long time. He looked right through me.
    'You have a well-stocked mind,' He said. 'But your heart is empty. You need a helpmate.'
    'Sounds good to me,' I said. 'When will it arrive?'
    'Making you a helpmate isn't as simple as making a worm or a wren,' said God. 'Adam, I'm going to give you the first general anesthesia.'
    And God caused me to fall into a deep sleep. And when my body was asleep, my spirit climbed out and flew straight to the well, and jumped in, and came back with all this stuff that the well had made down in the depths. Emerald winds. Tiger lilies. So now I knew how God made things. God wasn't the only one who could dream. God wasn't the only one who could invent. But He was the only one who could bring it all back.
    In the first fragile moments between waking and sleeping, I thought I had brought something back, perhaps a little corner of the emerald wind, speaking in wild green syllables. What I heard on waking was neither bird nor bell nor angel, and it sounded like nothing else in Eden.

> 'I will give my love an apple without any core,
> I will give my love a house without any door,
> I will give my love a palace wherein he may be
> and he may unlock it without any key.'

'What's that marvelous sound?' I exclaimed.

'That's singing,' said God.

How can I say what the singing was like? It was not like words rising from the well into my mouth. It was as if the well itself were singing. And hearing that sound for the first time in my life, I was—for the first time in my life—lonely. The singing changed course, the way a river does, but it did not end.

> 'O, western wind, when wilt thou blow
> that the small rain down may rain?
> Christ, that my love were in my arms
> and I in his bed again!'

I sprang up, wide awake now. And God took my hand and said, 'Adam, meet Eve. This is your helpmate.'

She sang *lullay, lullay* and the birds and beasts tucked their heads under their wings and slept, and she sang Hallelujah! and everything woke up full of praise. Nobody had ever made those words before. She sang, and the words answered with rhythms of their own. One was like a heartbeat, another like a dance step. As I recognized the different rhythms, I knew that without realizing it, I'd been hearing them since the day I was born. I tried to name them, so I could ask for the ones I liked best. Iamb. Anapest. Trochee. I'd say to Eve, 'Sing me something in anapests.'

'You mean something that sounds like a stone skipping?'

Sometimes in the middle of her song she'd throw in *lullay, lullay* or *hey nonny nonny* or *fiddle dee dee*. And I'd look all over creation for a nonny or a dee, and finally I'd have to ask her, 'What's a fiddle? What's a dee? What's a nonny?' And she'd laugh and say,

'I don't know. It's what the well sings to itself early in the morning. Ask the well.'

Oh, when she laughed! The stars in their spheres started humming, the morning stars sang together. What were riddles and metaphors to her? She could never remember the names of the iambs and anapests. But let her draw a song around the simplest thing in the world, and I would be filled with joy. And long after I'd forgotten the tune, long after I'd forgotten the words, I could still hear the rhythm of the words, the hum they make when they dance and sing in the well. Who can explain singing? It is a bell weeping and it is a procession of butterflies chanting and it is the tender tread of an elephant walking in its sleep. And whenever I heard Eve singing, I said to myself, 'Though I have the secret names of the angels, if I have not music, I have nothing.' Whenever I made metaphors, I tried to please the ear of God as well as His eye."

Adam stopped talking. It was very quiet in my office. Even the janitor had gone home. I cleared my throat and shuffled my papers and tried to remember why I'd ended up in the insurance business. The reasons eluded me, and I resolved to start looking for another job tomorrow. Eve blew her nose and wiped her eyes.

"Everyone liked my singing," said Eve, "except the serpent. He'd come by in the morning and listen to me, though. There was one song he always asked for, a song I'd sing when I was off tending the roses in the western bower. I sang it so Adam would know where to find me.

>'It is late last night the dog was speaking of you;
>the snipe was speaking of you in her deep marsh.
>It is you are the lonely bird through the woods;
>and that you may be without a mate until you find me.'

One evening when I sang that song for the serpent, he said,

'It's nice. But something is missing. You sing everything in the same key.'

'Key?'

'Key,' said the serpent. 'Key is what locks the tune to itself and locks it into your heart. You are singing in the key of C major.'

'What other key is there?' I asked.

'Why, there are more keys for tunes than roses on that bush. When you've found all the major keys, you haven't even started to discover the noble sorrows of the minor keys. Let me sing your song in one of the minor keys and you'll see what you're missing.

> When I go by myself to the Well of Loneliness,
> I sit down and I go through my trouble;
> when I see the world and do not see my boy,
> he that has an amber shade in his hair.

> My heart is as black as the blackness of the sloe,
> or as the black coal that is on the smith's forge;
> or as the sole of a shoe left in white halls;
> it was you put that darkness over my life.

> You have taken the east from me; you have taken the west
>   from me;
> you have taken what is before me and what is behind me;
> you have taken the moon, you have taken the sun from me;
> and my fear is great that you have taken God from me!'

Well, I shivered all over when I heard how the serpent's singing changed things. It was just as if somebody had opened a door in the garden and showed us what we were going to do tomorrow and tomorrow and tomorrow, just as if we could know what only God knew, that our little garden was called out of a sea of darkness, and it could be called back to that darkness. I'd never thought much about the Void, though God had told us a little about how it was before the garden came, when darkness covered the face of the deep.

'Wise serpent, wily serpent,' I whispered, 'what is the secret of your singing?'

'Loss,' hissed the serpent. 'Change. Sorrow. You and Adam live forever in Eden. When he's gone, you don't miss him. You just misplace him.'

'And where I can get loss, change, and sorrow?' I begged.

'From the Tree of Knowledge,' replied the serpent.

'God said if we eat of that tree we shall surely die,' I said.

The serpent laughed his flat little breathy laugh.

'Did God tell you what death means?' he asked.

'He said something about falling asleep forever,' I said. 'To tell you the truth, I didn't pay very much attention.'

'Believe me, you won't fall asleep,' the serpent assured me. 'I know. I've eaten from the tree myself. You will be more alive than ever. You will savor every moment. And you will sing the song that makes your bones shiver and your spirit ache with longing.'

'But will we fall asleep forever after the song is sung?' I asked.

'Eve,' said the serpent, 'you will turn into the greatest gift the tree can offer. Your life will have a beginning and an end. Your life will be a story in the mouths of millions.'

'Story,' I repeated. It wasn't a word I knew. 'Did you find that word in the well?'

'I put it there myself,' replied the serpent.

'And what does a story look like?' I asked.

'Like me,' said the serpent. 'I am the very shape of a story. Story is the thread on which all the other words are strung. It pulls them along, it gives them a purpose in life.'

'Is it as good as singing? Is it as good as metaphor?' I asked.

'My dear little Eve, story is the river on which metaphor moves and has its being. But it can only live in the fullness of time. That's why God, who lives outside of time, can't tell stories. To Him the alpha and the omega, the once-upon-a-time and the happily-ever-after, are features on a single face. But you, Eve, shall tell stories. When you have eaten the fruit of the Tree of Knowledge, you shall know the beginning of your life but not the end of it, only that it must end. You'll tell stories whose endings will surprise you, though you are their teller and creator. The Tree of Knowledge will make you wonderfully ignorant.'

'And can I sing stories?' I asked.

'Your most beautiful stories will be those you sing,' the serpent assured me. 'And when you sing them, broken lives and broken promises will become as lovely and whole as a tear of crystal.'

'Sing me a story,' I begged the serpent. 'Sing me a story made of such healing.'

So the serpent sang,

> There lived a wife at Usher's Well,
>   And a wealthy wife was she;
> She had three stout and stalwart sons,
>   And sent them o'er the sea.
>
> They hadna been a week from her,
>   A week but barely ane,
> When word came to the carline wife
>   That her three sons were gane.
>
> They hadna been a week from her,
>   A week but barely three,
> When word came to the carline wife
>   That her sons she'd never see.
>
> 'I wish the wind may never cease
>   Nor fashes in the flood,
> Till my three sons come hame to me,
>   In earthly flesh and blood.'
>
> It fell about the Martinmass,
>   When nights are lang and mirk,
> The carline wife's three sons came hame,
>   and their hats were o' the birk.
>
> It neither grew in syke nor ditch,
>   Nor yet in ony sheugh;
> But at the gates o Paradise,
>   That birk grew fair enough.
>
> 'Blow up the fire, my maidens!
>   Bring water from the well!
> For a' my house shall feast this night,
>   Since my three sons are well.'

And she has made to them a bed,
   She's made it large and wide,
And she's ta'en her mantle her about,
   Sat down at the bed-side.

Up then crew the red, red cock,
   And up and crew the gray;
The eldest to the youngest said,
   ''Tis time we were away.'

The cock he hadna craw'd but once,
   And clapp'd his wings at a',
When the youngest to the eldest said,
   'Brother, we must awa'.

'The cock doth craw, the day doth daw,
   The channerin' worm doth chide;
Gin we be mist out o' our place,
   A sair pain we maun bide.

'Fair ye weel, my mother dear!
   Fareweel to barn and byre!
And fare ye weel, the bonny lass
   That kindles my mother's fire!'

'I don't understand the story,' I said, 'but I believe it. What's it about?'

'It's about you,' said the serpent. 'The wife is you, the maids are you, the lassie by the fire is you. They're all you. When you have eaten the fruit of the Tree of Knowledge, little Eve, no story will be closed to you.'

'Give me knowledge,' I pleaded.

'What God calls knowledge I call ignorance,' said the serpent. 'What God calls ignorance, I call story. Help yourself to an apple from the tree that stands in the center of the garden.'"

Silence again fell over the three of us. It would be getting dark outside the office, I thought. I don't have a window; you don't get a window till someone who has one quits or dies.

"So you ate the apple, Madam, and you gave a piece to your husband, and God put you both out of the garden with nothing but your fig leaves," I said, trying to sum up the legalities of the case. "You wish to declare a total loss?"

"No," said Adam, "because we didn't lose everything. When the avenging angel took us to the East Gate, just before he opened it, he turned and said to me,

'You lost eternal life. How could you be so dumb?'

'Eternal life never seemed that great,' I said humbly. 'We'd never known anything else. What I really hate to lose is that well.'

The angel looked surprised.

'Why, that's the only thing you haven't lost,' he said. 'God doesn't want the well. What use is it to God? So He's letting you take it with you.'

'Where is it?' I asked.

'The well is inside you,' replied the angel. 'Much more convenient to carry it that way. Of course it's not going to be as easy to find as it was in the garden, when you could just lean over and take a drink. Sometimes you'll forget the words you're looking for, or you'll call and the wrong ones will answer. Sometimes they'll be a long time coming. But everything the well gave you it will give you again. Or if not to you, to your children. Or your great great great great grand-children. And since God created you in His image, you have His dream power. By the grace of dreams we may meet again, blown together by an emerald wind. And I hope you'll remember me with metaphors and make a lovely web of words about me. I hope you'll make some marvelous—what do you call it?'

I said the first word that came into my head: 'Poetry.'"

Hilma Wolitzer

MOTHER

Despite what everyone said, Helen wasn't sure that she'd seen the baby. Maybe the ether had taken her memory of recent events or maybe she simply couldn't believe that anything this important had really happened to her. Ten years before, she'd been a spinster, working in a typing pool at a textile company, and still living at home in Brooklyn with her father. How he must have pitied and despised her for having his broad, ruddy face, and such a sorry awkwardness in the world of men and women. It was to escape his sympathy that she'd gone to the dance that night, and met Jon. Her father had come to the doorway of her room and caught her posing in the mirror, trying on her mother's crystal beads. When she saw him standing there, stout and pink in his uniform, she felt her face and throat blotch in that awful way. He smiled and said, "Going out tonight, Helen?" She'd had no intention of going anywhere. Nellie, another typist in the pool, had told her about a get-acquainted dance a single women's club was holding, to celebrate Harding's election. Helen wasn't interested—she knew the political event was only an excuse for the social one, and she hated standing on the sidelines, wearing a frozen smile of expectation when she expected nothing. But she told her father that she was going out. "Just to a dance," she muttered.

"Well, that's nice, dear, that sounds like fun," he said. He touched his forehead, his breast, and his holster in a kind of nervous genuflection and pushed their hopeless conversation further. "Mother loved to dance in her heyday, you know," he said. He indicated the box of her mother's jewelry on the dresser. "Maybe you ought to wear some of that stuff . . . gussy up a little."

She pitied and hated him then, too, for pretending that twenty-eight was not a desperate age for a woman, that "gussying up" was the secret of fatal attraction, that he believed her capable of abandoned fun. Her mother had probably never danced. Maybe she'd never made love, either, with that great, aching hulk in the doorway. Maybe Helen had been born of some chaste, clothed act that produced only lesser beings. Her face blazed up again. Maybe she was going crazy at last, the way they said all lustful virgins eventually did. Her father continued to stand there, smiling.

The very worst thing, she was certain, was not human misery, but its nakedness, and the naked witness of others. And as her father knew her secret heart, so she knew his. She'd seen him standing for minutes in front of the open, smoking icebox, staring inside as if he expected something beyond butter or milk to be revealed. Then, with a heaving sigh, he always settled for butter and milk. His whole life had whizzed by like a bullet from the gun he'd never fired off the firing range, and here he was: long-widowed, still a foot patrolman, and with a sullen old-maid daughter on his hands. She'd inherited his homely looks, and out of spite she'd deny him his immortality. Her mother had died of pneumonia when Helen was two years old, and all she could recall were a few real or imagined impressions—breast, hair, shadow.

Lying now in the maternity ward at Bellevue Hospital, she couldn't conjure up even the vaguest image of the living child they'd said she'd delivered. All the other women in her ward, but one, had infants at their breasts at regular intervals. The nurses wheeled them in in a common cart, like the vegetables sold by street peddlers. The woman in the bed opposite Helen's had given birth to a stillborn son. Before the wailing babies were distributed among the new mothers, a three-sided screen was arranged discreetly around her bed, and she could be heard weeping behind it.

Helen felt remote from the celebration around her, as she had felt remote from the festive possibilities of the dance the night she'd met Jon. The ballroom had been romantically lit for the occasion, and adorned with political banners and posters. As soon as she walked in, she knew that her dress was wrong—she would disappear in the shadows. It was November and cold, and everyone, all the magazines, said that simple black was always smart and always right. Yet even Nellie and Irene, who lived by the dictates of fashion, wore gaily-colored dresses and matching headbands. Oh, what difference did it make? There were so many women, in bright noisy clusters, and only a few men, aside from the band that was just warming up.

Irene glanced around and said, "Boy, I bet we'd find more fellas at a convent. She and Nellie leaned together, giggling. Helen didn't see what was so funny. They weren't beautiful or in such hot demand, either, and the Great War had diminished all of their chances even further. But she was rallying to laugh along with them, to be a good sport, when the huge mirrored ball suspended from the center of the ceiling began to slowly revolve. Facets of light ricocheted off every surface and struck her painlessly on her arms, her dress, her shoes. The band started to play the lively melody of some popular song she couldn't name, but that she found herself humming. Everyone was wearing the same restless pattern of light. In that way they were all united, like jungle beasts marked by the spots or stripes of their species. Helen felt that something was about to happen. It was in the very air. President Harding gazed down at her from the enormous posters like a stern, but benevolent chaperone. And look, the ballroom was filling up—so many men were coming in! Irene said it was because *they* only had to pay half-price, but who cared? Couples went whirling by in one another's arms. Before long, Nellie was pulled into the maelstrom, and a few minutes later Irene was gone, too. Soon someone would come for her, would know intuitively her concealed qualities: that she'd been golden blond as a child, and her body skin attested to it; that she had lovely breasts; that she could type sixty flawless words a minute.

A man seemed to be coming purposefully in her direction. She felt an immediate affinity with the gawkiness of his stride, the way his cowlick had resisted combing. He appeared hell-bent in his mission and a quivery thrill traveled through her body. Then she saw that he'd meant someone else, the gyrating flapper in fringed pink standing next to her, who shook her head no at him and turned to another man. Helen drew her breath in deeply and put up her arms, as if he'd meant her all along. He hesitated for the barest moment before he held out his own arms. She was careful not to lead.

They were married on Inauguration Day, and Jon moved in with Helen and her father. He was a typesetter for *The Sun*, with a modest salary. Their living arrangement enabled them to save money for the house they'd buy after they'd begun their own family. Helen stored their wedding gifts neatly in the walk-in cedar closet, so that everything would still be new no matter when they moved. The closet's cool, scented interior was like a little forest glade, and she often just stood there and daydreamed, surrounded by the artifacts of her future.

Helen didn't become pregnant, though not for want of trying. Each disappointing month she wept in the privacy of the cedar closet, wiping her eyes carefully on a corner of one of the monogrammed wedding sheets. Old Dr. Kelly insisted she was fine, that nature would take its course, wait and see. When Helen asked if she should see a specialist, he laughed and shook his head. "Isn't the family doctor best when you want to start a family?" he said. "Didn't I deliver herself in my little black bag?"

Oh, yes, she thought, and took my mother away in it. He was like a gentle, cheerful priest, his undaunted cheer shaking her faith, but she gave him the tremulous smile he wanted. Finally, though, they did consult a specialist, in his Gramercy Park offices. She gasped during his examination and fainted during the first treatment to expand her fallopian tubes. He prescribed a nerve powder and told Jon that it was inadvisable for Helen to continue working in her condition.

She stayed home for two years, prowling the house like a high-strung watchdog. She'd left her job, but her fingers refused to give up typing. They tapped out imaginary letters about late shipments and damaged goods, on the tabletops and the walls. She played game after game of Patience, telling herself that if the next hand worked out she would become pregnant that month. It was a relief to go back to work at last, to give up hope, if not the longing that had impelled it.

Helen and Jon developed the peculiar exclusive closeness of childless couples. After Helen's father died, walking the orbit of his beat, they became even closer, and insulated from the world of real families. Jon's parents and sisters were far away, on a farm in Minnesota he'd left years before. He and Helen had friends, of course, but their only important connection was to one another, a wondrous and scary thing. Once they'd stopped trying so hard to conceive, though, they made love less often, and it became more a matter of mutual comfort than a passionate pursuit.

When the Depression began, Jon's salary was cut in half and Helen lost her job, but they told themselves how lucky they were not to have to worry about anyone else during such difficult times. Helen took inordinate pride in her resourcefulness and her capacity for thrift. She made filling soups out of battered produce and scraps of meat, and screwed low-wattage light bulbs into all the lamps and fixtures. Going from door to door, she found various kinds of piecework they could do at home. She typed envelopes and stuffed them with flyers, and they both pasted glitter onto celluloid Kewpie dolls. The stuff got into everything; it stuck to their fingers and was scattered in the carpets and on their clothing. At night, Helen saw a trace of phosphorescent glitter on the pillows, like a sprinkling of celestial dust. It reminded her of the fairy tales her father had read to her years ago, in which worthy wishes were granted and deprivation was ultimately rewarded. The story she'd loved best was *The Goose Girl*, about an orphan who carried around a cambric stained with three drops of her mother's blood. Helen had always favored the most morbid stories: *The Goose Girl* with her bloody cambric and decapitated talking horse,

The Hardy Tin Soldier melting away for love and heroism; and, of course, *Sleeping Beauty*. But even happy endings couldn't dispel the essential melancholy of Grimm and Anderson. The Goose girl would lament, "Alas dear Falada, there thou hangest," and the horse's head would answer, "Alas, Queen's daughter, there thou gangest. If thy mother knew thy fate, her heart would break with grief so great." Helen wasn't quite sure what gangest meant, or cambric, for that matter, but her own heart always broke on cue. Had she loved those stories because she was a miserable child? Or had they helped to make her that way?

When she did become pregnant, after ten years of marriage, she decided never to read those stories to her child. *Her child*. How extraordinary that a living creature could be made accidently in darkness. That a reprieve could come so long after the end of hope. Helen experienced bliss that seemed dangerous. Jon was as happy as she was, although she knew he'd pretended acceptance of their childlessness out of a kind of gallantry, just as he continued to pretend she was the girl he'd meant to dance with.

One morning, in Helen's seventh month of pregnancy, there were a few drops of blood on the sheet, and Dr. Kelly ordered her to bed. He came to examine her at home each week, and it was like being a child again—his minty, medicinal smell in the room, the black leather bag gaping on the dresser top. Sometimes, after he'd listened to her belly with his stethoscope, he would put it to her ears. What a marvelous din! It denied what she had feared most about herself, that she was inferior and unfinished, incapable of this simple biological purpose. She rested, luxuriating in fantasy, as she used to do in the cedar closet, and willed her body to wait out its sentence. It didn't, though.

Two weeks into her eighth month, she woke during the night with her waters flooding the bed. "Oh, Jesus," Jon said. "It's too soon!" While he went to fetch Dr. Kelly, their next-door neighbor came in in her nightgown. She worked dry blankets under Helen and crooned, "All right, dear. All right, all right."

It wasn't all right at all. Everything was happening so fast: the waters, and then the pain—accelerating, intensifying. Why had she ever thought she'd wanted a baby? The neighbor crossed Helen's legs tightly and said, "Don't push! Lie still!"

Dr. Kelly came and he hoisted her from the bed, ordering Jon to take her feet and the other woman to carry his bag and throw the doors wide. They struggled down the stairs like barflies with a soused buddy, but they managed to get Helen to the street and into Dr. Kelly's car.

At Bellevue she was separated from Jon. The last thing she remembered of that night was his diminishing figure as she was wheeled down a hallway. When she woke, it was another day. Her mouth was sweet with ether and sour with sleep. They told her she'd had a daughter. They said that Jon had been to see her soon after, and that she'd spoken to him, but she didn't really remember that, either. She missed the baby in a physical way, with an emptiness that was not unlike hunger. Her breasts ached and leaked until a nurse came with a lethal-looking pump and expressed the milk. Helen was assured that the baby was alive, that this very milk would be fed to her soon in the nursery.

"Now you saw her, Helen," Dr. Kelly scolded, "just before we sent her down. You said she looked like a little drowned rat." And the nurse who gave her a sponge bath said, "Turn on your side for me now, Mother." They promised that she would be taken to the special nursery in the basement for another look as soon as she could tolerate a wheelchair ride. She'd lost a lot of blood, they told her, and she wasn't even ready yet to dangle.

An aide propped Helen up for supper and she found herself facing the grieving woman, who sat immobile over her own tray. They looked at one another in the cheerful clamor of silverware. The woman's eyes returned Helen's commiseration, like a mirror, and her mouth twitched into a bitter, conspiratorial smile. Helen couldn't eat her supper. She was almost glad when the babies were brought in again, and the three-sided screen came between her and that knowing gaze.

That evening, Jon was in the herd of visitors who carried the chill of winter in on their clothes. Helen questioned him about the baby and he said that she was doing well, breathing nicely and taking nourishment. "What did Dr. Kelly say?" she asked. Jon glanced nervously away before he said, "He told me she's holding her own." Helen knew that was only a partial truth, that the fate of premature infants was shaky, at best. They were meant to stay inside longer and develop. Their hearts and lungs might be too weak to sustain them, and they had no defenses against the slightest infection. She imagined the special nursery with its tiny, perishable occupants ticking away like homemade bombs.

"Well, what shall we name her, Helen?" Jon asked.

She had made up names, and even careers, for the unborn baby during those weeks in bed. She'd drawn up secret lists, under "Girl" and "Boy," but now she said, sullenly, "I don't know, I haven't thought about it."

"They need it for the certificate," Jon said.

She had a sudden, dreadful image of the small, toppled tombstones in the old churchyard near their house. Some of them were over the graves of infants whose chiseled names and dates could still be read. "I don't want to name her yet," she said in a rising voice, and Jon quickly said, "All right, dearest, don't worry about it," which only made her feel worse.

He sat at her bedside, helpless against her mood. He held her hand and she was touched by the familiar sight of his ink-stained fingers. She thought of how he'd apologized for them the night of the dance, explaining that he'd come straight from work, that his hands weren't actually dirty. He'd worked so hard recently, and had never complained, even when she withdrew into the pleasure of her secret interior life. Yet there were times he'd enraged her with that glance of mournful sympathy he might have learned from her father. Now she felt a swell of love for him at the same time that she felt impatience and a desire for him to go.

At last visiting hours were over, and Jon was ushered away with the other outsiders. In a while, the babies were brought in for their last feeding of the day. Whey they were taken out again, the overhead lights went off and a few of the bed lamps were switched on. Some of the women whispered together in the cozy dimness. Others combed their hair. This was the strangest hour, a time in the real world when only children are put to bed. Helen was very tired, but not sleepy. She couldn't find a comfortable position under the tight, starched sheets.

"Goodnight! Goodnight!" the happy mothers called to each other. One by one the lamps were shut off and the only visible light was outside the room at the nurse's station. The woman in the bed next to Helen's coughed and someone at the far end giggled. Someone else said, "Shhh!" Soon there was a chorus of slow, even breathing, the counterpoint of snoring. The shadow of the night nurse fell across the threshold as she stood and peered in at them.

After the nurse went down the hall, Helen sat up and worked her way out of the sheets' bondage. She turned carefully on the high hospital bed and let her legs hang over the side. She became dizzy, and had to sit still for a few moments. Then she slipped down until her feet were shocked by the cold floor. She found her slippers and stepped into them, and she put on her flannel robe. No one, not even the mother of the stillborn baby, stirred. Helen's bottom hurt and the thick sanitary pad she wore felt clumsy. She walked stiffly, sliding her feet along like someone learning to ice-skate. At the sink she paused and looked at herself in the mirror—a pale wraith with glints of silver in its tousled hair, as if childbirth had aged her. She peered more closely and saw that it was only the Kewpie dolls' glitter. She whispered "Mother," just to try it out, but it felt strange on her tongue, a foreign food for which she hadn't yet cultivated a taste. When she came to the doorway she stopped again, breathless from so much exertion, and leaned against the frame. The nurse's station was empty, and there was nobody in the corridor.

It took a long time to walk the few yards to the stairway. Behind her the phone on the desk rang and rang. In the stairwell, Helen wondered what floor she was on. It didn't matter. They'd said the nursery was in the basement; she would go down and down until there were no more stairs. I've done this before, she thought, at the second or third landing. And then she knew it was school she was thinking of, the empty, echoing stairwell when she'd carried a note from one teacher to another while everyone else was in class. How privileged she'd felt, and free! But once she was punished in front of the whole assembly for talking when the flag was being carried in. She could never remember the joy without the shadow of humiliation. It was the danger of all happiness, and what she had willed to her mortal child. Alas, Queen's daughter.

There were two orderlies in the basement corridor, wheeling a squeaking stretcher and laughing. Helen waited until they'd turned the corner, and then she shuffled out in the other direction. She smelled something cooking, the strong, beefy odor of institutional soup or gravy. It made her feel hungry and a little sick. She looked through the glass panel of one of the swinging doors that led to the kitchen. It was as brightly lit in there as the delivery room—she remembered *that* now, the impossible glare. She'd tried to say something about the stingy light they suffered at home, and then the mask had come down, dousing her voice and the lights at once.

In the kitchen, witches' cauldrons were bubbling on the giant stoves. Three women in hair nets chopped onions and wept, and an angry chef attacked a slab of meat. It was the landscape of nightmares, and here she was in her nightclothes, but awake. Feeling lightheaded, she went past the kitchen and at the corner of the corridor found a sign, its arrow pointing the way to the *Laboratory, X-Ray*, and the *Morgue*. The nursery had to be somewhere beyond them.

The locked laboratory door had a glass panel, too. There was no one inside; the small light might have been left on for the animals. She could see a few of them crouched in their cages: quivering brown rabbits, white rats squinting suspiciously back at her. She had surely never said that awful thing about the baby. It was only one of Dr. Kelly's silly bedside jokes. The rats scurried in their limited space and Helen shuddered and moved on.

There was no one in sight, and she longed to sit for a moment on one of the wooden benches on either side of the door to the X-ray room. But she was afraid that if she sat down, she'd be unable to get up again. Instead she slumped against the black door. It felt cold and solid. Years ago, when she was about thirteen, Helen developed a bad cough that Dr. Kelly's syrups and tonics couldn't cure. Her father took her to the clinic of one of the big uptown hospitals to have a picture taken of her chest. It was a brand-new procedure, and she could still recall the anxious darkness, and the icy pressure of the machine against her beginning breasts. After she was dressed, the doctor invited Helen and her father into the consultation room, where the back-lit X-ray was hung. Astonished, she saw her own tiny, lurking heart, and the delicate fan of ribs that housed her lungs. With a pointer the doctor showed them a faint shadow he said was a touch of wet pleurisy. Her father was so relieved it wasn't pneumonia, he grasped the doctor's hand, making him drop the pointer. Helen should have been relieved, too, but she harbored a secret fury that there could no longer be any secrets. Her father could already read her evil mind, and now the last stronghold of privacy had fallen.

Later, she opened herself gladly to Jon, and then to the baby. Leaning against the door to the X-ray room, she was stirred by the memory of the child inside her, the thrill of its quickening. "Push!" the nurse in the delivery room had said, just as Helen's neighbor had ordered her not to push when her labor first began. And then her body had made its own willful choice. She could hear herself grunting, those deep animal grunts of colossal effort. You were never supposed to really remember the pain—that's what all the women she knew had said. They'd told her it was the worst pain in the world, and they said it with a kind of religious fervor. But they promised that she'd forget it afterward, as if it had all taken place in another life. Then why was it coming back to her here in the basement corridor, an echo of the pain and thrusting she'd believed she could not survive? Then she remembered *everything* that had happened under that brilliant sun: being shackled to the table, the grunts changing to screams, the mask she'd risen to meet as if it were a lover's mouth. The missing part was still the birth itself—that happened in a long tunnel of dreamless sleep—and the baby. Where was the baby?

A child was crying somewhere, and Helen's breasts ran. The crying got louder and closer, and she slid along the wall to one of the benches and sat down. But it wasn't an infant's sound—these wails smothered language, and there were footsteps hurrying toward her. There was no place to hide, no time to even stand up. Two people, a man and a woman, half-carrying, half-dragging the shrieking child between them, turned the corner. Helen shrank against the bench in terror of being discovered. The child banged his ear with his fist. The parents didn't seem to notice Helen's robe and slippers—the man shouted at her, "Where's the emergency room?" She was unable to answer him, although her mouth worked in spasms. They hurried past her, struggling with their struggling burden, their footsteps and the child's screams receding as they all disappeared at the next corner. God, she had wet herself! But when she looked down, she saw blood flowering her pink slippers and puddling the floor. She stood and stared down in amazement. The child with the earache still screamed in the far distance. "Help me," Helen said. "Help me!" she said, louder. Of course no one responded; she had to get back to the kitchen where there were people. She stood there in confusion before she was able to push off. Then it was as if the walls moved past her, and she walked on a treadmill. She was on fire, she was melting. "Papa," she whimpered. "Jon!" When she came to the morgue, she knew she had gone in the wrong direction. Her fists were soft against the door and they tingled with pins and needles, as if she had just woken and had to wait for them to wake, too. She thought she heard someone in there, or a radio playing, but she might have been hearing noises inside her own head.

She was afraid to look at her slippers now, and she was shivering with cold. "*Please,*" she said, and turned to follow the drunken, slithery trail of blood. The first of it on and near the bench had already started to darken. It looked like the remains of an accident after the victims have been carted away. She staggered past the bench and went like a moth to the lighted window of the laboratory. The rats looked back at her. She gasped, as she had gasped during the last earth-shaking pain of her waking labor. When she'd emerged from the tunnel she saw the glistening blue-pink baby hung by its feet, girdled by the thick, pulsing cord. "Oh!" she had cried. "Oh! It looks like a little drowned rat!" That wasn't what she'd meant to say. She meant words of welcome and consolation for the terrible gift of the world. There thou gangest.

She fell through the double doors of the kitchen and saw the three women and the chef in a sudden, frozen tableau. She came to once more, somewhere else, with Dr. Kelly looming above her saying, "No! Oh, Christ, damn it!" Then she felt her soul folding end on end on end, like the flag from her father's coffin, like the wedding sheets in the cedar closet, until it was small enough to slip through the open mouth of the waiting black leather bag.

BIBLIOGRAPHY OF RECENT WORK

Ann Beattie, WHERE YOU'LL FIND ME (1986) and LOVE ALWAYS (1984)

Harold Brodkey, WOMEN AND ANGELS (1985)

Rosellen Brown, CIVIL WARS (1984) and TENDER MERCIES (1978)

Raymond Carver, FIRES (1984) and CATHEDRAL (1983)

Nicholas Delbanco, THE BEAUX ARTS TRIO (1985) and ABOUT MY TABLE (1983)

Richard Ford, A PIECE OF MY HEART (1985) and QUEST FOR THE FARADON (1983)

Gail Godwin, THE FINISHING SCHOOL (1985) and THE ODD WOMAN (1983)

Ron Hansen, THE ASSASSINATION OF JESSE JAMES BY THE COWARD ROBERT FORD (1983) and DESPERADOES (1980)

Mark Helprin, WINTER'S TALE (1983) and THE REFINER'S FIRE (1981)

Robert Houston, THE NATION THIEF (1984) and THE SIXTEENTH OF SEPTEMBER GAME (1985)

David Huddle, ONLY THE LITTLE BONE (1986) and PAPER BOY (1975)

John Irving, THE CIDER HOUSE RULES (1985) and THE HOTEL NEW HAMPSHIRE (1984)

Joyce Johnson, MINOR CHARACTERS (1983)

David Madden, CAIN'S CRAFT (1985) and BIJOUX (1976)

Mary Morris, THE WAITING ROOM (1986) and THE BUS OF DREAMS (1985)

Joyce Carol Oates, RAVEN'S WING (1986) and MARYA (1985)

Tim O'Brien, THE NUCLEAR AGE (1985) and GOING AFTER CACCIATO (1979)

Cynthia Ozick, ART AND ARDOR (1983) and THE CANNIBAL GALAXY (1984)

Francine Prose, HUNGRY HEARTS (1983) and HOUSEHOLD SAINTS (1981)

Lynne Sharon Schwartz, ACQUAINTED WITH THE NIGHT (1984) and DISTURBANCES IN THE FIELD (1983)

John Updike, ROGER'S VERSION (1986) and THE WITCHES OF EASTWICK (1985)

Nancy Willard, THINGS INVISIBLE TO SEE (1985) and ANGEL IN THE PARLOR (1983)

Hilma Wolitzer, IN THE PALOMAR ARMS (1983) and HEARTS (1980)

Acknowledgments *(continued)*

"A Good Deal" by Rosellen Brown first appeared in *The Massachusetts Review*.
"Boxes" by Raymond Carver first appeared in *The New Yorker*.
"Fireworks" by Richard Ford first appeared in *Esquire*.
"Over the Mountain" by Gail Godwin first appeared in *Antaeus*.
"The Pacific" by Mark Helprin first appeared in *The Atlantic Monthly*.
"Apache" by David Huddle first appeared in *Denver Quarterly*.
"The Fall of Texas" by Joyce Johnson first appeared in *The New Yorker*.
"Willis Carr at Bleak House" by David Madden first appeared in *The Southern Review*.
"The Things They Carried" by Tim O'Brien first appeared in *Esquire*.
"The Shawl" by Cynthia Ozick first appeared in *The New Yorker*.
"Other Lives" by Francine Prose first appeared in *Antaeus*.
"Poker Night" by John Updike first appeared in *The New Yorker*.

Passages quoted in "How Poetry Came into the World and Why God Doesn't Write It" are from the following sources: *p. 304*, Walt Whitman ("Song of Myself," section 6, *Leaves of Grass*); *pp. 304–5*, William Blake ("The Tyger," *Songs of Innocence and Experience*); *pp. 305–6*, two riddles from *The Oxford Nursery Rhyme Book*, ed. Iona and Peter Opie (London: Oxford University Press, 1967); *p. 307*, Linda Pastan ("Egg," in *PM/AM*, New York: W. W. Norton & Co., 1982); *pp. 308, 310–11, and 313–14*, adaptations from Anon., "The Names of the Hare," "I Will Give My Love An Apple With E'er A Core," "Donal Og," and "The Wife of Usher's Well," in *The Rattle Bag*, ed. Seamus Heaney and Ted Hughes (London: Faber and Faber, 1984); and *p. 309*, "Western Wind," in *Early English Lyrics*, ed. F. Sidgwick and E. K. Chambers (London: Chatto Windus, 1907).